Anna Ella Carroll: Secret Strategist

Anna Ella Carroll

Anna Ella Carroll: Secret Strategist

Genius, Feminist and Military Mastermind for the
Union during the American Civil War

A Military Genius

and

Life and Writings

Sarah Ellen Blackwell

LEONAUR

Anna Ella Carroll: Secret Strategist
Genius, Feminist and Military Mastermind for the Union during the American Civil War
A Military Genius
and
Life and Writings
by Sarah Ellen Blackwell

FIRST EDITION

First published under the titles
A Military Genius. Life of Anna Ella Carroll, of Maryland Volume 1
and
Life and Writings of Anna Ella Carroll, Volume 2

Leonaur is an imprint of Oakpast Ltd

Copyright in this form © 2017 Oakpast Ltd

ISBN: 978-1-78282-600-2 (hardcover)
ISBN: 978-1-78282-601-9 (softcover)

http://www.leonaur.com

Publisher's Notes

The views expressed in this book are not necessarily
those of the publisher.

Contents

A Military Genius

Contents

The long years come and go,
And the Past,
The sorrowful splendid Past,
With its glory and its woe,
Seems never to have been.
Seems never to have been!
O sombre days and grand,
Plough ye crowd back once more,
Seeing our heroes graves are green
By the Potomac, and the Cumberland
And in the valley of the Shenandoah!

When we remember how they died,
In dark ravine and on the mountain side,
In leaguered fort .and fire-encircled town,
And where the iron ships went down.
How their dear lives were spent
In the weary hospital tent,
In the cockpit's crowded hive,
            ———it seems
Ignoble to be alive!

Thomas Bailey Aldrich.

Preface

In commencing the attempt to portray a very remarkable career I had hoped for the cooperation of the person concerned so far, at least, as the supervision of any statements I might find it necessary to make. But it was decided by her friends that it would not be well for her at present to be troubled with new projects, or even informed of them. It was at first a serious disappointment to me and seemed to increase my difficulties, but as I was allowed access to sources of family information I have been enabled to present a sketch, slight and inadequate, but authentic, and greatly desired by many distant friends. With continued improvement in health I trust that the wishes of Miss Carroll's friends may be better met by an autobiography taking the place of the present meagre and imperfect sketch.

It should be at once understood that this is *not* a plea for Miss Carroll.

Her work has but to be fairly presented to speak for itself.

Her claim was settled once and forever by the evidence given before the first Military Committee of 1871, met to consider the claim, and reporting, through Senator Howard, unanimously endorsing every fact. The Assistant Secretary of War, Thomas A. Scott, the Chairman of the Committee for the Conduct of the War, Benjamin F. Wade, and Judge Evans, of Texas, testifying in a manner that was conclusive. These men knew what they were talking about and human testimony could no farther go. Congress, through its committees, has again and again endorsed the claim, and never denied it, being "adverse" only to award as involving national recognition.

Our great generals have left us one by one without ever antagonising the claim, and General Grant advised Miss Carroll to continue to push her claim for recognition.

But this work is to be considered rather in the light of an historical research bearing on questions of the day.

Are our present laws and customs just toward women? Are women ever pre-eminently fitted for high offices in the State? Is it for our honour and advantage when so fitted to avail ourselves of the whole united intellect and moral power of men and women side by side in peril and in duty? Such a life as this gives to all these questions the authoritative answer of established facts.

New York, April 21st, 1891. (Summer address, Lawrence, Long Island, N.Y.)

Miss Carroll's address is 931 New Hampshire Avenue, Washington, D. C.

A Search for the Documents

Arriving as a stranger in Washington, knowing nothing of libraries and document rooms, Secretaries offices, and War departments, I was at first greatly at a loss. For many years, I had had in my possession two very important documents, the last memorial of 1878 and the report of the Military Committee thereon under General Bragg in 1881. With these two in my hand I proceeded to consult the Descriptive Catalogue of the Congressional Library. To my surprise, I found that these two very important documents had been omitted from the index. Calling attention to the fact, we looked them up in the body of the volume and Mr. Spofford immediately added them in pencil together with the other important documents, in Miss Carroll's favour, which had also been omitted.

When I made my way to the Senate document room I found that this important Miss. Doc. 58 had been omitted there also, having been set down under another name. Looking it up in the volume of Miscellaneous Documents I again obtained the admission by Mr. Amzi Smith. In the list at the Secretaries office Miss. Doc. 58 was also omitted together with the last report by a Military Committee, under General Bragg, endorsing the claim in the most thorough going way. The index ending with an intermediate report mistakenly designated as *adverse*, though the previous reports were not thus heralded as favourable.

After the first report, as made by Senator Howard and the repeated endorsements made by Wilson and Williams of succeeding Congresses, these two documents are by far the most important and interesting.

The memorial of '78, containing additional evidence explaining some things, otherwise unaccountable, and making some very singular revelations. It is a mine of wealth for the future historian. At the secretary's office, I showed the documents and stated that their exclusion must have been unfavourable to the presentation of the case. I was not equally fortunate in obtaining their immediate admission, but trust the mistake has since been rectified.

The report marked as "adverse" would be more truly described as "admission of the incontestable nature of the evidence in support of the claim," admitting the services in every particular and being "adverse" only to award involving national recognition.

At the Secretary's office, I obtained permission to see the file of the 41st Congress, 2nd. session. There I saw the first short memorial with the plan of campaign attached as described by Thomas Scott. Then my investigations were temporarily ended by the outside of a document being shown me stating that the papers had been withdrawn by Samuel Hunt, thus agreeing with the statement made by him in Miss. Doc. 58, that they had been stolen from his desk while the committee were examining the claim.

I found it very difficult to obtain the earlier documents. "Supply exhausted" being the answer that has long been given, but all can be looked up in the bound volumes.

When, at length, fairly started in my work I was disturbed by a rumour that Miss Carroll's papers, formerly placed on file at the War Department, were no longer to be found there. I set out as far as possible to investigate. Provided with an excellent letter of introduction to the Secretary of War I made my way, on March 6, 1891, to the vast building of the War Department and sent in my letter with a list of the documents I wanted to see. Miss Carroll's Military papers, given in the Miss. Doc. 58, and a list of letters from the same memorial by Wade, Scott, and Evans.

The permission being kindly accorded I was transferred to the Record office and told that the file should be ready for me on the following day.

Taking with me the Miss. Doc. 58, an unpublished manuscript of Miss Carrolls, and specimens of the handwriting of Wade and Scott, I punctually put in an appearance, was transferred to the office of the Adjutant General, and Miss Carroll's file produced for my inspection. I met with all possible courtesy and every facility for the examination. I found two of the papers on my list in her now familiar handwriting, and some others.

A letter to Secretary Stanton, of May 14, 1862, recommending the occupation of Vicksburgh and referring to Pilot Scott, stating that she had derived from him some of the important information which had lead to her paper to the War Department on Nov. 30, 1861, which had occasioned the change of campaign in the southwest and proved of such incalculable benefit to the national cause.

A paper of May 15th, 1862, advising that Memphis and Vicksburgh should be strongly occupied and the Yazoo River watched. Another letter to Stanton concerning her pamphlets and proposing to write another one in aid of Mr. Lincoln, unjustly assailed. There was a portion of a letter written in great haste from St. Louis. There was an interesting letter from Robert Lincoln when Secretary of War. A petition from a group of ladies, asking for information concerning Miss Carroll's services and several other documents, but most of the important papers on my list were not on the file.

After examining the papers for some time, I asked to see the originals of the letters of Wade and Scott. I was told they were in another department and would take some time to look up, but a gentleman was politely detailed to conduct me there and look up the letters. I opened my Miss. Doc. 58 and pointed out the long list of letters of Mr. Wade's, on pages 23, 24, 25, and 26, and asked to see those first.

The gentlemen expressed his astonishment that, with *such* a document in my hand, I should ask for *originals*. He said that the documents printed by order of Congress were to all intents and purposes the same as the originals, as they were never so printed until those letters and papers had been examined and proved to be genuine. I asked if the printing was also a guarantee for Miss Carroll's papers as printed in that document, though we were now unable to find the originals. He replied assuredly it was; that I could positively rely upon all that had been so printed. There was no going back upon the Congressional records. Other gentlemen came up and confirmed the statement.

Under these circumstances it seemed unnecessary to carry the investigation any further, so with thanks for the great friendliness and courtesy that I had met with I took up my precious Miss. Doc. 58 and departed with a slight intimation that if anything more should be needed they might have the pleasure of seeing me again.

The missing documents, after being on file for 8 years, were sent on one or more occasions from the War Department to the Capitol for examination by committees.

On page 30 of the Miss. Doc. 58 we learn the reason, on testimony of Wade and Hunt (keeper of the records), why they are there no longer.

Miss Carroll's Military Maps

On page 178 of the memorial of '78 Judge Evans, in one of the many repeated letters and statements of great interest that I have been obliged to omit for want of space, relates how he stood beside Miss Carroll in her parlour at St. Louis when she was gathering the information for the preparation of her paper to the War Department of November 30, 1861, and its accompanying map. He says:

> I have a very distinct recollection of aiding her in the preparation of that paper, tracing with her upon a map of the United States, which hung in her parlour, the Memphis and Charleston railroad and its connections southward, the course of the Tennessee, the Alabama, and the Tombigbee Rivers, and the position of Mobile Bay; and when Henry fell she wrote the Department, showing the feasibility of going either to Mobile or Vicksburg.

In his testimony given on page 85 of Miss. Doc. 179, he says:

> On Miss Carroll's return from the West she prepared and submitted to the deponent, for his opinion, the plan of the Tennessee River expedition, as set forth in her memorial. Being a native and resident of that part of the section and intimately acquainted with its geography, and particularly with the Tennessee River, deponent was convinced of the vast military importance of her paper, and advised her to lose no time in laying the same before the War Department, which she did on or about November 30, 1861. The accompanying map, rapidly prepared by Miss Carroll, was made on ordinary writing paper. An unpretentious map, but fraught with immense importance to the national cause.

Assistant Secretary of War Thomas A. Scott, the great railroad magnate and a man of remarkably acute mind, saw at a glance the immense importance of the plan; he hastened with it to Lincoln, and when her plan of campaign was determined on he studied her map with the greatest care before going West to consolidate the troops for the coming campaign.

The second map sent in with Miss Carroll's paper of October, 1862, when the army before Vicksburg was meeting with disastrous failure, was made on regular map paper, representing the fortifications at Vicksburg, demonstrating that they could not be taken on the plan then adopted and indicating the right course to pursue. Miss Carroll bought the paper for the map at Shillington's, corner of Four-and-a-Half Street and Pennsylvania Avenue; sketched it out herself with blue and red pencils and ink and took it to the War Department.

On page 24 of Miss. Doc. 58, Judge Wade writes:

Referring to a conversation with Judge Evans last evening he called my attention to Colonel Scott's telegram announcing the fall of Island No. 10 in 1862 as endorsing your plan, when Scott said, the movement in the rear has done the work. I stated to the judge, as you and he knew before, that your paper on the reduction of Vicksburg had done the work on that place, after being so long baffled and with the loss of so much life and treasure by trying to take it from the water; that to my knowledge your paper was approved and adopted by the Secretary of War and immediately sent out to the proper military authority in that Department.

On April 16, 1891, by permission of the kindly authorities of the War Department, search was made in the office of the Chief Engineer to see if, by chance, these maps might have come to the War Department. No trace or record was found and it seemed to be agreed that, considering the circumstances of extreme secrecy attending the in auguration of the campaign, it was unlikely that they should come there. Time, which so often corroborates the truth, may possibly bring those maps to light. At present, I cannot trace them.

It is proposed to follow this volume with another, entitled *Civil War Papers in Aid of the Administration*, by Anna Ella Carroll, with notes by the author.

CHAPTER 1

Ancestry and Old Plantation Life

In looking at the map of Maryland we find that the configuration of the State is of an unusual character. The eastern portion is divided through the middle by the broad waters of Chesapeake Bay, leaving nine counties with the State of Delaware on the long stretch between the Chesapeake, Delaware Bay, and the Atlantic Ocean. Of late years, the great tide of population has set toward the western side of Chesapeake Bay, leaving the widely divided eastern counties in a comparatively quiet and primitive condition. But in the earlier history of our country these eastern counties, with easy access to the Atlantic Ocean, were of greater comparative importance to the State, and were a centre of culture and of hospitality. It was in Somerset, one of the two southernmost of these eastern counties, that Sir Thomas King, coming from England about the middle of the eighteenth century, purchased an extensive domain.

Landing first in Virginia with a group of colonists, he there married Miss Reid, an English lady also highly connected and of an influential family. The estate which he subsequently purchased in Maryland embraced several plantations, extending from the county road back to a creek, a branch of the Annemessex River, then and since known as King's Creek.

Standing well back and divided from the county road by extensive grounds, Sir Thomas King built Kingston Hall, a pleasant and commodious residence. An avenue of fine trees, principally Lombard poplars and the magnificent native tulip tree, formed the approach to the Hall, and its gardens were terraced down to the creek behind.

On one of the outlying plantations Sir Thomas King also established the little village of Kingston, of which he built and owned every house. He brought hither settlers, but the little place did not thrive. Plantation life and proprietary ownership were not conducive to the growth of cities. As the old settlers died out the houses were abandoned, and the post office was removed to a corner of the Hall plantation, then known as Kingston Corner. A new settlement grew up there, and since emancipation has changed the conditions of life it has grown and thriven. It is now a promising little place of 250 inhabitants. It has assumed to itself the name of the older village and is known as Kingston on the present maps.

At the Hall Sir Thomas King established his family residence. Here he lived and here his wife died, leaving but one child, a daughter, heiress to these wide estates, the future mother of Governor Thomas King Carroll and the grandmother of Anna Ella Carroll, whose interesting career is the subject of our present relation.

Through all the early history of Maryland the contests between Catholic and Protestant form one of its most conspicuous features. Early settled by Lord Baltimore, a Catholic proprietary, his followers were at once involved in a struggle with still earlier settlers at Kent Island, in the Chesapeake Bay, and the Protestants who followed, while condemning Catholicism as a rule of faith, associated it also with the doctrine of divine right and arbitrary rule. Bitter contests followed. The most active minds of the colony enrolled themselves enthusiastically in the opposing parties.

St. Mary's, a little town on the western side of the Chesapeake, was the ancient capital of the State and the head quarters of Catholicism.

Sir Thomas King, on his side, was a staunch Presbyterian. This household was strictly ruled in conformity to his faith, and by liberal contribution and personal influence he was largely instrumental in building the first Presbyterian meeting-house, at the little town of Rehoboth, a few miles from his own domain, a great barn-like structure of red brick, which remains to this day. The marriage of Miss King with her cousin, young Mr. Armstead, of Virginia, the ward of Sir Thomas King, was an event that had been planned for in both families, and was looked forward to with great satisfaction on all sides.

One may well imagine, then, the consternation which ensued to the proprietor of the Hall, to his relatives and friends, and all the neighbours of that staunch Presbyterian region, when Colonel Henry James Carroll, of St. Mary's, of the old Catholic family of the noted Charles Carroll, and himself a Catholic by profession, came across the waters of the Chesapeake, courting the only daughter of Sir Thomas King, the heiress to all these estates and the reigning *belle* of the county.

21

In vain was the bitter opposition of father and friends. The wilful young heiress insisted on giving to the handsome officer from St. Mary's the preference over all her other admirers. It may be that a reaction from the strict rules and the severe tenets of her education gave to this young scion of another faith an additional charm. However, that may be, love won the day.

The father was compelled to yield, and the young heiress became the wife of the intrepid Colonel Henry James Carroll. It could hardly have been expected that Sir Thomas King should associate with himself under the same roof a son-in-law of principles so opposed to his own; but he established the young couple on the adjacent estate of Bloomsborough, which he also owned, and here their little son, Thomas King Carroll, first saw the light of day.

The old proprietor, in his great empty hall, coveted this little grandson and proposed to adopt him as his own child and make him the heir to all his estates.

In course of time a younger son, Charles Cecilius Carroll, was born to the Bloomsborough household, the grand father's proposition was accepted, and little Thomas King Carroll, then between five and six years of age, became an inmate of Kingston Hall and the object of Sir Thomas King's devoted affection and brightest hopes.

Governor Carroll, in after times, used to relate to his children how they spent the winter evenings alone in the old Hall. His grandfather, in his spacious armchair, on one side of the open hearth, with a blazing wood fire and tall brass andirons; the little boy, in a low chair, on the opposite side, listening to the tales that his grandfather related of ancient times and heroic deeds. By these means Sir Thomas King strove to amuse his youthful heir and to train his mind to high principles and brave aspirations. But Sunday must have been a terrible day to the little boy, attending long services in the red brick meeting-house and occupying himself as he best could between whiles with the old English family Bible, with pictures of devils and lakes of fire and brimstone, calculated to inspire his youthful mind with horror and alarm.

At an early age the young heir was sent to college, to the Pennsylvania University at Philadelphia, then the most famous seat of learning for those parts. Here he graduated with distinguished honours, at the age of seventeen. Among his classmates and intimate friends were Mr. William M. Meredith, of Philadelphia; Benjamin Gratz, of St. Louis, and the father of Mr. Mitchell, the author of Ike Marvel.

Returning to Maryland, Thomas King Carroll began the study

of law with Ephraim King Wilson, who had been named after Sir Thomas King. He was the father of the late United States Senator for Maryland. His studies being completed, arrangements were made to associate him as partner with Robert Goodloe Harper, the son-in-law of Charles Carroll, of Carrollton, in his lucrative law practice, and a house was engaged for his future residence in Balti more.

During the studies of Thomas King Carroll, his aged grandfather, Sir Thomas King, having died, Colonel Henry James Carroll and his family were residing at Kingston Hall and managing the estate for the young heir.

An old friend of the family was Dr. Henry James Stevenson, one of the prominent physicians of Baltimore. Dr. Stevenson had come over formerly as a surgeon in the British Army. He had married in England Miss Anne Henry, of Hampton. Settling in Baltimore, he acquired a large estate, then on the outskirts, now, (1894), in the centre of Balti-more. On Parnassus Hill, he built a very spacious and handsome residence. During the Revolutionary War Dr. Stevenson remained loyal to his British training and was an outspoken Tory. The populace of Baltimore were so incensed against him that they mobbed his residence, threatening to destroy it.

The doctor showed his military courage by standing, fully armed, in his doorway and threatening to shoot the first man who attempted to enter. The mob were so impressed by his determined attitude that they finally retired, leaving the owner and his property uninjured. Dr. Stevenson afterwards became much beloved through his devotion and care, bestowed alike on the wounded of both armies. He became noted in the profession from his controversy with Dr. Benjamin Rush, of Philadelphia, the one advocating and the other opposing inoculation for smallpox. Dr. Stevenson was so enthusiastic that he gave up, temporarily, his beautiful residence as a hospital for the support of his theory.

An ivory miniature in a gold locket, now in possession of Miss Carroll, represents Dr. Stevenson in his red coat and white waistcoat, and at the back of the locket there is a picture of Parnassus Hill, crowned by the doctor's residence, with a perpendicular avenue straight up hill, and a negro attendant opening the gate at the foot for Dr. Stevenson, mounted on his horse and returning home. It is a very quaint and valuable specimen of ante-revolutionary art.

The daughter of this valiant doctor was a beautiful and accomplished girl, Miss Juliana Stevenson. She is described as having very regular features, a complexion of dazzling fairness, deep blue eyes, and auburn hair flowing in curls upon her shoulders. She was a good musician, playing the organ at her church, and educated carefully in every respect. Her knowledge of English history was considered something phenomenal.

Thomas King Carroll early won the affections of this lovely girl, and they were married by Bishop Kemp before the youthful bridegroom had completed his twentieth year.

Those that care for heraldry may be interested to know that at Baltimore may be seen the eight coats-of-arms be longing to the King-Carroll family, of which Miss Anna Ella is the eldest representative.

When the question came of Miss Stevenson leaving home, her especial attendant, a bright coloured woman, had been given her choice of remaining with Dr. Stevenson's family or accompanying her mistress. The poor woman was greatly exercised in choosing between conflicting ties.

Mrs. Carroll was accustomed to describe to her children, with much feeling, the scene which followed. Sitting in her room she heard a knock at the door and in rushed Milly, with her face bathed in tears, and throwing herself at Miss Stevenson's feet she exclaimed "Oh, mistis, I cannot, cannot, leave you!" It was a moment of deep emotion for both mistress and maid. Milly followed Mrs. Carroll to her new home and became the old mammy, the dear old mammy of all the Carroll children.

Her daughter Leah was born on the Kingston plantation, and then her granddaughter Milly, who in later times clung to the changing fortunes of the Carroll family, and is at this day, (1891), a devoted attendant on her invalid mistress, Miss Anna Ella Carroll. A visitor to the modest home in Washington, now occupied by the Carroll sisters, is met at the door by the comely face and pleasant smile of this same faithful Milly. The life-long devotion of the affectionate "Mammy" illustrates one of the most touching features of the old plantation life; but the shadow of slavery was over it all. To follow the fortunes of her adored mistress, Mammy left behind her in Baltimore her husband, a free coloured man. But what was the marital relation to a slave! The youthful couple set out on a wedding tour, but were un expectedly recalled by the sudden death of Colonel Henry James Carroll. It was necessary for his son to return at once and take possession his of inheritance.

The coming home of the proprietor and his youthful bride was a great event at Kingston Hall. There were at that time on the plantation 150 slaves, besides the children. They are described as a fine and stalwart people, looking as if they belonged to a different race from the coloured people that we now meet with in cities. They seemed like a race of giants. The men were usually as much as six feet in height, and broad and muscular in proportion. All these numerous dependents were drawn up in lines on the long avenues, dressed in their livery of green and buff, and must have presented an imposing appearance as the stately family carriage was seen approaching through the long vista of fine old trees. The arrival was heralded by a roar of welcome and demonstrations of joy.

And thus, the youthful couple took possession of the home that was to be the scene of so many joys and so many sorrows, ending in troublous times that completely changed the existing order of things, and which witnessed the conclusion of the reign of the Kings and the Carrolls at Kingston Hall.

Shortly after his return with his bride Thomas King Carroll was elected to serve in the Legislature. He only attained the requisite age of 21 years on the day before he took his seat. His birthday was celebrated at Kingston Hall after the old English fashion, and he was *fêted* and toasted and received congratulations on all sides. It is said that he was the youngest member ever elected to the Legislature.

Thomas King Carroll commenced life not only with wide social advantages, but with great natural gifts. He was striking in appearance, and of so graceful and dignified a demeanour that it is said that he never entered a crowd without a movement of respect and appreciation showing the impression that he created.

He was a good orator and of unimpeachable integrity and lofty character. This was early exemplified when as still very youthful he was sent to represent his county at a political caucus in Baltimore. The question of raising money for the approaching campaign came up, and he was asked in his turn how much would be needed for his county of Somerset. He arose and said: "With all due deference, Mr. President, *not one cent*. We can carry our county without any such aid!"

There was a general laugh, and Robert Goodloe Harper, who was present, said, "Very well, young gentleman, you will tell a different tale a few years hence." He went home and related the proceedings to his constituents, who applauded his answer, and that year Somerset was the banner county of the State.

The early years succeeding the marriage were years of peace and prosperity.

The young bride won all hearts by her beauty and the sweetness of her disposition.

In time a lively group of children filled the old Hall with life and gayety.

Thomas King Carroll, like many another Maryland planter, was fully convinced that in itself slavery was wrong. The early settlers of Maryland would gladly have excluded it, but the institution was forced upon them by the mother country, the English monarch and his court deriving large incomes from the sale of slaves and cancelling every law made by the early settlers to prevent their introduction into the colony. Slavery had now become a settled institution, on which the whole social fabric was built, and individual proprietors, however they might disapprove of the system, could see no way to change it. All that Thomas King Carroll knew how to do was to seek as far as possible the happiness and welfare of his slaves, and slavery showed itself on the Kingston plantation in its mildest and most attractive form.

Not much money was made usually upon plantations, but everything was produced upon the estate that was needed to feed and clothe the great group of dependents. And this was the state of things at Kingston Hall.

There was Uncle Nathan, the butler, whose wife was Aunt Susan, the dairywoman; Uncle Davy, the shoemaker; Saul, the blacksmith; Mingo, the old body servant of Colonel Carroll; Fortune, the coachman, etc., etc.—all very powerful men.

Every trade was represented upon the estate. There were blacksmith shops; there were shoemakers, tanners, weavers, dyers, etc. All the goods worn by the servants, male and female, were manufactured on the place. The wool was sheared from the sheep, and went through every process needed to produce the linsey-woolsey garments of men and women. The women were allowed to choose the colours of their dresses, and the wool was dyed in accordance with their tastes. Two of these dresses were allowed for a winter's wear, and each woman was furnished with a new calico print for Sundays.

There were few local preachers among them at that time, but two were noticeable during the childhood of the Carroll children, Ethan Howard and Uncle Saul. And there was an Uncle Remus, too, in Fortune, the coachman, who told the children the stories of Brer Rabbit and the Tar-baby quite as effectively as the Uncle Remus of our popular magazines.

The servants had their own rivalries and class distinctions. One portion of the house servants prided themselves as being the old servants—born on the place. Another group plumed themselves as having come in with the "Mistis," and having seen outside regions and a wider range of life. But all the house servants considered themselves vastly superior to the field hands and treated them with condescension.

The house servants, though slaves, in fact, were absolute despots in their own department. The Carroll children would not have dared to touch a knife or a fork without the permission of the butler, and if they had attempted to enter the cellar or the dairy without leave from their respective guardians a revolutionary war would have been the result.

Mammy, too, was the absolute ruler over every shoe and stocking, and was expected under all circumstances to be responsible for every article of the children's toilet.

The largest quarter devoted to the slaves was a great circular structure, with a central hall surrounded by partitions, giving to each field-hand a separate sleeping birth. The hall in the centre was devoted to those who were old or unfitted for work, and here the young children were deposited while their parents were pursuing their tasks, and they were expected to wait upon the "Grannies" and be cared for in return.

Behind this central apartment was one in which the food was prepared, and there was a great hand-mill, where the corn was ground for the daily use.

The children at the Hall were seldom allowed to enter these quarters, but were occasionally granted permission to go there when delicacies for the sick or new caps and dresses for the babies were furnished from the Hall.

There were also quarters for the married slaves, each family having its little cottage and garden, which it was allowed to cultivate on its own account, and great was the pride of its occupants if by dint of especial care, they could raise the spring vegetables earlier than in the master's gar den, and carry them up to the Hall in triumph. There they always found a customer ready to purchase their produce. Every Monday morning rations were given out for a week by the overseer and they were cooked by the families in their own quarters.

The hours of work were moderate, and on Saturday they had a half holiday.

Sometimes there were parties and merry-makings at the negro

quarters. On great occasions, such as the marriage of a house servant, the family at the Hall, by their presence, gave dignity to the festivities, and inwardly they greatly enjoyed the fantastic scene.

At Kingston Hall, open house was kept, and numerous visitors and entertainments made life gay for the children, who grew up in an atmosphere of ease and hospitality, little anticipating the vicissitudes of the future and the stormy and heart-rending times in which their country was about to be involved.

CHAPTER 2

Childhood and Early Life

On August the 29th, 1815, Anna Ella Carroll was born, at Kingston Hall. By this time a little brick Episcopal church had also been built at Rehoboth, but the congregation was too small to support a resident clergyman, and it had to alternate with other churches in its services. At this infant church, in due course of time, Anna Ella was christened by the Rev. Mr. Slemmonds. She was the eldest child, and thenceforth the pride of her distinguished father, who viewed with delight her remarkable intelligence, and early made her his companion in the political interests in which he took such an active part. It soon became evident that this was a child of decided and unusual character. When but three years old she would sit on a little stool at her father's feet, in his library, listening intently as he read aloud his favourite passages from Shakespeare.

All Mr. Carroll's children were so drilled in Shakespeare that there was not one of them who could not, when somewhat older, repeat long passages by rote, and they made the rehearsal of scenes from Shakespeare's plays one of their favourite amusements. Anna Ella showed no taste for accomplishments; cared neither for dancing, drawing, music, or needlework. She used to boast to her sisters that she had made a shirt beautifully when ten years old; but they would smile at the idea, as they had never seen her handle a needle and could associate her only with books.

These were to her of absorbing interest, and books, too, of a grave and thoughtful character. Alison's *History* and Kant's *Philosophy* were her favourite reading at eleven years of age. She read fiction to some extent, under her father's direction; but, with the exception of Shakespeare and Scott, she never cared for it. While other girls of her age were entranced by Sir Charles Grandison and fascinated by the he-

KINGSTON HALL, BIRTHPLACE OF ANNA ELLA CARRLL

roes of Bulwer's earlier novels, she turned from them to read Coke and Blackstone with her father, and followed with him the political debates and discussions of the day. She studied with lively interest the principles and events which led to the separation of the Colonists from the Mother Country, and buried herself in theological questions. At a very early age her letters bore reference to the gravest subjects. Imagination was never prominent; her mind was essentially analytical. Pure reason and clear consecutive argument delighted her, and works of that nature were eagerly sought by her.

Her life passed largely in her father's excellent library, which was well stocked with classic works, both history, biography, philosophy, and poetry, and her education was to him a constant delight.

Miss Carroll's early associates were the children of the neighbouring proprietors, the Handys, the Wilsons, the Gales, the Henrys, etc., and she early made acquaintance with the distinguished men who where her father's associates.

Mr. Carroll continued to serve in the Legislature until elected Governor of Maryland, in 1829. On this occasion, he received an interesting letter from Charles Carroll, of Carrollton, congratulating him and expressing his pride and gratification at the event. When Governor Thomas King Carroll went to Annapolis, in performance of the duties of his office, he was accompanied by Mrs. Carroll, with the younger children and a group of servants under the superintendence of the invaluable Mammy. Mrs. Carroll, by her beauty and accomplishments, was well fitted to adorn her station. When the weather became warm she returned with her children to Kingston Hall.

The following charming letters from Miss Carroll, then a girl of fourteen, show the tenderness of the relation between father and child, and at how early an age she interested herself in politics and entered into the questions of the day:

Kingston Hall, Jan. 20, 1830.

My Precious Father:

My dearest mother received your letter on Monday, and we were all happy to know you had arrived safely at the seat of government, although the Annapolis paper had previously announced it.

Oh! my dear father, if I could but see you! I miss you—we all miss you—beyond measure. The time passes tediously without you.

I have just read Governor Martin's last message. (He was Governor Carroll's predecessor). I think it quite well written. I wondered to see it published in the *Telegraph* (an opposition paper, I suppose). I am anxious to see what the Eastern papers say of your election. Please, dear father, when anything relating to your political action is published, whether in the form of a message, in pamphlet, or in newspaper, do not fail to let us have them. I read with so much pride your letter in the Annapolis paper. It merits all the distinction and fame it has brought you. Too much could not be said in praise of my noble father. Dr. K—— was here today. He says they feel "quite exalted" to be so near neighbours to a governor.

When do you think the Legislature will rise? But I must not write on political subjects only. Brother is delighted with his new horse. The little children are begging dearest mother to write you for them. May every blessing attend you, my precious father. Be sure and write me a *long* letter.

Your devoted daughter,

A. E. Carroll.

Kingston Hall, Feb. 17, 1830.

My Beloved Father:

Again, we are disappointed in your arrival home! *and how* disappointed no tongue can tell. Dearest mother thought it possible you might come on a little visit, even if the Legislature did not rise. (At that time the sessions of the Legislature were not restricted, as now they are, to sixty days). You said in your last letter to me that this was "probable." Why did you not say "*certain?*" Then I would rejoice, for when my father says a thing is certain, I *know* it is certain. I am happy to tell you that I am much better; have had a long and tedious spell. I would lie for hours and think of you away from me, and if I had not the kindest and tenderest mother to care for me and for us all, what should we do.

I understand that your appointments have not been generally approved by the milk-and-water *strata* of the party, of course, for no thorough Jackson man would denounce, even if he did not approve. It is my principle, as well as that of Lycurgus, to avoid "mediums"—that is to say, people who are not decidedly one thing or the other. In politics, they are the inveterate enemies of the State. I hear there has been a committee appointed to visit you on your return to the Hall and present a petition for the removal of some whom you have recently appointed. They call themselves reformers. I want reform, too, even in court criers, but to be for ever reforming reform is absurd. I know whatever you do is *right*, and needs no reform, my wisest and dearest of fathers.

Write as soon as you can to your loving child,

A. E. Carroll.

Mrs. Carroll was a devoted member of the Church of England, as was natural in the daughter of staunch Dr. Stevenson.

As there were no Sunday schools in those days, Mrs. Carroll gathered her children around her on Sunday afternoons and drilled them in the church catechism until it was as familiar to them as their ABC; but Anna Ella always inclined to the Westminster Confession and the tenets in which her father's childhood had been so rigorously educated.

When about fifteen Miss Carroll was sent to a boarding school, at West River, near Annapolis, to pursue her studies with Miss Margaret Mercer, an accomplished teacher.

Thomas King Carroll, at the same age, had been sent to the University of Pennsylvania, and afterward to the law school; but for this girl of gifts so remarkable, and of a character so decided, the best thing that the world of those times offered was a young ladies' boarding school of the olden time. Well it was for her and her country that her exceptional position as the cherished daughter of a man of such education and talent, occupied with political affairs, secured for her an education that would otherwise have been unattainable to her.

However, she made the best possible use of such education as a ladylike school permitted, was noted for her intelligence, and made many friends; but her true education began and continued with Governor Carroll at home.

Miss Carroll had early shown an intense interest in moral and religious questions, following her father's views on these subjects. She became interested in the ministrations of Dr. Robert J. Breckenridge, of Kentucky, then settled over a Presbyterian church in Baltimore.

Dr. Breckenridge was the uncle of John C. Breckenridge, afterward one of the leading secessionists, utterly opposed to his uncle in political views, and one of the candidates for the Presidency in 1860.

Dr. Robert J. Breckenridge was a valued friend of Governor Carroll.

Miss Anna Ella became a communicant and earnest member of his church, and a mutual friendship arose, terminated only by the death of the aged minister, who has left on record his high appreciation of the mental abilities and the great services afterward rendered by his remarkable parishioner.

We will give in part two letters from this excellent man to Miss Carroll, written from Kentucky in after years. For want of space we must greatly shorten them.

Danville, Ky., December 6, 1864.

My Excellent Friend:

It is very seldom I have read a letter with more gratification than yours of November 29th. How kind it is of you, after so many events, to remember me; and how many people and events and trials and enjoyments, connected with years of labour, rush through my heart and my brain as you recall Maryland and Baltimore so freshly and suddenly to me; and how noble is the picture of a fine life, well spent, which the modest detail of some of your efforts realises to me. It is no extravagance, not even a trace of romance; it is a true enjoyment, and deeply affecting, too, that you give me in what you recount and what is recalled thereby. For what is there in our advanced life more worthy of thankfulness to God than that our former years were such that if we remember them with tears they are tears of which we need not be ashamed.

My life during the almost twenty years since I left Maryland has been, as the preceding period had all been, a scene of unremitting effort in very many ways; and now, if the force of invincible habit permitted me to live otherwise, I should hardly escape by any other means a solitary if not a desolate old age. Solitary, because of a numerous family all, except one young son, are either in the great battle of life or in their graves. Desolate, because the terrible curse which marks our times and desolates our country has divided my house, like thousands of others, and my children literally fight in opposite armies and my kindred and friends die by each other's hands.

There is no likelihood, in my opinion, that our Legislature will send me to the Senate of the United States; and will you wonder if I assure you that I have never desired that they should. Was it not a purer, perhaps a higher, ambition to prove that in the most frightful times and through long years a simple citizen had it in his power by his example, his voice and his pen, by courage, by disinterestedness, by toil, to become a real power in the State of himself; and have not you, delicately nurtured woman as you are, also cherished a similar ambition and done a similar work, even from a more difficult position? . . . . . I beg to be remembered in kind terms to your father, and that you will accept the assurances of my great respect and esteem.

Robert J. Breckenridge.

Danville, Ky., April 27, 1865.

My Dear Miss Carroll:

. . . . You will easily understand how much I value the good opinion you express of my past efforts to serve our country, and of my ability to serve it still further; and it is very kind of you to report to me with your approbation the good opinion of others, whom to have satisfied is in a measure fame. . . . . Many years ago, without reserve and with a perfect and irrevocable consecration, I gave myself and all I had to Him, and have never, for one moment, regretted that I did so. The single principle of my existence, from that day to this, has been to do with my might what it was given to me to see it was God's will I should do.

You see, my dear Miss Carroll, that I, who never sought anything, am not now capable of seeking anything, nor even permitted to do so; and, on the other hand, that I, who never refused to undertake any duty, am not allowed now to hesitate, if the Lord shows me the way, nor permitted to refuse what my country might demand of me. This is all I can say—all I have cared to say for nearly my whole life. I would not turn my hand over to secure any earthly power or distinction. I would not hesitate a moment to lay down my life to please God or to bless my country.

Mr. Lincoln was my personal friend and habitually ex pressed sentiments to me which did me the highest honour.

It gives me pleasure to learn that you propose to publish annals of this revolution, and I trust you will be spared to execute your purpose.

Make my cordial salutations to your father and accept the assurance of my high respect and esteem.

Your friend, &c.,

R. J. Breckenridge.

Miss Carroll was very pleasing, with a fine and intelligent face, an animated and cordial manner, and great life and vivacity, roused into fire and enthusiasm on any topic that appealed to her intellect and her sympathies. Naturally, in so favourable a social position and with such gifts, she received early in life much attention and had offers of marriage from many distinguished parties; but she never seemed inclined to change her condition or to give up the beloved companionship of her father. A literary life and his congenial presence seemed to be all-sufficient for her, and she remained his devoted companion until his death, in 1873, when she also, the child of his youth, was well advanced in life.

After Governor Carroll's term of office had expired he returned to his estate, and shortly after he was waited upon by a deputation, who had been sent to enquire if he would accept a nomination as United States Senator. But at that time Mrs. Carroll was dangerously ill. His extensive plantation and group of children required his presence, and he declined to serve. He was devoted to his wife, and their marriage was one of unbroken harmony until her death, in 1849. Governor Carroll devoted himself thereafter to the necessities of his family and estate.

Anna Ella Carroll frequently visited her friends at Washington, and early commenced an extended relation with the press, writing usually anonymously on the political subjects of the day. A friend of her father, Thomas Hicks, considered that he owed his election as Governor of Maryland largely to the articles which she contributed in his favour, and he retained through life a strong personal friendship and high admiration for her intellectual powers. At his death, he left her his papers and letters, to be edited by her—a labour prevented by her subsequent illness. In 1857 Miss Carroll published a considerable work, entitled *The Great American Battle*, or Political Romanism, that being the subject of immediate discussion at that time. This work was compiled from a series of letters contributed by her to the press, and her family knew nothing of the project until she surprised them by the presentation of the bound volume.

Old Sir Thomas King would certainly have been greatly gratified if he could have known how vigorously his great-granddaughter was to uphold the banner of religious and political freedom. This work was accompanied by an excellent portrait of the authoress in the prime of life, which we here reproduce for our present readers.

In the following year Miss Carroll published another considerable work, entitled *The Star of the West*, relating to the exploration of our Western Territories, their characteristics, the origin of the National claims, and our duties towards our new acquisitions, and she urged the building of the Pacific railroad. This seems to have been one of her most popular works, as it went through several editions, and greatly extended her acquaintance with leading men.

The following letter, written by the Hon. Edward Bates, is very descriptive of Miss Carroll and evinces the admiration and esteem which she inspired among those best fitted to appreciate her high character, her uncommon cultivation, and natural gifts.

Washington, D. C., October 3, 1863.

To Hon. Isaac Hazlehurst, of Philadelphia.

My Dear Sir: I have just received a note from Miss Anna Ella Carroll, of Maryland, informing me she is going to Philadelphia, where she is a comparative stranger, and desiring an introduction to some of the eminent publicists of your famous city. I venture to present her to you, sir, first, as an unquestionable lady of the highest personal standing and family connection; second, as a person of superior mind, highly cultivated, especially in the solids of American literature, political history, and constitutional law; third, of strong will, indomitable courage, and patient labour. Guided by the light of her own understanding, she seeks truth among the mixed materials of other minds, and having found it, maintains it against all obstacles; fourth and last, a writer fluent, cogent, and abounding with evidence of patient investigation and original thought.

I commend her to your courtesy, less for the delicate attentions proper for the drawing room than for the higher communion of congenial students, alike devoted to the good of the Commonwealth.

With the greatest respect, I remain, sir, your friend and servant.

Edward Bates.

As time went on, Thomas King Carroll, now advanced in years, many of his children married and scattered, began to find his estate and great group of dependents a burden some and unprofitable possession.

Under a humane master, unwilling to sell his slaves, they were apt to increase beyond the resources of the plantation to sustain them. Ready-money payment was not the general rule upon plantations. Abundance of food was produced, but money was not very plentiful when markets were distant and trade very limited.

It was not unusual for debts to accumulate and even to be handed down from father to son. The creditors rather favoured this state of things, as the debt drew interest. As long as there were plenty of slaves, their ultimate payment was secure whenever they chose to press for it. If the money was not then forthcoming, their redress was certain— a descent followed of that brutal intermediary, "the nigger dealer," loathed and dreaded alike by master and servant. A sufficient amount of the human property was speedily secured and driven off for sale to satisfy the creditor. To the slave, torn from his home and his life-long ties, it was despair. To the master's family, often a bitter grief. They might shut themselves up and weep at the outrage, but they were powerless in the face of an inexorable system.

To the master, therefore, as the slaves increased, there could often be no alternative between ruthless sale and financial ruin. Thomas King Carroll, honourable, humane, unwilling to sell his slaves, immersed during the best years of his life in political affairs, found in later years his burdens increasing, and his kindness of heart had involved him also in some especial difficulties. He had on several occasions allowed his name to be used as security for friends in difficulty. Two or three of these debts remained unpaid and the responsibility came upon him. One especially, of an unusually large amount, involved him in embarrassment which led him to determine on the sale of his plantation. A neighbour and intimate friend, Mr. Dennis, was desirous to purchase, and very sorrowfully Thomas King Carroll came to the resolution to give up his ancestral home. As he was accustomed to say, he loved every corner and every stone upon the place, but the burden had become too great for his declining strength.

The sale was effected and Mr. Carroll removed to Dorchester County, on the eastern side of the Chesapeake, with his unmarried children, and here he died, in 1873, in his 80th year.

Governor Carroll is described in the annals of the State as "one of the best men Maryland has ever produced," a man of *character unsullied* and of lofty integrity.

At the breaking out of the civil war Mr. Carroll was already an elderly man. At first his sympathies were with his own section, but after the attack on Fort Sumter they were steadily enlisted for the National cause, though he foresaw that its triumph would lead to the destruction of his own fortunes and those of his children.

Most of the slaves had been left on the plantation, but some had always been considered the especial property of each of his children.

Thus, Anna Ella Carroll had her own group. At the very outset of the war she fully realised that slavery was at the root of the rebellion, and she at once liberated her own slaves and devoted her time, her pen, and all her resources to the maintenance of the National cause. She immediately commenced a series of writings of such marked ability that they speedily attracted the attention of Mr. Lincoln and the Administration. Governor Hicks, too, placed in a situation of unusual difficulty, turned to his able friend for consultation and for moral and literary support.

Jefferson Davis, who was aware of Miss Carroll's great literary and social influence, wrote to her early in the secession movement adjuring her to induce her father to take sides with the South.

"I will give him any position he asks for," wrote Mr. Davis.

"Not if you will give him the whole South," replied Miss Carroll. A visitor to her in 1861 says:

Her room was lined with military maps, her tables covered with papers and war documents. She would talk of nothing but the war. Her countenance would light up most radiantly as she spoke of the Union victories and the certainty that the great Nation must win an ultimate success.

When fresh news from the army came in she would step up to one of her charts and, placing a finger on a point, she would say:

Here is General ———'s detachment; here is the rebel army; such and such are the fortifications and surrounding circumstances; and she would then begin thoughtfully to predicate the result and suggest the proper move.

We will give a sketch of the situation in the early days of the secession movement, mainly in the words of Miss Carroll's own able account, afterwards published by order of Congress.

List of Documents in Relation to Services Rendered by Anna Ella Carroll

(Descriptive Catalogue, page 911.)

Petition for compensation for services. Anna Ella Carroll. March 31, 1870. Senate Mis. Doc. No. 100, 41st Congress, 2nd session.

(Catalogue, page 928.)

Report on memorial of Miss Carroll. Senator Howard. February 2, 1871. Senate report No. 339, 41st Congress, 3rd session.

(Catalogue, page 962.)

Memorial for payment of services. June 8, 1872. Senate Mis. Doc. No. 167, 42nd Congress, 2nd session, vol. 2.

(Catalogue, page 1058.)

Petition for compensation for services. Anna Ella Carroll. February 14, 1876. House Mis. Doc. No. 179, 44th Congress, 1st session, vol. 9.

(Catalogue, page 1099.)

Memorial of Anna Ella Carroll. October 22, 1877. Senate Mis. Doc. No. 5, 45th Congress, 1st session, vol. 1.

(Catalogue, page 1128.)

House of Representatives. Mis. Doc. No. 58, 45th Congress, 2nd session. Claim of Anna Ella Carroll. Memorial of Anna Ella Carroll, of Maryland, praying for compensation for services rendered to the United States during the late civil war. May 18, 1878.

(Catalogue, page 1149.)

Report on claim of Anna Ella Carroll. Senator Cockrell February 18, 1879. Senate Report No. 775, 45th Congress, 3rd session, vol. 2.

(Catalogue, page 1241.)

Report of claim of Anna Ella Carroll. Representative E. S Bragg. March 3, 1881. House report No. 386, 46th Congress, 3rd session, vol. 2.

Note.—Most of these only to be seen by consulting the bound volumes in the Congressional library.

★★★★★★

(All the following letters, reports, etc., concerning Miss Carroll's literary and military services are reproduced from these Congressional documents.)

Thomas A. Scott

CHAPTER 3

Rise of the Secession Movement

On the election of Mr. Lincoln, in 1860, the safety of the Union was felt to be in peril and its perpetuity to depend on the action of the border slave States, and, from her geographical position, especially on Maryland.

In the cotton States the Breckenridge party had conducted the canvass on the avowed position that the election of a sectional President—as they were pleased to characterize Mr. Lincoln—would be a virtual dissolution of the "compact of the Union;" whereupon it would become the duty of all the Southern States to assemble in "sovereign convention" for the purpose of considering the question of their separate independence.

In Maryland, the Breckenridge electors assumed the same position, and as the Legislature was under the control of that party, it was understood that could it assemble they would at once provide for a convention for the purpose of formally withdrawing from the Union. The sessions, however, were biennial, and could only be convened by authority of the governor.

It therefore seemed for the time that the salvation of the Union was in the hands of Governor Hicks. Although he had opposed the election of Mr. Lincoln and all his sympathies were on the side of slavery, his strong point was devotion to the Union. With this conviction, founded upon long established friendship, Miss Carroll believed she might render some service to her country, and took her stand with him at once for the preservation of the Union, come weal or woe to the institution of slavery.

Governor Hicks had been elected some three years before as the candidate of the American party, and to the publications Miss Carroll had contributed to that canvass he largely attributed his election. It was therefore natural that when entering on the fierce struggle for the preservation of the Union, with the political and social powers of the State arrayed against him, that he should desire what ever aid it might be in her power to render him.

A few days after the Presidential election Miss Carroll wrote Governor Hicks upon the probable designs of the Southern leaders should the cotton States secede, and suggested the importance of not allowing a call for the Legislature to be made a question. That she might be in a position to make her services more effective, she repaired to Washington on the meeting of Congress in December, and soon understood that the Southern leaders regarded the dissolution of the Union as accomplished. The leading disunionists from Maryland and Virginia were on the ground in consultation with the secession leaders in Congress, and the emissaries from the cotton States soon made their appearance, when it was resolved to make Maryland the base of their operations and bring her into the line of the seceding States before the power of the Democratic party had passed away, on the 4th of March, 1861.

Hence every agency that wickedness could invent was industriously manufacturing public opinion in Baltimore and all parts of the State to coerce Governor Hicks to convene the Legislature.

With Maryland out of the Union they expected to in augurate their Southern Confederacy in the Capitol of the United States on the expiration of President Buchanan's term, on the 4th of March, and by divesting the North of the seat of Government and retaining possession of the public buildings and archives, they calculated with great confidence upon recognition of national independence by European powers. About the middle of December Miss Carroll communicated to Governor Hicks their designs on Maryland and suggested the propriety of a public announcement of his unalterable determination to hold Maryland to the Union.

After his address on the 3rd of January, 1861, resolutions and letters from men and women endorsing his cause were received from Maryland and from all quarters of the United States.

Governor Hicks at that time was willing to abide by any terms of settlement that would save a conflict between the sections.

He favoured the compromise proposed by the border States committee, that slavery should not be forbidden, either by Federal or territorial legislation, south of 36° 30', and he was strongly inclined to base his action on the acceptance or rejection of the Crittenden resolutions by Congress.

On the 19th of January, 1861, he urged Miss Carroll to exert whatever influence she was able to induce Congress to adopt some measure of pacification; but she was soon satisfied that no compromise that Congress would adopt would be accepted by the cotton States, and, perceiving the danger should the governor commit himself to any impossible condition, informed him on the 24th of January that the Crittenden proposition would by no possibility receive the sanction of Congress.

All efforts to move the steadfastness of the governor having failed, the President of the Senate and Speaker of the House of Delegates issued their call to the people to act independently of him and elect delegates to a convention. This was a most daring and dangerous proceeding, and had the plan succeeded and a convention assembled they would immediately have deposed the governor and passed an ordinance of secession. The governor was powerless in such an emergency to defend the State against the revolutionary body, as the State militia were on their side and Mr. Buchanan had declared that the National Government could not coerce a sovereign State.

The gravity of the situation was appreciated by the governor and the friends of the Union. Miss Carroll addressed articles through the press and wrote many letters to prepare the public mind in Maryland for the struggle. Fortunately, the people (thus warned) failed to endorse this call; consequently, the leading statesmen of the disunion party abandoned their cherished expectation of inaugurating their government in the National Capitol.

Many of the conspirators, however, still sought to seize Washington and forcibly prevent the inauguration of the President elect on the 4th of March. The military organisations of the South were deemed sufficient for the enter prise, and a leader trained in the wars of Texas was solicited to lead them. The more sagacious of their party, however, discountenanced the mad scheme. They assured Miss Carroll that no attempt would be made to seize the Capitol and prevent the inauguration of

Mr. Lincoln, so long as Maryland remained in the Union.

The ruthless assault upon the Massachusetts troops in Baltimore, as they were passing through on their way to Washington, on the 19th of April, with the antecedent and attendant circumstances, roused to the highest degree the passions of all who sympathized with the secession movement, and the mob became for the time being the controlling force of that city. So largely in the ascendant was it and so confident were the disunionists in consequence that they, without warrant of law, assumed the responsibility of issuing a call for the Legislature of Maryland to convene in Baltimore. Governor Hicks, fearing that the Legislature would respond to the call, and that if it did it would yield to the predominant spirit, give voice to the purpose of the mob, and adopt an act of secession, resolved to forestall such action by convening that body to meet at Frederick City, away from the violent and men acing demonstrations of Baltimore.

The Legislature thus assembled contained a number of leading members who were ready at once for unconditional secession. There were also others who, with them, would constitute a majority and would vote for the measure could they be sustained by public sentiment, but who were not prepared to give that support without that assurance. The field of conflict was, therefore, transferred from the halls of legislation to the State at large, and to the homes of their constituents, and there the battle raged during the summer of 1861. In that conflict of ideas Miss Carroll bore an earnest and prominent part, and the most distinguished men have given repeated evidence that her labours were largely instrumental in thwarting the secessionists and saving Maryland to the Union.

The objective point of the labours of the disunion leaders was a formal act of secession, by which Maryland would become an integral portion of the Confederacy, not only affording moral and material aid to the Southern cause, but relieving the rebel armies in crossing the Potomac from the charge, which at that stage of the conflict the leaders were anxious to avoid, of ignoring their vaunted doctrine of State rights by invading the territory of sovereign States. With the usual arguments that were urged to fire the Southern heart and to reconcile the people to the extreme remedy of revolution, special prominence was given to what was stigmatised as the arbitrary and unconstitutional acts of President Lincoln. To place the people in possession of the true theory of their institutions and to define and defend the war powers of the Government were the special purposes of Miss Carroll's labours during these eventful months.

It would not be possible in the compass of this paper to set forth circumstantially all the important questions that arose in the progress of the war, in the discussion of which Miss Carroll took part; but it is proper to say that on every material issue, from the inception of the rebellion to the final reconstruction of the seceded States, she contributed through the newspapers, in pamphlet form, and by private correspondence to the discussion of important subjects. Governor Hicks bore the brunt of this terrible conflict, greatly aided by Miss Carroll's public and private support, and stimulated by such inspiring letters as the following:

Washington House,
Washington City, Jan. 16, 1861.

My Dear Governor:

I have for some days intended to write and express my cordial admiration and gratitude for the noble stand you have now taken in behalf of the Union by the public address issued on the 3rd instant. An extended relation with the leading presses of the country has enabled me in a public and more efficient manner to testify to this and create a public opinion favourable to your course of patriotic action throughout the land. Many of the articles you have seen emanated from this source.

I feel it will be a gratification to you, in the high and sacred responsibilities which surround your position, to know from one who is incapable of flattering or deceiving you the opinion privately held in this metropolis concerning your whole course since the secession movement in the South was practically initiated.

With all the friends of the Union with whom I converse, without regard to section or party, your course elicits the most unbounded applause. I might add to this the evidences furnished from private correspondence, but you doubtless feel already the sympathy and moral support to be derived in this way. I am often asked if I think you *can* continue to stand firm under the frightful pressure brought to bear upon you. I answer, *yes*; that my personal knowledge enables me to express the confident belief that nothing will ever induce you to surrender while the oath to support the Constitution of your country and the vow to fulfil the obligations of your God rest upon your soul.

As a daughter of Maryland, I am proud to have her destiny in the hands of one so worthy of her ancient great name; one who will never betray the sacred trust imposed upon him. "*When God is for us, no man can be against us,*" is the Christian's courage when the day of trial comes.

I shall continue to fight your battle to the end.

Your sincere friend,

A. E. Carroll.

Well might Governor Hicks say to her again and again, as in a letter to her in 1863:

> Your moral and material support I shall never forget in that trying ordeal, such as no other man in this country ever went through.

A little further on, Governor Hicks writes as follows:

Annapolis, MD., December 17, 1861.

My Dear Miss Carroll:

In the hurry and excitement incident to closing my official relations to the State of Maryland I cannot find fitting words to express my high sense of gratitude to you for the kind and feeling manner in which you express your approval of my whole term of service in doing all in my power to uphold the honour and dignity of the State; but especially do I thank you for the personal aid you rendered me in the last part of my arduous duties.

When all was dark and dreadful for Maryland's future, when the waves of secession were beating furiously upon your frail executive, borne down with private as well as public grief, you stood nobly by and watched the storm and skilfully helped to work the ship, until, thank God, helmsmen and crew were safe in port.

★★★★★★

With great regard, I have the honour to be ever your obedient friend and servant.

T. H. Hicks.

Thus, it was that, supported by Miss Carroll, this high-minded and sorely tried man held fast to the end. He went into the struggle a rich man, in a position of worldly honour and prosperity. He came out of it reduced in prosperity, having, like other faithful Southern Unionists, lost his worldly possessions in that great upheaval. Thenceforth he lived, and he died, comparatively a poor man, but one of the noble and faithful who had acted an immortal part in the salvation of his country. All honour to brave and true-hearted Governor Hicks of Mary land!

Thus, by her powerful advocacy and influence Miss Carroll largely contributed to securing the State of Maryland to the Union and saving the National Capital, and her writings also had a great effect upon the border States, Besides her numerous letters and newspaper articles, she began writing and publishing, at her own expense, a remarkable series of war pamphlets, which speedily became an important element in the guidance of the country.

Senator John C. Breckenridge, in the July Congress of 1861, made a notable secession speech. Miss Carroll replied to this in a pamphlet containing such clear and powerful arguments that the War Department circulated a large edition, and requested her to write on other important points then being discussed with great diversity of opinion.

The following letters give some indication of the timely nature and value of the Breckenridge pamphlet:

My Dear Miss Carroll:
Your refutation of the sophistries of Senator Breckenridge's speech is full and conclusive. I trust this reply may have an extended circulation at the present time, as I am sure its perusal by the people will do much to aid the cause of the Constitution and the Union.

Caleb B. Smith.

(Caleb B. Smith was Secretary of Interior in Mr. Lincoln's Cabinet and an old friend of Miss Carroll).

Globe Office, Aug. 8, 1861.

Dear Miss Carroll:
Allow me to thank you for the privilege of reading your admirable review of Mr. Breckenridge's speech. I have enjoyed it greatly. Especially have I been struck with its very ingenious and just exposition of the constitutional law bearing on the President, assailed by Mr. B., and with the very apt citation

of Mr. Jefferson's opinion as to the necessity and propriety of disregarding mere legal punctilio when the source of all is in danger of destruction. The gradual development of the plot in the South to over throw the Union is also exceedingly well depicted and with remarkable clearness. If spoken in the Senate your article would have been regarded by the country as a complete and masterly refutation of Mr. B.'s heresies. Though the peculiar position of the *Globe* might preclude the publication of the review, I am glad that it has not been denied to the editor of the *Globe* to enjoy what the *Globe* itself has not been privileged to contain.

I remain, with great respect, your obedient servant,

Sam'l T. Williams.

(Samuel T. Williams was at that time chief editor of the *Globe,* the Congressional Record of the day, and son-in-law of Mr. Rives, the owner of the *Globe.*)

September 21, 1861.

Dear Miss Carroll:

I have this moment, 11 o clock Saturday night, finished reading your most admirable reply to the speech of Mr. Breckenridge; and now, my dear lady, I have only time to thank you for taking the trouble to embody for the use of others so much sound constitutional doctrine and so many valuable historic facts in a form so compact and manage able. The President received a copy left for him and requested me to thank you cordially for your able support.

The delay was not voluntary on my part. For some time past my time and mind have been painfully engrossed by very urgent public duties, and my best affections stirred by the present condition of Missouri, my own neglected and almost ruined State; and this is the reason why I have been so long deprived of the pleasure and instruction of perusing your excellent pamphlet.

I remain, with great respect and regard, your friend and obedient servant,

Edward Bates.

(Edward Bates was the Attorney General of Mr. Lincoln's Cabinet and an intimate friend of Miss Carroll.)

Appleby, Sept. 22, 1861.

My Dear Miss Carroll:

I will thank you very much if you will send me a couple of hundred copies of your reply to Breckenridge, with bill of expenses for the same. I do not think it is right that you should furnish your publications *gratis* any longer. I told our friends in Baltimore last week that the Union State Committee must go to work and send your documents over the entire State if they expect to carry this election. Mr. Mayer and Mr. Fickey, of the committee, said they would make application to you immediately and pay for all you can supply.

No money can ever pay for what you have done for the State and the country in this terrible crisis, but I trust and believe the time will come when all will know the debt they owe you. With great respect, your friend and obedient servant,

Thos. H. Hicks.

Baltimore, Oct. 2, 1861.

Miss Carroll:

If you could let me have more of your last pamphlet in answer to Breckenridge, I could use them with great effect. I have distributed from my house on Camden Street all the committee could furnish me. I set my son at the door with paper and pencil, and five hundred men called for it in one day. These are the bone and sinew of the city, wanting to know which army to enter. Please send as many as you can spare. They go like hot cakes.

Yours very respectfully,

James Tilghman.

A. S. Diven, in the House of Representatives, January 22, 1862:

She signs herself Anna Ella Carroll. I commend her answer on the doctrine of the war power to those who have been following that phantom and misleading the people, and I recommend it to another individual, a friend of mine, who gave a most learned disquisition on the writ of *habeas corpus* and against the power of the President to imprison men. He will find that answered. I am not surprised at this. The French Revolution discovered great political minds in some of the French women, and I am happy to see a like development in our women.

51

Judge Diven subsequently addressed the following letter to Miss Carroll:

Washington, February 9, 1862.

I thank you for the note of the 6th. Your pamphlet I have read with satisfaction, as I had your former publication. I have no desire to appear complimentary, but can not forbear the expression of my admiration of your writings. There is a cogency in your argument that I have seldom met with. Such maturity of judicial learning with so comprehensive and concise a style of communication surprises me. Ladies have certainly seldom evinced ability as jurists—it may be because the profession was not their sphere—but you have satisfied me that at least one might have been a distinguished lawyer. Go on, madam, in aiding the cause to which you have devoted your talent; your country needs the labour of all her defenders. If the time will ever come when men will break away from passion and return to reason your labours will be appreciated; unless that time soon arrives, alas for this Republic; I have almost despaired of the wisdom of men. God's ways are mysterious, and my trust in Him is left me as a ground of hope.

I have the honour to be, madam, your obedient servant,

A. S. Diven.

(A. S. Diven was Member of Congress from New York, a railroad man, and, I think, is still living, as at 1894).

Baltimore, May 9, 1874.

Miss Carroll:

After the Presidential election in 1860 a Union Association was formed in Baltimore and I was elected chairman, which position I held until the Union party was formed in Maryland in 1861, when Brantz Mayer was made chairman and I was appointed treasurer, and held the position until 1863. We commenced at once to circulate your publications and sent them broadcast over the entire State.

When we appealed to you, you furnished them most liberally, and to our surprise and the relief of our treasury you informed us you made no charge.

All were disposed to give your articles a careful perusal, and many instances came to my knowledge of the great positive good they effected in keeping men within the Union party when the first blow of secession had been struck.

Fred. Fickey, JR.

May 15, 1862.

I have never read an abler or more conclusive paper than your war-power document in all my reading. . . . .

Richard S. Coxe.

(Richard S. Coxe was a very eminent lawyer from the District of Columbia).

Washington, May 22, 1862.

I most cheerfully indorse the papers respecting your publications under the authority of the War Department. Mr. Richard S. Coxe, I can say, is one of the ablest lawyers in this District or in the country. In his opinion of your writings I entirely concur as with other men who have expressed one. I regret that I am without the influence to serve you at the War Department, but Mr. Lincoln, with whom I have conversed, has, I know, the highest appreciation of your services in this connection. Judge Collamer, whom I regard as among the first of living statesmen and patriots, is enthusiastic in praise of your publications, and, indeed, I have heard but one opinion expressed by all the able men who have referred to them.

Sincerely yours,

R. J. Walker.

(R. J. Walker was long a Representative in Congress, Secretary of the Treasury under James K. Polk, and was acknowledged as the best financier of his day).

In September of 1861 Miss Carroll prepared a paper on "the Constitutional powers of the President to make arrests and to suspend the writ of *habeas corpus*." In December, 1861, she published a pamphlet entitled *The War Powers of the Government.*

This was followed by a paper entitled *The Relation of Revolted Citizens to the National Government.* This was written at the especial request of President Lincoln, approved by him, and adopted as the basis of his subsequent action.

Washington, January 25, 1861.

My Dear Miss Carroll:

I read the address of Governor Hicks, which gave me great

pleasure. I have been overwhelmed with work and anxiety for North Carolina. I franked all the papers you sent me. It is a great matter for the Union that you hold Maryland firm now. Go on in your great work. I wish you would say a word for S—— in some of your articles; he is doing us good, but needs encouragement.

I wish to talk with you on these matters as soon as I can find a moment.

Respectfully and sincerely your friend,

John A. Gilmer.

(John A. Gilmer was Member of Congress from North Carolina, but a Union man throughout the war).

Washington City, March 11, 1861.

My Dear Miss Carroll:

I will be pleased to see you tomorrow, any time convenient to yourself, after nine o clock. I am not seeing anyone just yet on the matter to which you refer, but, of course, will see *you*. You have my grateful thanks for the great and patriotic services you have rendered and are still rendering to the country in this crisis.

I have the honour to be your friend and servant,

S. P. Chase.

(Salmon P. Chase was U. S. Senator, Governor of Ohio, Secretary of the Treasury, and Chief Judge of the Supreme Court).

Washington City, April 15, 1862.

My Dear Lady:

I thank you for sending me the last number of your able essays in the New York *Times*. The President paid you a very handsome compliment in the Cabinet meeting yesterday, in reference to your usefulness to the country. He handed your views on colonisation and the proper point to initiate the colony, which he said he had requested of you, to Secretary Smith, and said you had given him a better insight into the whole question than any one beside, and you had, on his inquiry, suggested the Interior Department as proper to look after the matter, and advised the Secretary to get into communication with you. This was no more than your desert, but, coming from the President in Cabinet meeting, it was as gratifying to me to hear as it is now to communicate this to you.

With great regard, your obedient servant,

Edward Bates.

House of Representatives, May 13, 1862.

Miss Carroll:

I send a package by your servant which came here yesterday, I suppose, as I had the honour to frank some of your documents from here. If you will excuse my poor writing I will tell you what Mr. Lincoln said about you last night.

I was there with some seven or eight members of Congress and others, when a note and box came from you with products from Central America. He seemed much delighted and read your letter out to us and showed the contents of the box. He said, "This Anna Ella Carroll is the head of the Carroll race. When the history of this war is written, she will stand a good bit taller than ever old Charles Carroll did." I thought you might like to hear this.

Wm. Mitchell.

Washington, D. C., September 9, 1863.

My Dear Miss Carroll:

I have read with great pleasure the manuscript left with me. Like all that emanates from your pen, it is profound and able, and I concur with you that its publication would now be timely. As you requested, I forward the package to New York.

Very sincerely and respectfully your friend,

S. P. Chase.

The Hon. B. F. Wade (then President of the United States Senate) writes from Washington:

March 1, 1869.

Miss Carrll:

I cannot take leave of public life without expressing my deep sense of your services to the country during the whole period of our national troubles. Although the citizen of a State almost unanimously disloyal and deeply sympathising with secession, especially the wealthy and aristocratic class of the people, to which you belonged, yet, in the midst of such surroundings, you emancipated your own slaves at a great sacrifice of personal interest, and with your powerful pen defended the cause of the

Union and loyalty as ably and effectively as it ever has been defended.

From my position on the Committee on the Conduct of the War I know that some of the most successful expeditions of the war were suggested by you, among which I might instance the expedition up the Tennessee River.

The powerful support you gave Governor Hicks during the darkest hour of your State history prompted him to take and maintain the stand he did, and thereby saved your State from secession and consequent ruin.

All these things, as well as your unremitted labours in the cause of reconstruction, I doubt not are well known and remembered by the members of Congress at that period. I also well know in what high estimation your services were held by President Lincoln, and I cannot leave this subject without sincerely hoping that the government may yet confer on you some token of acknowledgment for all these services and sacrifices.

Very sincerely, your friend,

B. F. Wade.

Baltimore, September 28, 1869.

I have known Miss Carroll many years; she is a daughter of Governor Carroll, and by birth and education entitled to the highest consideration.

She writes exceedingly well, and during the late war published several pamphlets, etc., which I have no doubt proved most serviceable to the cause of the Union. Her own loyalty was ardent and constant through the struggle.

Reverdy Johnson.

(Reverdy Johnson a distinguished lawyer from Maryland, U. S. Senator, Attorney General in Taylor's Cabinet, and Minister to England during Johnson's Administration).

Dayton, Nov. 23, 1869.

My Dear Miss Carroll:

Your letter finds me in the midst of care, labour, and preparation for removal to Washington.

Pardon me, therefore, if I write briefly. You must see me when the session of Congress commences, that I may say much for which there is not space or time on paper. Nobody appreciates more highly than I do your patriotism and your valuable services with mind and pen through so many years.

Yours faithfully and truly,

Robert C. Schenck.

(Robert C. Schenck General through the war, Member of Congress, and Minister to England).

London, E. C., July 30, 1872.

Dear Miss Carroll:

I have read with pleasure the pamphlet you were so kind as to send me, and am glad to see that your claim is so strongly endorsed—so strongly that it can hardly be ignored by Congress.

Very truly yours,

H. McColloch.

(Hugh S. McCulloch was Secretary of the Treasury under Lincoln, Johnson, and Arthur.)

Washington City, January 20, 1873.

My Dear Miss Carroll:

I owe you an humble apology for not calling to pay my respects to you, as I intended to do; but I have been so occupied with numerous engagements that the purpose indicated escaped my recollection until I was on the point of leaving for my home in Connecticut, and can only now proffer to you my cordial and heartfelt wishes for your health, prosperity, and happiness.

I have too much respect for your name and character to address you in the accents of flattery, and I presume you will not suspect me of any such purpose when I say that of the many characters, both male and female, of whom I have formed a favourable opinion since I was introduced into public life, there is no one for whom I cherish a higher esteem than Miss Carroll, of Maryland.

May the richest of Heaven's blessings rest upon your ladyship, and may the inappreciable services which you rendered your country in the dark hour of its peril be recognised by your countrymen, and to a just extent rewarded.

I have the honour to be and to remain, my dear Miss Carroll, most faithfully and truly your friend,

Truman Smith.

Truman Smith was a Member of Congress from Connecticut for a long time.

Greensburg, Pa., May 3, 1873.

Miss Carroll:

I do remember well that Mr. Lincoln expressed himself in wonder and admiration at your papers on the proper course to be pursued in legislating for the crisis.

In this connection, I know that he considered your opinions sound and, coming from a lady, most remarkable for their knowledge of international law.

Edgar Cowan.

Edgar Cowan was U. S. Senator from Pennsylvania during the whole war.

Quincy, Illinois, Sept. 17, 1873.

Miss A. E. Carroll:

During the progress of the War of the Rebellion, from 1861 to 1865, I had frequent conversations with President Lincoln and Secretary Stanton in regard to the active and efficient part you had taken in behalf of the country, in all of which they expressed their admiration of and gratitude for the patriotic and valuable services you had rendered the cause of the Union and the hope that you would be adequately compensated by Congress. At this late day, I cannot recall the details of those conversations, but am sure that the salutary influence of your publications upon public opinion and your suggestions in connection with the important military movements were among the meritorious services which they recognised as entitled to remuneration.

In addition to the large debt of gratitude which the country owes you, I am sure you are entitled to generous pecuniary consideration, which I trust will not be withheld.

    With sentiments of high regard, I am,

        Your obedient servant,

O. H. Browning.

(O. H. Browning, of Illinois, was Senator during the war, in confidential relations with President Lincoln and Secretary Stanton).

Washington, D. C., May 13, 1874.

Miss A. E. Carroll:

I am gratified to have the opportunity of expressing my knowledge and appreciation of the valuable services rendered by you to the cause of the Union at the beginning of and during the late war. Being a Marylander and located officially in Baltimore in 1861, 1862, 1863, and 1864, I can speak confidently of the important aid contributed by you to the government in its struggle with the rebellion. I recollect very distinctly your literary labours, the powerful productions of your pen, which struck terror into the heart of the rebellion in Maryland and encouraged the hopes and stimulated the energies of the loyal sons of our gallant State.

Especially do I recall the eminent aid you gave to Governor Hicks, and the high esteem he placed upon your services. Indeed, I have reason to know he possessed no more efficient coadjutor, or one whose co-operation and important service he more justly appreciated. I can say with all sincerity I know of no one to whom the State of Maryland—I may say the country at large—is more indebted for singleness of purpose, earnestness, and effectiveness of effort in behalf of the government than to yourself.

A failure to recognise these services will indicate a reckless indifference to the cause of true and unfaltering patriotism, to which I cannot think a just government will prove ungrateful.

I am, dear Miss Carroll, always, most sincerely and truly yours,

Chris. C. Coxe.

(Christopher C. Coxe held many offices of trust throughout the war, was quite eminent as a poet and man of letters, and was pension agent at Baltimore).

Petersboro', N.Y., May, 1874.

Miss Anna Ella Carroll:

Surely nothing more can be needed than your pamphlet, entitled *Miss Carroll's Claim before Congress*, to insure the prompt and generous payment of it. Our country will be deeply dishonoured if you, its wise and faithful and grandly useful servant, shall be left unpaid.

Gerritt Smith.

(Gerritt Smith was a noted philanthropist, Member of Congress, one of the first so-called Abolitionists, and a man of immense wealth).

Washington, D. C., June 5, 1874.

Dear Miss Carroll:

I did not receive your polite note and the pamphlet in relation to your claim till this morning. The statement of your case is very strong, both as to the clear proof of "value received" from you by the government, and on which was founded its promise to pay, and as to the favourable opinions of your literary and military services expressed by leading men. I know of no instance in which a woman not born to sovereign sway has done so much to avert the impending ruin of her country, and that not by cheap valour, like Joan of Arc, but by rare mental ability. As a Marylander, I am proud that the "Old Maryland line" was so worthily represented by you in the struggle for the Union.

You would have had your substantial reward long ago but for the very absurd opinion that by some fixed, mysterious law of nature the labour done by women is worth less than precisely similar work done by men. You should persist in your just claim, if only to establish the principle that the value of work should be estimated according to its merits and not with reference to the worker; but, whatever may be the fate of your demand on the Government, you cannot fail to receive the thanks of the people.

Very respectfully,

Sam'l T. Williams.

Princess Anne, Md., August 22, 1874.

My Dear Miss Carroll:

I have read with interest and gratification the publication respecting your claim now pending before Congress.

I well remember that you were an earnest supporter of the Union in the hour of its trial, and that you did much by word and pen to encourage and sustain those who battled against the rebellion, and for such services you are entitled to high consideration and reward.

The proofs adduced are very full and direct. I don't see how its payment can be resisted without impeaching the evidence of Mr. Scott, the late Assistant Secretary of War, and of Judge Wade, Chairman of the Committee on the Conduct of War—an alternative which their official and personal characters forbid, even in cases where their personal interests were involved.

With, my best wishes, I have the honour to be very truly yours, &c.,

J. W. Crisfield.

(J. W. Crisfield was a Representative from Maryland during the war).

Cumberland, Md., August 25, 1874.

My Dear Miss Carroll:

You may feel assured that I read with exceeding interest everything from your pen and every reference in the press to yourself and interests. I have no doubt your contribution to the history of Maryland at the eventful crisis referred to will be a most valuable and interesting one.

H. W. Hoffman.

(Henry W. Hoffman was a Representative from Maryland, lawyer, and Member of the House of Representatives).

Lima, Peru, September 12, 1874.

My Dear Miss Carroll:

It affords me great pleasure to have an opportunity to testify to the valuable assistance rendered by yourself to the cause of the Union at the commencement and during the progress of the late war. Your private conversations and your publications in the newspapers and pamphlets all tended to inspire that ardent patriotism which a grave crisis in public affairs imperatively demanded.

Every Marylander who felt called upon to support the endangered Government of the United States must have been encouraged and cheered in the discharge of a painful duty by that earnest enthusiasm which was at that time displayed by yourself in support of the measures forced upon the government by the rebellion.

I am gratified to hear that you propose to publish a book that will do justice to the memory of the late Governor Hicks; and offering my best wishes for the success of your undertaking and for your personal health and happiness,

I am sincerely your friend,

Francis Thomas.

(Francis Thomas was a Member of Congress from Maryland, Governor of Maryland, and Minister to Peru under Grant).

Newark, Sept. 28, 1874.

Dear Miss Carroll:

I have carefully read your pamphlet, and I do not hesitate to say your claim is a strong one. You could not have a better witness than Colonel Scott, a man of the highest character. His testimony is clear and unequivocal, and if your claim is rejected I can attribute it to but one cause—you are a woman—a relic of barbarism against your sex; but still I believe you will succeed. I am satisfied that a large majority of the members of both Houses are fair-minded, honourable men, disposed to do what is right. I should be glad to meet you and talk with you about your proposed life of Governor Hicks. There are several matters I should be pleased to discuss with you.

Very truly your friend,

Wm H. Parnell,
President Delaware College.

Chestertown, Md., Oct. 9. 1874.

My friend Miss Carroll has two claims against the government growing out of services rendered to the country during the civil war—the one of a literary and the other of a military character. Miss Carroll is a daughter of the late Hon. Thomas King Carroll, one of the best men Maryland has ever produced.

George Vickers.

Princeton, October 13, 1874.

Miss Carroll:

I thank you for your letter of the 19th *ultimo* and for the two pamphlets that accompanied it, which I read with great interest. I think they clearly establish your claim on the gratitude of the country and on a suitable remuneration by Congress by proving that you rendered the government very important service during the crisis of the late war. As that service involved great labour and sacrifice on your part and saved the country a great amount of useless expenditure in men and money, justice as well as gratitude demands that it should be liberally rewarded. Hoping that those in authority will recognise the debt which the country owes you,

I am very respectfully yours,

Charles Hodge,
President of Theological Seminary.

Washington, D. C., December 16, 1874.

Dear Miss Carroll:

I have not the vanity to suppose that my commendation can add to the high estimate placed by all upon your services to the Union in the late war; but as you have done me the honour to ask a candid expression of my opinion I venture to say that any statesman or author of America might be justly proud of having written such papers as the able pamphlets produced by you in support of the government at that critical period.

As to your military services in planning the Tennessee campaign, you hold and have published too many proofs of the validity of your claim to require further confirmation.

I shall rejoice in your success in procuring a formal recognition of your labours if only it will aid in establishing the just rule that equal services, whether performed by man or woman, must always command equal recognition and reward.

As a Marylander, I am proud that in the war of the rebellion "the Old Maryland line" was so worthily represented by you.

Samuel T. Williams.

The letters of eminent men in admiration of Miss Carroll's papers, published and unpublished, would fill a volume. These are only a portion of those published by order of Congress.

Senator Jacob Howard, of the Military Commission appointed to inquire into Miss Carroll's services, in his report of the 42nd Congress, states:—

> She did more for the country than all the military generals. She showed where to fight and how to strike the rebellion on the head, possessing withal judicial learning so comprehensive and concise in its style of argument that the government gladly sat at her feet to learn the wisdom of its powers.

This allusion to military services leads us to a still more remarkable record of Miss Carroll's work.

BENJAMIN F. WADE.

CHAPTER 4

The Military Situation

Early in the fall of 1861 a gunboat fleet was under preparation to descend the Mississippi. It was a time of extreme peril, when the continuance of the Union depended on immediate military success. The Union Armies had met with repeated reverses. The Confederates were exultant and the European nations were expectant of the approaching downfall of the United States Government. France had already put forth her hand to control Mexico, and although in England the Union had warm friends who still hoped for its success, the general impression was that its defeat might be considered a foregone conclusion. Financial ruin also seemed inevitable. The Northern Army was costing the nation two million dollars a day. The Hon. Mr. Dawes, in a speech in Congress, had declared it "impossible for the United States to meet this state of things sixty days longer."

"An ignominious peace," he predicted, "was upon the country and at its very doors."

At that time, there was nothing in the attitude of the Union cause very strongly to appeal to English sympathy. It was openly set forth that the war was not waged for the extermination of slavery. Devotion to the Union could not excite especial interest in any but an American. On the contrary, the prevalent opinion in England was that the United States was a dangerous and rather unscrupulous power, and that it would be for the interests of humanity that it should be divided; consequently, the general sympathy was largely with the Confederates and the desires of the governing classes for their success openly avowed.

After the emancipation proclamation, it was different. The Union cause had thereafter the incalculable advantage of a well-defined moral position—a position always keenly felt by the English masses.

The desires of the governing class at that period and the dangers of the position from a military point of view are well indicated in extracts given by Miss Carroll in her successive memorials from the English journals and from diplomatic correspondence.

In an extract from the London *Times,* brought to the notice of the Senate by Mr. Howe, the command of the waters of the southwest is pointed out as the essential matter, and it is stated by Mr. Grimes that "the British Government has sent over into all the British colonies of North America some thirty thousand men."

London *Times,* September 27 1861.
Whatever may be the assertions of the Northerners, they must look upon the permanent separation of the Southern States and the formation of a second republic as at least highly probable, and in the action of England and France toward Mexico Mr. Lincoln, perhaps, only sees an intervention in the affairs of a country which is soon to be divided from his own by the territory of a rival. . . . . It is said the three European powers have taken advantage of the dissensions of the American Union to carry out plans upon a violation of the Monroe doctrine.

London *Shipping Gazette,* February 1 1862.
A semi-official note is sent by Napoleon to the British Government respecting the blockade, to the effect that the emperor cannot longer allow French commerce to be injured.

Diplomatic Correspondence—Clay to Seward.
Jan. 24, 1862.
Prince Gortchakoff expresses his fears should any reverse happen to us that England would at once make common cause with the South, acknowledge her independence, and finally break down the power of the Republic. I must confess I very much fear England's influence. My first impression is not weakened, but rather strengthened. Nothing but great and decisive success will save us from foreign war. I would prepare for war with England as an essential means to prevent the independence of the South before the first of April.

★★★★★★

Note:—Cassius M. Clay, Minister to St. Petersburg during the Civil War, has been from first to fast one of Miss Carroll's warm supporters. He says, "Be that as it may, your case stands out unique, for you towered above all our generals in military genius, and it would be a shame upon our country if you were not honoured with the gratitude of all and solid pecuniary reward." (See batch of memorials.)

★★★★★

Seward to Dayton.

Jan. 27, 1862.

. . . . You see our army and our fleet are at Cairo. You see another army and another fleet are behind Columbus, which alone is relied upon to close the Mississippi against us on the north. Though you may not see it, another army and another fleet are actually on their way to New Orleans.

At this time of intense anxiety, it was suggested to Miss Carroll by the War Department that she should go West and endeavour to form an opinion as to the probable result of the proposed descent of the Mississippi by the gunboats, upon the success of which the continuance of the Union depended. Accordingly, she went to St. Louis, and remaining for a month or more at the Everett House, in that city, by means of maps and charts procured from the Mercantile Library she made careful study of the topography of the proposed line of advance. She became convinced that this intended expedition would result in disaster, and that the Tennessee River, not the Mississippi, would be the true pathway to success.

Again, we will turn to Miss Carroll's able account in the Congressional Records of the military position at that time:—

It became evident, in the autumn of 1861, that if the unity of the United States could be maintained by military force, the decisive blow upon the Confederate power must be delivered within sixty or ninety days. To that period the tide of battle had been steadily against the Union, and the military operations had not met the expectations of the country. Nothing is more certain than that this rebel power was able to resist all the power of the Union upon any of the lines of operation known to the Administration; for operating on any safe base, on any of these known lines, the Union Armies were not numerically strong enough to reach the vital point in the Confederate power.

The enemy were in strong force on a line extending from the Potomac, westward through Bowling Green, to Columbus, on the Mississippi, and was complete master of all the territory to the Gulf. Kentucky and Missouri had been admitted formally into the Confederacy, and they had resolved to move the Capital to Nashville and extend their battle lines to the northern limits of those States, and the Secretary of War, after a tour of inspection, reported that these States had not sufficient force to hold them to the Union.

The war had then been waged seven months, and between 700,000 and 800,000 men had been mustered in the field; the public debt aggregated over $500,000,000; and the daily average expenses of maintaining the army was upward of $2.000,000, besides the hundreds of precious lives which were being daily sacrificed.

Thus, while the two armies were confronting each other in sight of Washington, events were rapidly pressing in the Southwest which, if unchecked, would change the destiny of the American people for ages to come.

Thus, in that ominous silence which preceded the shock and storm, the two sections stood, each watching and awaiting the movements of the other. Both were confident; the South greatly strengthened from her successes and impregnable position; the North strong in its large excess of numbers, wealth, and the justice of its cause.

The Army of the Potomac and the Army of the West were the two expeditions on which the Administration relied.

All others were auxiliary to these great movements. The first named, though seeming to the country of such signal moment, occupied a position of comparative insignificance when contrasted with the army of the Southwest, and had chance thrown Richmond under national control at an earlier day it could not have materially affected the destiny of the war. Capitals in an insurgent and unrecognised power can have but very little strategic value, and from the geographical position of Richmond it had none at all, and they were ready to move it any day.

They could have surrendered all the Atlantic States to Florida and yet maintained their independence; indeed, it was upon this theory that the disunion party had ever based its expectations of separate and independent nationality. Could the Confederates have held their power over the Mississippi Valley but a few more months they would have so connected themselves with France through Texas and with England through the States of the great northwest as not only to have made good their own independence but to have dwarfed the United States to the area of their old thirteen and taken the lead as the controlling political power on this continent.

With the Mississippi in their possession to the mouth of the Ohio, the presence of the English and French fleets at New Orleans would have brought about that result.

The Army of the Potomac, after having been put upon a scale of the rarest magnificence consistent with mobility, and with several changes of commanders, took three years and a half to reach Richmond, and was not then halfway to a decisive point, and never would have been strong enough had the expedition to open the Mississippi been executed on the plan as originally devised.

Strategically an invasion always leads to deep lines of operations which, on account of the difficulty of maintaining communications with its base, are always dangerous in a hostile country, and every mile the national armies advanced, every victory they gained, carried them farther from their base, and required an increase of force to protect their communications; while every retreat of the enemy brought him nearer to his resources, and it is mathematically certain that he would soon have reached the point on that line where he would have been the superior power. Nothing but the results of the Tennessee campaign prevented Lee from recruiting his army and extorted from him his sword at Appomattox Court-House.

The Mississippi expedition was designed by the aid of the one from the Gulf to clear the river to the mouth, etc. Could it succeed? Could it open the Mississippi to its mouth? These momentous questions and the military delay were weakening the confidence of the people and confirming foreign powers in the belief that the government had neither the strength nor the ability to conquer the rebellion. And even could the expedition have opened the river, was there any point on that river where a decisive blow could have been dealt the Confederacy?

The Memphis and Charleston railroad, the only complete interior line of communication, would not necessarily have been touched. So long as the Confederacy could maintain its interior lines of communication complete, the United States could neither destroy its armies in the east nor open the Mississippi River. The National Government could only escape annihilation by reaching the centre of the Confederate power and striking a fatal blow upon its resources. Geographically, there was but one mode of attack by which this could be accomplished, and this was unthought of or unknown to all connected with the prosecution of the war.

Mr. Lincoln saw from the beginning the vital importance of regaining the Mississippi and controlling the resources of its great valley, and therefore reserved to himself the direction of this expedition as commander-in-chief. He was fully alive to the perils that now environed the Government, and he and his advisers looked imploringly to the army for relief as the agency absolutely essential to the nation's life. This and this only could strike the blow that must then be struck, if ever.

No display of military genius could have extorted from Lee his sword so long as his resources were un wasted. No valour on the part of our navies and armies could have opened the Mississippi so long as the Confederates could keep open the lines of communication.

The Memphis and Charleston railroad was their only complete bond of connection between their armies of the east and the armies of the Mississippi Valley. There was but one avenue by which this bond could be reached and effectually severed, and that was the Tennessee River. The people had responded grandly; their uprising in behalf of their endangered government had astonished the world. It now remained for the army to supplement by its valour in the field what the administration and the people had done at home.

Never was the stress and strain of a nation more severe; never when another defeat would have been so perilous and a victory so desirable as then. So long as the Confederates were undisturbed in the possession of the southwest, and men and munitions of war sent uninterruptedly to the east, the Army of the Potomac could not advance. Something had to be done to cripple or engage the rebel armies in that section.

As the weary months of October and November wore away, the darkness grew more and more intense and the anxiety more oppressive. A blow had to be inflicted quickly that would be sharp and mortal, to ward off intervention and invasion by European powers, to smother the spirit of secession in southern Illinois and Indiana, and to prevent financial bankruptcy, which of itself must destroy the nation.

And yet neither Mr. Lincoln nor his generals knew or had in mind any plan other than that of forcing a passage down the Mississippi, bristling with batteries that frowned from its bluffs, while swamps and bayous skirted and pierced its banks, affording defences in the rear little less formidable and forbidding.

And thus, the nation stood as in the hush that precedes the storm or the crash of battle, apprehending not so much any particular movement of the Confederate Armies as the threatening elements generally with which the air seemed surcharged, and knowing not how or when or where the blow would fall. Military success was of all things most desired; military delay of all things most dreaded. With the South to standstill was their strength; time was power, and every day's delay increased the thickening dangers that were closing around the Union cause. With the North, not to advance was to recede; not to destroy was to be destroyed.

The exigencies of the situation made it imperative that the decisive blow should be struck thus early in the war. How to make that advance and deliver that fatal blow was the great problem to be solved. Omniscience only was then able to know whether the last sun had set to rise no more on the Union of these States. The country was clamorous for military successes, but not half so troubled as was Mr. Lincoln and his advisers, for the people did not know, as they did, how much depended thereon; how the beam trembled in the balance and what irremediable evils were involved in delay.

Congress met; the Committee on the Conduct of the War was at once created. How great were the dangers which at that supreme moment made the continued existence of the Government a question of doubt, and the fact that the military successes in the West which followed were not achieved a day too soon is made evident by the speeches of many of the most distinguished statesmen of that period, in both houses of Congress, some of them occupying positions on the most important committees connected with the prosecution of the war and necessarily possessed of the most reliable information. The utterances in the halls of Congress sustain every fact as here described.

In this same Congressional document of 1878 Miss Carroll thus describes her inception of the plan of the Tennessee campaign:—

In the autumn of 1861 my attention was arrested by the confidence expressed by Southern sympathizers in the southwest, that the Mississippi could not be opened before the recognition of Southern independence. I determined to inform myself what the pilots thought of the gunboat expedition then preparing to descend the river. On inquiry, I was directed to Mrs. Scott, then in the hotel, whose husband was a pilot, and learned from her that he was then with the expedition that had moved against Belmont; and the important facts she gave me increased my wish to see Mr. Scott. On his arrival in St. Louis I sent for him. He said that it was his opinion, and that of all the pilots on these waters, that the Mississippi could not be opened by the gunboats.

I inquired as to the navigability of the Cumberland and the Tennessee. He said at favourable stages of water the gunboats could go up the former as high Nashville, and the latter, at all stages, as high as the Muscle Shoals in Alabama. The moment he said the Tennessee was navigable for gun boats the thought flashed upon me that the strongholds of the enemy might be turned at once by diverting the expedition in course of preparation to open the Mississippi up the Tennessee; and having had frequent conversations with Judge Evans on the military situation, I left the room to communicate this thought—as he had just then called at the hotel—and asked him if it would not have that effect. He concurred that it would, and that it was the move if it was a fact that the Tennessee afforded the navigation; and he accompanied me to interrogate Mr. Scott, to be satisfied as to the feasibility of the Tennessee. The interview was prolonged some time.

At the close I told Mr. Scott it was my purpose to try and induce the government to divert the Mississippi expedition up the Tennessee, and asked him to give me a memorandum of the most important facts elicited in the conversation, as I wished them for this object. I further stated my intention to pen the history of the war, and requested him to write from time to time all the valuable information he might be able, and I would remember him in my work. The same day I wrote again to As-

sistant Secretary of War Thomas A. Scott, to whom I had promised to communicate the result of my observations while in the
West, and also to Attorney General Bates; to both of whom I
urged the importance of a change of campaign.

★★★★★★

(Note:—Thomas A. Scott was the great railroad magnate, was
Assistant Secretary of War when Stanton was Secretary, and was
sent by Stanton to inaugurate the Tennessee campaign which
saved the Union).

★★★★★★

A letter from Judge Evans, who chanced to be in St. Louis on other
business, at the time gives a precisely similar account of this interview
with the pilot, and the ideas then suggested by Miss Carroll uttered, as
he relates, "in a very earnest and animated manner!"

Even though it involves some repetition, we will here give also an
account written by Miss Carroll in the winter of 1889. It will possess an especial interest, as it may be the last literary exertion that the
invalid authoress will ever be asked to make.

It was called forth by a wish expressed by a leading magazine to
have a fresh account written directly by Miss Carroll. With fingers
lamed by paralysis the following account was written, showing the
clearness of Miss Carroll's memory in her seventy-fifth year.

In the beginning of the rebellion public opinion gave the victory to the Southern cause, and no one shared in this conviction to a greater extent than President Lincoln and the War
Department. The first effort made by me was in an unpreten-
tious pamphlet, which fell into the hands of Mr. Lincoln and so
pleased him (it did not appear with my name) that he suggested
its adoption as a war measure, and the satisfaction it gave was so
general that Governor Bates, then Attorney General, urged that
I should continue to write in the interest of the government.
Fired by enthusiasm in a noble cause, I accepted the suggestion,
and followed soon with what some have considered my best
work, *The War Powers of the Government*, and other pamphlets.
About this time, I had thought of visiting St. Louis, and mentioned my intention to Col. Thomas A. Scott, Assistant Secretary of War. He urged me to go, asking me to write him fully of
every point and fact investigated. These facts I communicated
as requested, both to him and to Governor Bates.

The clouds were dark and lowering. Despair had well-nigh possession of the bravest hearts. After my arrival, I soon saw and felt that the sentiment of the West was decidedly against the Union, or rather in favour of the Southern cause.

I visited the various encampments *en route* and in St. Louis and found but little difference among leading minds as to the result anticipated. All in a measure believed the struggle useless.

Finding the sentiment prevalent that the Union must fall and feeling in my soul that it *must not* fall, I began revolving an escape from the threatened doom. Just then, while I was in St. Louis, the Battle of Belmont was fought. When I saw the dead and dying as they lay upon that field and witnessed the sad sight of the ambulance wagons bearing the wounded to the hospitals, my heart sank within me. The future of the war with these awful scenes repeated was a picture not to be endured, and my anxiety as to the result grew still more intense.

In reflecting upon the dangers of the proposed expedition it came upon me, as by inspiration, that the sailors—the pilots— might offer some suggestion. I knew that the military leaders would never avail themselves of this humble source of information. I thought the pilots, of all others, should know the strategic points. Sending for the proprietor of the hotel where I was stopping, I asked him how I could get into contact with any of these men. He told me that the wife of a pilot named Scott was then in the house. I called on her at once and, finding her well informed, I questioned her as to the harbours, coast defences, etc. Mrs. Scott was just about to leave the city, but she promised to send her husband to me.

I could not wait for this chance, but wrote to him for the information I desired. He called upon me in response, and during our conversation he said it would be death to every man who attempted to go down the Mississippi." Yet no other route had been dreamed of. I then asked him, "What about the Cumberland and Tennessee Rivers;" whether they were fordable for gunboats? He replied, "Yes, the Tennessee especially. Of course, he did not at first know of any ulterior purpose in the questions which I was asking, other than the information of an ardent lover of our country. As he mentioned the Tennessee it flashed upon me with the certainty of conviction that I had seen my way to the salvation of my country.

I left the pilot and sent immediately for Judge Evans, of Texas, who was stopping at the same hotel. I was almost overcome with excitement and shall never forget the moment that I rushed to him exclaiming, "What do you think of diverting the army from the Mississippi to the Tennessee!"

★★★★★★

(Note:—Judge Evans himself, describing this eventful scene, said "that for a moment it seemed as if a halo of glory surrounded Miss Carroll, and that she looked like one transfigured." One hesitates in these matter-of-fact days to repeat such words as these, but as my reliable informant, to whom they were addressed, assures me that such were his words it seemed worthwhile to record them. In all times, it has seemed that the human countenance wholly possessed by a great idea could assume a radiance only to be described by the spectator by some such words as these, and the fact was so symbolised in ancient art. The human soul is no less potent in these days than in the times of old).

★★★★★★

I waited breathlessly for his reply. It came in measured tones. "It may be so. I had never thought of it."

That night I wrote to Governor Bates, who had planned the Mississippi gunboat scheme. He presented the letter at once to the Acting Secretary of War, Mr. Scott. They both opposed it at first as impracticable. I returned immediately to Washington, prepared a paper on that basis and took it to Mr. Scott, who was really Acting Secretary of War, General Cameron's time being largely consumed in Cabinet meetings. After reading my plan and hearing my verbal arguments, Mr. Scott's countenance brightened and he exclaimed, "Miss Carroll, I believe you have solved the question." He hurried at once, with the plan in his hands, to the White House and with much excitement gave it to the President. Mr. Lincoln read it with avidity, and when he had finished it Mr. Scott told me that he had never witnessed such delight as he evinced.

General McClellan was then in command. He opposed the plan, but Mr. Lincoln quietly gave the orders himself for a change of base as soon as possible. Up to that time no plan for the close of the struggle, except down the Mississippi, had ever occurred to the mind of any living man or woman, as far as known; but from that moment Mr. Lincoln thought of nothing else. He hastened to send Mr. Scott to investigate, and went himself at once to St. Louis to aid in putting the plan in motion. Just after the fall of Fort Henry I called at the War Dpartment and saw Mr. Tucker, then Assistant Secretary of War. He told me that Mr. Scott stated to him on leaving for the West, "This is Miss Carroll's plan, and if it succeeds the glory is hers."

General Wade, then chairman of the Committee on the Conduct of the War, was consulted in the matter. He recognised it at once as the right move and openly and boldly approved the plan. Every effort was made to hasten the completion of the gunboats. As soon as they were finished, which was not until February, action was commenced on the Tennessee line. Mr. Wade at the same time made it known to Hon. Wm. Pitt Fessenden, chairman of the Finance Committee in the Senate, that there was then a movement on foot, to be executed as soon as the gunboats, then building at St. Louis, were ready, which would satisfy the entire country and astound the world; and he so re assured the Senate that they calmly waited until the time arrived for the execution of the plan.

Colonel Thomas A. Scott was sent to the West to make all things ready and expedite the movement.

He gave his orders from one point to another, so that when General Halleck, who was then in military command, was notified by Mr. Lincoln that the whole force was to be moved from the Mississippi up the Tennessee River he stood ready for the movement. In February, 1862, the armies moved up the Tennessee, then to Fort Donelson, and then back up the Tennessee to Hamburgh, and two miles from there they fought the Battle of Pittsburgh Landing, as pointed out in my plan. Had the movement been strictly carried out from the foot of the Muscle Shoals, in Alabama, Vicksburgh could have been reduced, or Mobile, and the whole thing ended in the spring of 1862 as easily as in 1865, and with the same result. In a recent publication, General Sherman has admitted this fact.

At the fall of Fort Henry, the country was thoroughly aroused as it never had been before. It was clearly seen that the end was approaching. Richmond was then within reach through Tennessee. For this General McClellan had been waiting. Before this no power on earth could have captured Richmond, and no one knew this better than General McClellan. When the National armies had penetrated into the heart of the South, within two miles of the Memphis and Charleston railroad, the result was plain to every mind.

The old flag displayed in the presence of a million of slaves, who had before been necessarily on the side of their owners, made the fact doubly secure. All hearts were jubilant, and Roscoe Conkling then offered his celebrated resolutions in the House of Representatives to ascertain who it was that had designed these military movements so fruitful in great results; whether they came from Washington or elsewhere; by whom they were designed and what they were intended to accomplish. Judge Olin replied that if it was Mr. Conkling's design to find out who had done this work he could learn by inquiring at the War Department, for certainly the Secretary of War or the President must know all about it; but it was sufficient for the present to know that someone had designed these movements, and that the country was now in the enjoyment of the blessings that had resulted from them.

Hon. Thaddeus Stevens moved that the resolutions of Mr. Conkling, making inquiry, be referred to the Military Committee of the House. During the discussion, the plan was attributed to one person and another, but no satisfactory proof could be given on any side. I was present through it all and could at any moment have satisfied Congress and the world as to the authorship of the plan, but from prudential reasons I refrained from uttering a word. It was decided to refer the question to the Military Committee of the House, and there the matter slept.

It is worthwhile to pause for a moment in our narration to introduce upon the scene one of the most useful and remarkable men of the time, who became one of Miss Carroll's principal coadjutors; this was Senator Wade, of Ohio. He was successively justice of the peace, prosecuting attorney, State senator, judge of the circuit court, and United States Senator for three terms; he was also Acting Vice-President of the United States after Lincoln's death. If President Johnson's impeachment had been carried through he would have been the President for the rest of the term, and it was feared by his opponents that in that case he would have secured the Chicago nomination for the coming term, of which he was one of the candidates.

The first encounter of the Union Army, a crowd of raw, undisciplined recruits, under new and inexperienced officers, with the better prepared Confederate Army naturally resulted in a tremendous panic. Two carriages were present on the battlefield; one contained Senators Wade, Chandler, and Brown, Sergeant-at-arms of the Senate, and Major Eaton; in the other was Tom Brown, of Cleveland, Blake, Morris, and Riddle, of the House. Near the extemporised hospital, Ashley's Black Horse sweeping down on the recruits caused the panic. One of the gentlemen present thus described the scene. (The description can be met with in Coxe's *Three Decades* and in Riddle's *Life of Wade*, a work that should be more widely published.)

It seemed as if the very devils of panic and cowardice had seized every mortal officer, soldier, teamster, and citizen. No officer tried to rally a soldier or do anything but spring and run toward Centerville. There was never anything like it for causeless, sheer, absolute, absurd cowardice—or rather panic—on this miserable earth before. Off they went, one and all off—down the highway, across the fields, towards the woods, anywhere, everywhere, to escape. The further they ran the more frightened they grew, and though we moved as fast as we could the fugitives passed us by scores. To enable themselves better to run they threw away their blankets, knapsacks, canteens, and finally their muskets, cartridge-boxes—everything. We called to them; told them there was no danger; implored them to stand. We called them cowards; denounced them in the most offensive terms; pulled out our heavy revolvers, threatened to kill them—in vain. A cruel, crazy, hopeless panic possessed them and infected everybody, front and rear.

The two carriages were blocked up in the awful gorge of Cub's Run and were for a time separated. When they again met, Mr. Wade shouted, "Boys, we'll *stop* this damned runaway!"

They found a good position, where a high wall on one side and a dense impassable wood secured the other side. The eight gentlemen leaped from their carriages and put Mr. Wade in command. Mr. Wade, with his hat well back and his famous rifle in his hand, formed them across the pikes all armed with heavy revolvers and facing the onflowing torrent of runaways, who were ghastly sick with panic, and this little band, worthy of the heroes of Thermopylae, actually kept back the runaway army, so that:—

For the fourth of an hour not a man passed save McDowell's bearer of dispatches, and he only on production of his papers. The rushing, cowardly, half-armed, demented fugitives stopped, gathered, crowded, flowed back, hedged in by thick-growing cedars that a rabbit could scarcely penetrate. The position became serious. A revolver was discharged, shattering the arm of Major Eaton, from the hand of a mounted escaping teamster (who had cut loose from his wagon).

At that critical moment the heroic old Senator and his friends were relieved and probably saved by Colonel Crane and a part of the Second New York, hurrying toward the scene of the disaster, and then the party proceeded. Naturally the exploit of Mr. Wade in stopping a runaway army caused much talk at Washington and increased the great confidence and admiration with which he was a ready regarded. (A few days ago, the present writer was conversing with one of the survivors of the party and received from him a detailed account of this singular episode).

In consequence of this disaster and the following one at Ball's Bluff, it was evident that both soldiers and officers would have to be created, and that we were without a military commander competent to direct so vast a war. This led to the formation by Congress of a Committee for the Conduct of the War. It consisted of seven members, three from the Senate and four from the House; Wade, Chandler, and Andrew Johnson from the Senate; Julian, Covode, Gooch, and Odell from the House. (Johnson seems never to have acted.)

Nobody but Wade was thought of for chairman. Mr. Wade was absolutely fearless, physically and morally; absolutely regardless of self; absolutely devoted to his country. All parties agreed in boundless admiration and confidence in the heroic old Senator. It is said that Wade seldom missed a session of the committee. The most conscientious of known men; never ill; he never neglected a duty; failed of an engagement; was never waited for, and never failed to meet his foe, one or many.

The committee, by Mr. Wade, omitting Mr. Johnson's name, made their first report soon after the close of the 37th Congress, in April, 1863, which made three heavy volumes of over

2,000 printed pages.

Their second report was made May 22, 1865, a trifle more in bulk, six volumes in all. (Very valuable for future historians.)— *Life of Benjamin F. Wade* by A. G. Riddle.

President Lincoln, as commander-in-chief, with the assistance of this committee, thereafter directed the movements of the war, all the generals being subordinate and only enlightened step by step as to the accepted plan of campaign, great secrecy being, as Mr. Wade testifies, necessary or the plan would have been frustrated.

CHAPTER 5

Miss Carroll's Papers to the War Department

List of Miss Carroll's papers sent into the War Department in her own handwriting and signed with her name, originally on file at the War Department; all in the first division relating to the Tennessee campaign; sent on various occasions to the Capital to be examined by military committees, and printed by order of Congress in successive memorials and reports from 1870 to 1881.

The papers marked with a star are now on file at the War Department. With the permission of the Secretary of War, these were seen by me and carefully examined March 7th, 1891. They were sent by Robert Lincoln to the Court of Claims in 1885, and copies were put on file in the office of the attorney general, the original documents being returned to the War Department. One of these original documents at the War Department is now incomplete, but must have been in good order in 1885, as the copies then made are complete and in excellent condition. They were verified as true copies by the Secretary of War. These also were examined by me at the office of the attorney general March 23, 1891.

The absence of the other documents from the War Office is accounted for by the remark able testimony of Benjamin F. Wade and Samuel Hunt (keeper of the records), as given on page 30, 45th Congress, 2nd session, Misc. Doc. 58, both testifying that the papers were abstracted from the desk of the Secretary when the Military Committee were considering Miss Carroll's claim, in 1871. As Miss Carroll possessed the original draft of these letters, she quickly reproduced them.

The papers having been already examined by the Committee and by Mr. Hunt, the copies were accepted in place of the missing file and printed "by order of Congress," and thus guaranteed they became, to all intents and purposes, the same thing as the original documents; but apparently, they were not sent to the War Office, not being the original documents sent from there. On March 20, 1891, I examined the files of the 41st Congress, 2nd session, at the Secretary's office of the U. S. Senate, at the Capitol, and there I found Miss Carroll's first memorial, 1870, with the "plan of campaign" attached, just as described by Thomas A. Scott.

S. E. Blackwell.

First Division.

A paper usually designated as the "plan of campaign."

When given in at the War Office to Thomas A. Scott it was accompanied by a military map; the paper in Miss Carroll's own handwriting and signed with her name, the map unsigned.

1. November 30, 1862.
2. January 5, 1862.
3. March 26, 1862.
4. May 2, 1862.★
5. May 14, 1862.★
6. May 15, 1862.★
7. Following Monday, 1862.
8. September 9, 1862.★
9. October —, 1862.

The letter to Stanton is on file at the office of the Attorney General, certified as copied from the documents furnished by the War Department in 1885.

(The letter of October, 1862, was also accompanied by a military map, "approved and adopted by the Secretary of War and the President and immediately sent out to the proper military authority." See letter of B. F. Wade, page 24, Misc. Doc. 58, of Memorial, May 18, 1878.)

Second Division.

August 25, 1862.
January 31, 1863.
October 7, 1863.
January 11, 1864.
——— —, 1865.

A letter, on file from Robert Lincoln, states that the papers of the second division were returned to Miss Carroll, March 10, 1869.

Miss Carroll's first paper, addressed to the War Department, for a campaign on the Tennessee River and thence south, placed in the hands of Hon. Thomas A. Scott, Assistant Secretary of War, the 30th of November, 1861, with accompanying map, is as follows:—

> The civil and military authorities seem to be labouring under a great mistake in regard to the true key to the war in the southwest. *It is not the Mississippi, but the Tennessee River.* All the military preparations made in the West indicate that the Mississippi River is the point to which the authorities are directing their attention. On that river, many battles must be fought and heavy risks incurred before any impression can be made on the enemy, all of which could be avoided by using the Tennessee River. This river is navigable for middle-class boats to the foot of the Muscle Shoals, in Alabama, and is open to navigation all the year, while the distance is but two hundred and fifty miles, by the river, from Paducah, on the Ohio.
>
> The Tennessee offers many advantages over the Mississippi. We should avoid the almost impregnable batteries of the enemy, which cannot be taken without great danger and great risk of life to our forces, from the fact that our boats, if crippled, would fall a prey to the enemy by being swept by the current to him and away from the relief of our friends; but even should we succeed, still we will only have begun the war, for we shall then fight for the country from whence the enemy derives his supplies.
>
> Now an advance up the Tennessee River would avoid this danger, for *if our boats were crippled, they would drop back with the current and escape capture*; but a still greater advantage would be its tendency *to cut the enemy's lines in two by reaching the Memphis and Charleston railroad*, threatening Memphis, which lies one hundred miles due west, and no defensible point between; also, Nashville, only ninety miles northeast, and Florence and Tuscumbia, in North Alabama, forty miles east.
>
> A movement in this direction would do more to relieve our friends in Kentucky and inspire the loyal hearts in East Tennessee than the possession of the whole of the Mississippi River. If well executed *it would cause the evacuation of all these formidable fortifications* upon which the rebels ground their hopes for suc-

cess; and in the event of our fleet attacking Mobile, the presence of our troops in the northern part of Alabama *would be material aid to the fleet.*

Again, the aid our forces would receive from the loyal men in Tennessee would enable them soon to crush the last traitor in that region, and the separation of the two extremes would do more than one hundred battles for the Union cause.

The Tennessee River is crossed by the Memphis and Louisville railroad and the Memphis and Nashville railroad. At Hamburg, the river makes the big bend on the east, touching the northeast corner of Mississippi, entering the northwest corner of Alabama, forming an arc to the South, entering the State of Tennessee at the northeast corner of Alabama, and if it does not touch the northwest corner of Georgia comes very near it. It is but eight miles from Hamburg to the Memphis and Charleston railroad, which goes through Tuscumbia, only two miles from the river, which it crosses at Decatur, thirty miles above, intersecting with the Nashville and Chattanooga road at Stevenson. The Tennessee River has never less than three feet to Hamburg on the shoalest bar, and during the fall, winter, and spring months there is always water for the largest boats that are used on the Mississippi River.

It follows, from the above facts, that in making the Mississippi the key to the war in the West, or rather in overlooking the Tennessee River, the subject is not understood by the superiors in command.

Extracts from a second paper, January 5, 1862, giving additional particulars for the advance up the Tennessee:—

Having given you my views of the Tennessee River on my return from the West, showing that this river is the true strategical key to overcome the rebels in the southwest, I beg again to recur to the importance of its adoption. This river is never impeded by ice in the coldest winter, as the Mississippi and the Cumberland sometimes are. I ascertained, when in St. Louis, that the gunboats then fitting out could not retreat against the current of the western rivers, and so stated to you; besides, their principal guns are placed forward and will not be very efficient against an enemy below them. The fighting would have to be done by their stern guns—only two; or if they anchored by the stern they would lose the advantage of motion, which would prevent the enemy from getting their range. Our gunboats at anchor would be a target which the enemy will not be slow to improve and benefit thereby.

The Tennessee River, beginning at Paducah fifty miles above Cairo, after leaving the Ohio, runs across south-south east, rather than through Kentucky and Tennessee, until it reaches the Mississippi line directly west of Florence and Tuscumbia, which lie fifty miles east, and Memphis, one hundred and twenty-five miles west, with the Charleston and Memphis railroad eight miles from the river. There is no difficulty in reaching this point at any time of the year, and the water is known to be deeper than on the Ohio.

If you will look on the map of the Western States you will see in what a position Buckner would be placed by a strong advance up the Tennessee River. He would be obliged to back out of Kentucky, or, if he did not, our forces could take Nashville in his rear and compel him to lay down his arms.

Testimony of Thomas A. Scott, Assistant Secretary of War, to Hon. Jacob M. Howard, chairman of the Military Committee, to consider the claim presented by Miss Carroll in 1870:

Philadelphia, June 24, 1870.

On or about the 30th of November, 1861, Miss Carroll, as stated in her memorial, called on me, as the Assistant Secretary of War, and suggested the propriety of abandoning the expedition which was then preparing to descend the Mississippi, and to adopt instead the Tennessee River, and handed to me the plan of campaign, as appended to her memorial; which plan I submitted to the Secretary of War, and its general ideas were adopted. On my return from the southwest in 1862 I informed Miss Carroll, as she states in her memorial, that through the adoption of this plan the county had been saved millions, and that it entitled her to the kind consideration of Congress.

Thomas A. Scott.

To the Military Committee, appointed for that purpose in 1872: Hon. Jacob M. Howard, of the Military Committee of the United States Senate.

Again:

Philadelphia, May 1, 1872.

My Dear Sir:

I take pleasure in stating that the plan presented by Miss Carroll in November, 1861, for a campaign upon the Tennessee River and thence south, was submitted to the Secretary of War and President Lincoln, and after Secretary Stanton's appointment I was directed to go to the Western armies and arrange to increase their effective force as rapidly as possible. A part of the duty assigned me was the organisation and consolidation into regiments of all the troops then being recruited in Ohio, Indiana, Illinois, and Michigan, for the purpose of carrying through this campaign, then inaugurated. This work was vigorously prosecuted by the army, and as the valuable suggestions of Miss Carroll, made to the department some months before, were substantially carried out through the campaigns in that section, great success followed, and the country was largely benefited in the saving of time and expenditure.

I hope Congress will reward Miss Carroll liberally for her patriotic efforts and services.

Very truly yours,

Thomas A. Scott.

Letter from the Hon. Benjamin F. Wade, appended to the report of General Bragg, of the Military Committee, of March 3, 1881:—

Dear Miss Carroll

I had no part in getting up the Committee (on the Conduct of the War). The first intimation to me was that I had been made the head of it; but I never shirked a public duty, and at once went to work to do all that was possible to save the country. We went fully into the examination of the several plans for military operations then known to the government, and we saw plainly enough that the time it must take to execute any of them would make it fatal to the Union.

We were in the deepest despair, until just at this time Colonel Scott informed me that there was a plan already devised which, if executed with secrecy, would open the Tennessee and save the national cause. I went immediately to Mr. Lincoln and talked the whole matter over. He said he did not himself doubt that the plan was feasible, but said there was one difficulty in the way; that no military or naval man had any idea of such a movement, it being the work of a civilian, and none of them would believe it safe to make such an advance upon only a navigable river, with no protection but a gunboat fleet, and they would not want to take the risk. He said it was devised by Miss Carroll, and military men were extremely jealous of all outside interference.

I pleaded earnestly with him, for I found there were influences in his Cabinet then averse to his taking the responsibility, and wanting everything done in deference to the views of McClellan and Halleck. I said to Mr. Lincoln:

"You know we are now in the last extremity, and you have to choose between adopting and at once executing a plan which you believe to be the right one and save the country, or defer to the opinions of military men in command and lose the country."

He finally decided he would take the initiative; but there was Mr. Bates, who had suggested the gunboat fleet, and wanted to advance down the Mississippi, as originally designed; but after a little he came to see that no result could be achieved on that mode, of attack, and he united with us in favour of the change of expedition as you recommended.

After repeated talks with Mr. Stanton I was entirely convinced that, if placed at the head of the War Department, he would have your plan executed vigorously, as he fully believed it was the only means of safety, as I did. Mr. Lincoln, on my suggesting Stanton, asked me how the leading Republicans would take it; that Stanton was fresh from the Buchanan Cabinet, and many things were said of him.

★★★★★★

(Note:—Stanton had been the bitterest of Democrats. The Republicans then knew nothing certainly of his course in Buchanan's Cabinet. His appointment surprised the Senate. Wade knew and endorsed him there. That was sufficient.—*Riddle's Life of Wade.*)

★★★★★★

I insisted he was our man withal, and brought him and Lincoln into communication, and Lincoln was entirely satisfied. But so soon as it got out, the doubters came to the front. Senators and members called on me. I sent them to Stanton and told them to decide for themselves. The gunboats were then nearly ready for the Mississippi expedition, and Mr. Lincoln agreed, as soon as they were, to start the Tennessee movement. It was determined that as soon as Mr. Stanton came into the Department, then Colonel Scott should go out to the Western armies and make ready for the campaign in pursuance of your plan, as he has testified before committees. It was a great work to get the matter started; you have no idea of it. We almost fought for it.

If ever there was a righteous claim on earth, you have one. I have often been sorry that, knowing all this as I did then, I had not publicly declared you as the author; but we were fully alive to the importance of absolute secrecy. I trusted but few of our people; but to pacify the country I announced from the Senate that the armies were about to move, and inaction was no longer to be tolerated. Mr. Fessenden, head of the Finance Committee, who had been told of the proposed advance, also stated in the Senate that what would be achieved in a few more days would satisfy the country and astound the world.

As the expedition advanced, Mr. Lincoln, Mr. Stanton, and myself frequently alluded to your extraordinary sagacity and unselfish patriotism, but all agreed that you should be recognised for your most noble service and properly re warded for the same.

The last time I saw Mr. Stanton he was on his death bed; he was then most earnest in his desire to have you come before Congress, as I told you soon after, and said that if he lived he would see that justice was awarded you. This I have told you often since, and I believe the truth in this matter will finally prevail.

B. F. Wade.

Jefferson, Ohio, July 27, 1876.

My Dear Miss Carroll:

Yours of the 22nd is at hand and its contents noticed, but I cannot perceive, myself, that it is necessary for you to procure any further testimony to prove to all unprejudiced minds that you were the first to discover the importance of the Tennessee River in a military point of view, and was the first to discover that said river was navigable for heavy gun boats; and to ascertain these important facts you made a journey to that region, and with great labour and expense, by examination of pilots and others, and that with these facts you drew up a plan of campaign which you, I think, first exhibited to Colonel Scott, who was then Assistant Secretary of War, which was shown to the President and Mr. Stanton, which information and plan caused the immediate change of the campaign from the Mississippi to the Tennessee River, and this change, with all the immense advantages to the national cause, was solely due to your labour and sagacity.

I do not regard it as an impeachment of the military sagacity of the officers on either side that they had not seen all this before, but I suppose none of them knew or believed the Tennessee River to be navigable for such craft, for had the Confederate officers known all this it would have been easy for them to have so fortified its banks as to have made such an expedition impossible.

Now all the above facts are proved beyond doubt, unless the witnesses are impeached; but all should bear in mind that when the government had concluded to make this important change from the Mississippi to the Tennessee the utmost secrecy was absolutely necessary or the whole plan might have been frustrated by the enemy, and it was so kept that even members of Congress and Senators never could ascertain who was entitled to the honour of the plan, as can be seen by their endeavours to find out by consulting the *Congressional Globe*, etc. . . . . . . Where is Judge Evans and how is his health? I am anxious to hear from him, whom I regard as one of the best of men. Give him my best respects.

> Truly yours,
>
> B. F. Wade.

> Westminster Palace Hotel,
> London, November 29, 1875.

My Dear Miss Carroll:

I remember very well that you were the first to advise the campaign on the Tennessee River in November, 1861. This I have never heard doubted, and the great events which followed it demonstrated the value of your suggestions. This will be recognized by our government, sooner or later, I cannot doubt. On reaching home I hope to shake you by the hand once more.

> Sincerely your friend,
>
> Reverdy Johnson.

In the House, January 7, 1862.

Mr. Kelley: I think the condition of this Capital today invites war. It
is environed within a narrow circle of two hundred thousand men in
arms, and yet, sir, that short river which leads to the Capital of a great
and proud country, thus defended and encircled by patriot troops, is so
thoroughly blockaded by rebels that the government, though its army
has not an adequate supply of forage, cannot bring upon it a peck of
oats to feed a hungry horse. . . . Call it what you may, it is a sight at
which men may well wonder. We have six hundred thousand men in
the field. We have spent I know not how many millions of dollars, and
what have we done? What one evidence of determined war or military skill have we exhibited to foreign nations, or to our own people?
. . . We have been engaged in war for seven months. . . . . England does
respect power. . . . . Let her hear the shouts of a victorious army, and
England and the powers of the continent will pause with bated breath.

Sir, it was said yesterday the last days had come. My heart has
felt the last day of our dear country was rapidly approaching. Before
we have reached victory, we have reached bankruptcy. We are today
flooding the country with an irredeemable currency. In ninety days,
with the patriotism of the people paralyzed by the inaction of our
great army, the funded debt of the country will depreciate with a ra-
pidity that will startle us.

In ninety days more the nations of the world will, I fear, be justified
in saying to us, "You have no more right to shut up the cotton fields
of the world by a vain and fruitless effort to reconquer the territory
now in rebellion than China or Japan has to wall themselves in," and
in the eyes of international law, in the eyes of the world, and, I fear,
in the eyes of impartial history, they will be justified in breaking our
blockade and giving to the rebels means and munitions of war. . . . But,
sir, in less than ninety days, to come back to the point of time, we shall
be advancing in the month of April, when Northern men will begin
to feel the effects of heat in the neighbourhood of Ship Island and the
mouth of the Mississippi.

Looking at the period of ninety days, I say it is not a double but a
triple edged sword approaching, perhaps, the single thread of destiny
upon which the welfare of our country hangs. Bankruptcy and mias-
matic pestilence are sure to come within the lapse of that period, and
foreign war may add its horror to theirs.

Mr. Wright: We are gasping for life. This great government is upon the brink of a volcano, which is heaving to and fro, and we are not certain whether we exist or no.

Mr. F.A. Conkling: In this crisis of our history, when the very existence of the Republic is threatened, when in all human probability the next thirty days will decide for ever whether the Union is to maintain its place among the powers of the earth or whether it is to go down and constitutional liberty is to perish. . . . .

In the House, January 20, 1862.
Mr. Wright: There is one great abiding and powerful issue today, and that is the issue whether the country and the Constitution shall be saved or whether it shall be utterly and entirely annihilated. With Pennsylvania, it is a question of national existence, of life or death. . .
. . . The great heart of Pennsylvania is beating today for the cause of the Union. . . . . It is to decide the great question whether the liberty which has been handed down to us by our fathers shall be permitted to remain in the land, or whether chaos or desolation shall blot out the country and government forever.

In the Senate, January 22, 1862.
Mr. Wade: But, sir, though the war lies dormant, still there is war, and it is not intended that it shall stay in this quiescent state much longer. The committee to which I belong are determined . . . . . that it shall move with energy. If the Congress will not give us, or give themselves, power to act with efficiency in war, we must confide everything to the Executive Government and let them usurp everything. If you would not fix your machinery so that you might advise with me and act with me. . . . I would act independent of you, and you might call it what you please. This is for the suppression of the rebellion, and the measures that we are to sit in secrecy upon look to that end and none other. No measure rises in importance above that connected with the suppression of the rebellion. . . . . . We stand here for the people and we act for them. . . . . . There is no danger to be apprehended from any secrecy which, in the consideration of war measures, we may deem it proper to adopt. It is proper for us, as it is for the general in the field, as it is for your Cabinet ministers, to discuss matters in secret when they pertain to war.

In the House, January 22, 1862.
Mr. Thaddeus Stevens: . . . . Remember that every day's delay costs

the nation $1,500,000 and hundreds of lives. . . . . What an awful responsibility rests upon those in authority; their mistakes may bring mourning to the land and sorrow to many a fireside. . . . . . . If we cannot save our honour, save at least the lives and the treasure of the nation.

About this time Miss Carroll was spoken of by those conversant with her plans as "the great unrecognised member of Lincoln's Cabinet." But, glorious as was the success, Miss Carroll's plans were not fully carried out, to the great after regret of the War Department, who recognised that the war, which might then have been brought to a speedy termination, had been greatly prolonged through the omission.

Miss Carroll continued her communications to the War Department, endeavouring to rectify mistakes.

Extract from Miss Carroll's letter to the Department on the reduction of Island No. 10, and pointing out the advantages of the immediate seizure of the Memphis and Charleston railroad, March 26, 1862.

The failure to take Island No. 10, which thus far occasions much disappointment to the country, excites no surprise in me. When I looked at the gunboats at St. Louis and was informed as to their power, and considered that the current of the Mississippi at full tide runs at the rate of five miles per hour, which is very near the speed of our gun boats, I could not resist the conclusion that they were not well fitted to the taking of batteries on the Mississippi River if assisted by gunboats perhaps equal to our own. Hence it was that I wrote Colonel Scott from there that the Tennessee was our strategic point, and the successes at Fort Henry and Donelson established the justice of these observations.

Had our victorious army, after the fall of Fort Henry, immediately pushed up the Tennessee River and taken a position on the Memphis and Charleston railroad, between Corinth, Mississippi, and Decatur, Alabama, which might easily have been done at that time with a small force, every rebel soldier in Western Kentucky and Tennessee would have fled from every position to the south of that railroad; and had Buell pursued the enemy in his retreat from Nashville, without delay, into a commanding position in North Alabama, on the railroad between Chattanooga and Decatur, the rebel government at Richmond would have necessarily been obliged to retreat to the cotton

States. I am fully satisfied that the true policy of General H——
is to strengthen Grant's column by such force as will enable him
at once to seize the Memphis and Charleston railroad, as it is
the readiest means of reducing Island 10 and all the strongholds
of the enemy to Memphis.

Letter written from St. Louis, military headquarters for the Southwest, (copied by me, S. E. Blackwell, on March 23, 1891, from the file
at the office of the Attorney General):——

St. Louis, May 2, 1862.

I think the war on the approaches to the Tennessee River has
ended. I think the enemy will retreat to the Grand Junction,
some sixty miles nearer Memphis; and when our forces approach him there, he will go down the Central Mississippi railroad to Jackson, and if there is another great battle in the West it
will be there. I think they will try to postpone anything serious
until after the pending battles in Virginia. If they make the attempt now every leader would be taken in the event of defeat,
without fail, whilst if it is postponed until after the fate of Virginia is decided the leaders can bring what troops they have left
and, joining them to what they have here, make one last struggle for life, and if defeated they can escape across the Mississippi
into Arkansas, and through that into Texas and Mexico.

You may rest assured the *leaders* will not be caught if they can
get away with life; and as to *property*, they have that secured
already. The only way this plan can be frustrated is to occupy
Memphis and Vicksburg strongly, *particularly* the *latter*, and send
one or more of our gunboats up the *Yazoo* River *to watch every
creek and inlet*, so that they may be unable to get across the
swamps by *canoes* and *skiffs*.

I have heard that all the skiffs and canoes have been taken from
Memphis and Vicksburg to some point up the *Yazoo River* and
fitted up, for what purpose I do not know, but I can think there
is no other than what I name, for *one night's ride* from Jackson
will carry a man to the edge of the *Yazoo* River *swamps*, where
it would be impossible to follow unless equally well acquainted
and with boats like theirs. From there their escape would be
easy, as *they would have 400 miles* of the river to strike, at any part
of which they would find friends to assist them over to the Arkansas side of the river, and from *there* pursuit would be useless.

Letter from Miss Carroll to Secretary Stanton, (written to recommend Pilot Scott for information given):

May 14, 1862.

Hon. E. M. Stanton, Secretary of War:

It will be the obvious policy of the rebels, in the event of Beauregard's defeat, to send a large column into Texas for the purpose of holding that country for subsistence, where beef and wheat abound. Now, all this can be defeated by strongly occupying Vicksburg and plying a gun boat or two on the Yazoo River. I would also suggest a gunboat to be placed at the mouth of the Red and Arkansas Rivers. Whether the impending battle in North Mississippi should occur at Corinth or within the area of a hundred miles, a large part of the enemy's forces will retreat by the Yazoo River and by the railroad to Vicksburg, on the Mississippi, and will then take the railroad through Louisiana into Texas. I handed Honourable Mr. Watson on Monday a letter giving information that the canoes, skiffs, and other transports had been sent up the Yazoo River from Memphis and Vicksburg for the purpose, undoubtedly, of securing the rebels retreat from our pursuing army.

This information I obtained from Mr. Scott, a pilot on the *Memphis*, which conducted the retreat of the soldiers at the Battle of Belmont, and had been with the fleet in the same capacity up the Tennessee River. Until June last he resided in New Orleans, and for twenty years or more has been in his present employment. His wife stated this to me, and with a view of obtaining facts about that section of country I requested her to introduce him to me.

I was surprised at his general intelligence in regard to the war, and from the facts I derived from him and other practical men I satisfied myself that the Tennessee River was the true strategic point, and submitted a document to this effect to Hon. Thomas A. Scott, dated the 30th of November, 1861, which changed the whole programme of the war in the Southwest, and inured to the glory of our arms in that section and throughout the land. The government is not aware of the incalculable service rendered by the facts I learned from this pilot, and I therefore take the present occasion to ask his promotion to the surveyorship of New Orleans, for which I should think him well suited in this crisis.

I enclose you a letter describing the Battle of Pittsburgh Landing, which will interest you.

Very sincerely,

Anna Ella Carroll.

Extract from the letter to the Secretary of War on the 15th of May, 1862, advising the occupation of Vicksburg:—

. . . . . it will be the obvious policy of the rebels, in the event of Beauregard's defeat, to send a large column into Texas for the purpose of holding that country for subsistence, where beef and wheat abound. This can be defeated by strongly occupying Vicksburg and plying a gun boat, to be placed at the mouth of the Red and Arkansas Rivers. . . . . . Whether the impending battle in North Mississippi should occur at Corinth or within the area of a hundred miles, a large part of the enemy's forces will retreat by the Yazoo River, and by the railroad to Vicksburg, on the Mississippi, and will take the railroad through Louisiana into Texas.

On the following Monday Miss Carroll handed Mr. Watson a letter giving information that the canoes, skiffs, and other transports had been sent up the Yazoo from Memphis and Vicksburg for the purpose, undoubtedly, of securing the rebels retreat from our pursuing army.

Letter from the file of the Attorney General, Court of Claims, (copied by me, S. E. Blackwell, from the file at the office of the Attorney-General, March 23, 1891):—

Hon. E. M. Stanton, Secretary of War:

Sir: I find that the Secretary of War and the President are violently assailed for arresting certain parties in the loyal States and suspending the writ of *habeas corpus*. It is represented that a high judicial officer in the State of Vermont has taken issue with the Administration on this question. It is also intimated that the State authorities, in Vermont and elsewhere, are to be invoked for the protection of the citizen against military arrests. There is very great danger at this time to be apprehended to the country from a conflict between the military and the judicial authorities, because the opinion is almost universal that the authority to suspend the writ of *habeas corpus* rests with Congress. The reason that this opinion has so generally obtained is that in

England, whence we have derived much of our political and judicial system, the power to suspend the writ is vested alone in Parliament; and our jurists, without reflecting upon the distinction between the constitutions of the two governments, have erroneously made the English theory applicable to our own.

I believe in my work on the *War Powers of the Government*, etc., I was the first writer who has succeeded in placing the power of the government to arrest for political offences, and to suspend the writ of *habeas corpus*, on its true foundation. In the opinion of eminent men, if this work were now placed in the hands of every lawyer and judge it would stay the evil which threatens to arise from a conflict between the military and judicial depart ments of the country. I therefore respectfully suggest the propriety of authorising me to circulate a large edition of this work, or, what would be still better, that I should write a *new paper*, specially on the power of the executive to suspend the writ of *habeas corpus*, and to arrest political offenders.

Anna Ella Carroll.

In October, 1862, Miss Carroll wrote the following letter to the Secretary of War, through the hands of John Tucker, Assistant Secretary, on the reduction of Vicksburg:—

As I understand an expedition is about to go down the river for the purpose of reducing Vicksburg, I have prepared the enclosed map in order to demonstrate more clearly the obstacles to be encountered in the contemplated assault. In the first place, it is impossible to take Vicksburg in front without too great a loss of life and material, for the reason that the river is only about half a mile wide, and our forces would be in point-blank range of their guns, not only from their water batteries, which line the shore, but from the batteries that crown the hills, while the enemy would be protected by the elevation from the range of our fire.

By examining the map, I enclose you will at once perceive why a place of so little apparent strength has been enabled to resist the combined fleets of the upper and lower Mississippi. The most economical plan for the redaction of Vicksburg now is to push a column from Memphis to Corinth, down the Mississippi Central railroad to Jackson, the capital of the State of Mississippi.

The occupation of Jackson and the command of the railroad to New Orleans would compel the immediate evacuation of Vicksburg, as well as the retreat of the entire rebel army east of that line, and by another movement of our army from Jackson, Mississippi, or from Corinth to Meridian, in the State of Mississippi, on the Ohio and Mobile railroad, especially if aided by a movement of our gunboats on Mobile, the Confederate forces, with all the disloyal men and their slaves, would be compelled to fly east of the Tombigbee. Mobile being then in our possession, with 100,000 men at Meridian we would redeem the entire country from Memphis to the Tombigbee River. Of course, I would have the gunboats with a small force at Vicksburg as auxiliary to this movement.

With regard to the canal, Vicksburg can be rendered useless to the Confederate Army upon the first rise of the river; but I do not advise this, because Vicksburg belongs to the United States and we desire to hold and fortify it, for the Mississippi River at Vicksburg and the Vicksburg-Jackson railroad will become necessary as a base of our future operations. Vicksburg might have been reduced eight months ago, as I then advised, after the fall of Fort Henry, and with much more ease than it can be done today.

Washington, D. C., May 10, 1876.

My Dear Miss Carroll:

Referring to the conversation with Judge Evans last evening, he called my attention to Colonel Scott's telegram, announcing the fall of Island No. 10, in 1862, as endorsing your plan, when Scott said: "The movement in the rear has done the work." I stated to the judge, as he and you knew before, that your paper on the reduction of Vicksburg did the work on that place, after being so long baffled and with the loss of so much life and treasure, by trying to take it from the water; that to my knowledge your paper was approved and adopted by the Secretary of War and the President, and immediately sent out to the proper military authority in that department.

I remember well their remarks upon it at that time, and of all your other views and suggestions, made after we got the expedition inaugurated, and know the direction they took. These matters were often talked over as the campaign advanced, and in the very last interview with Mr. Stanton, just before his death, he referred to your services in originating the campaign in the strongest terms he could express, and, as I have informed you, stated that if his life was spared he would discharge the great duty of seeing your services to the country properly recognised and rewarded.

But why need I say more. Your claim is established beyond controversy, unless the witnesses are impeached, and I hardly think they would undertake that business. What motive could any of us have had to mislead or falsify the history of the war. Your claim is righteous and just, if ever there was one, and for the honour of my country I trust and hope you will be suitably rewarded and so declared before the world.

Yours truly,

B. F. Wade.

Miss Carroll's after papers, so far as I can learn, were mainly on emancipation, on the ballot, and on reconstruction.

CHAPTER 6

Congressional Revelations

Very curious is the picture revealed by the Congressional records. Fully as Lincoln and his Military Committee recognise the genius of the remarkable woman now taking the lead, it needs great courage to adopt her plans.

> Mr. Lincoln and Stanton are opposed to having it known that the armies are moving under the plan of a civilian, directed by the President as commander-in-chief. Mr. Lincoln says it was that which made him hesitate to inaugurate the movement against the opinions of the military commanders, and he says he does not want to risk the effect it might have upon the armies if they found that some outside party had originated the campaign; that he wanted the country and the armies to believe they were doing the whole business in saving the country.

Judge Wade alludes to a remark about the sword of Gideon, made by Secretary Stanton, and says that was done to maintain the policy of secrecy as to the origin of the plan. Strict silence is counselled as absolutely necessary, and Anna Ella Carroll is not the woman to allow a thought of self to interfere with her plans for the salvation of her country.

Rapid and brilliant is the success of that Tennessee campaign, planned and supervised by that able head. Her papers, as the campaign progresses, are as remarkable as the original plan. On the fall of Fort Henry, she prepares a paper on the feasibility of advancing immediately on Mobile or Vicksburg, without turning to the right or left. She carries it, in person, to the War Department and delivers it into the hands of Assistant Secretary Tucker, who takes it at once to the Secretary of War.

She exhibits also a copy of the original plan, submitted on the 30th of November, 1861.

Mr. Tucker remarks: "This is prophecy fulfilled so far," and says he knows her to be the author, Colonel Scott having so informed him before he left for the West.

Notwithstanding some blunders in the execution, the campaign progresses, as the authorities at the War Office testify, "mainly in accordance with Miss Carroll's suggestions."

The fall of Fort Henry having opened the navigation of the Tennessee River, its capture is followed by the evacuation of Columbus and Bowling Green. Fort Donelson is given up and its garrison of 14,000 troops are marched out as prisoners of war; Pittsburgh Landing and Corinth follow. The Confederate leaders discover with consternation that the key to the whole situation has been found. All Europe rings with the news of victories that have reversed the probabilities of the war.

On the 10th of April, four months after the adoption of Miss Carroll's plans, President Lincoln issues a proclamation thanking Almighty God for the "signal victories which have saved the country from foreign intervention and invasion."

THE FOREIGN MINISTERS ARE ENRAPTURED.

Seward to Dayton.

March 6, 1862.

It is now apparent that we are at the beginning of the end of the attempted revolution. Cities, districts, and States are coming back under Federal authority.

Adams to Seward.

March 6, 1862.

We are anxiously awaiting the news by every steamer, but not for the same reasons as before; the pressure for interference here has disappeared.

Dayton to Seward.

March 25, 1862.

The emperor said that he must frankly say that when the insurrection broke out and this concession of belligerent rights was made he did not suppose the North would succeed; that it was the general belief of the statesmen of Europe that the two sections would never come together again.

Dayton to Seward.

March 31, 1862.

I again called the emperor's attention to the propriety of his government retracing its steps in regard to its concession to the insurrectionists of belligerent rights, refer ring him to the consideration in regard thereto contained in your former dispatches. He said, 'It would scarcely be worthy of a great power, now that the South was beaten, to withdraw a concession made to them in the day of their strength.'

President Lincoln's Proclamation.

April 10, 1862.

It has pleased Almighty God to vouchsafe signal victories to the land and naval forces engaged in suppressing an internal rebellion, and at the same time to avert from our country the danger of foreign intervention and invasion.

Seward to Dayton.

May 7, 1862.

The proclamation of commerce which is made may be regarded by the maritime powers as an announcement that the Republic has passed the danger of disunion.

Great enthusiasm is felt at Washington and throughout the country, as it becomes evident that a brilliant and successful plan has been adopted, and great anxiety is evinced to find out and reward the author.

For this purpose, a lively debate takes place in the House of Representatives for the avowed purpose of finding out whether "these victories were arranged or won by men sitting at a distance, engaged in organising victory," or whether "they have been achieved by bold and resolute men left free to act and to conquer." No one knows.

Mr. Conkling proposes to "thank Halleck and Grant."

Mr. Washburne thinks "General McClernand and General Logan should be included."

Mr. Cox thinks "General Smith is entitled to an equal degree of the glory."

Mr. Holman thinks "General Wallace should have a fair share."

Mr. Mallory thinks "General Buell should not be for gotten."

Mr. Kellogg thinks all these suggestions derogatory to President Lincoln, as Commander-in-Chief. He desires "it to be remembered that subordinate officers by law are under the control and command of the Commander-in-Chief of the American Army." He believes "there is, emanating from the Commander-in-Chief of the American forces, through his first subordinates, and by them to the next, and so continuously down to the soldiers who fight upon the battlefield, a well digested, clear, and definite policy of campaign, that is in motion to put down this rebellion;" and he "here declares that he believes that the system of movements that has culminated in glorious victories, and which will soon put down this rebellion, finds root, brain, and execution in the Commanding General of the American Army and the Chief Executive of the American people."

Mr. Olin says:—

> If it be the object of the House, before passing a vote of thanks, to ascertain who was the person who planned and organised these victories, then it would be eminently proper to request the Secretary of War to give us that information. That would satisfy the gentle man and the House directly as to who was the party that planned these military movements. It is sufficient for the present that somebody has planned and executed these military movements. Still, if the gentleman has any desire to know who originated these movements, he can ascertain that fact by inquiring at the proper office, for certainly someone at the War Department must be informed on the subject. The Secretary of War knows whether he had anything to do with them or not; the Commanding General knows whether he had anything to do with them or not. If neither of them had anything to do with them, they will cheerfully say so.

But at the War Department it has been determined that the secret must be kept so long as the war continues, and this noble, silent woman sits in the gallery listening to all this discussion and makes no claim, knowing well the injury that it would be to the national cause if it should be known that the plan was the work of a civilian, and, above all, a *woman*—a creature despised and ignored, not even counted as one of "the people" in the sounding profession made of human rights a hundred years ago.

The House of Representatives having failed to discover the author of the campaign, on March 13th, 1862, the Senate makes a similar attempt.

Mr. Washburne and Mr. Grimes think "it is Commodore Foote who should be thanked." But no one knows.

Again, that wonderful, quiet woman in the gallery sits silently listening to all their talking and discussing.

She speaks of it afterwards to Colonel Scott; refers to the discussions which had taken place in Congress to find out who had devised the movement, and to the fact that she had preserved entire silence while the debate went on, claiming it for one and another of the generals of the war.

Colonel Scott says she has: "acted very properly in the matter; that there is no question of her being entitled to the vote of thanks by Congress; that she has saved incalculable millions to the country, etc., but that it would not do while the struggle lasted to make a public claim; "and also states that the War Power pamphlet has done much good, and he has heard it frequently referred to while in the West.

Judge Wade discusses the matter and says it greatly adds to the merit of the author that it was not made known. "Where is there another man or woman," says Judge Wade, turning to Judge Evans, "who would have kept silence when so much could have come personally from an open avowal." Judge Evans says he has reproached himself more than once that he had not in some way made known what he knew, but was constrained to silence by considerations of patriotism that were above all else at that time.

Hon. Benjamin F. Wade, Chairman of the Committee on the Conduct of the War, afterward writes to Miss Carroll:—

I have sometimes reproached myself that I had not made known the author when they were discussing the resolution in Congress to find out; but Mr. Lincoln and Mr. Stanton were opposed to its being known that the armies were moving under the plan of a civilian. Mr. Lincoln wanted the armies to believe that they were doing the whole business of saving the country.

Mr. Wade also writes to Miss Carroll:—

The country, almost in her last extremity, was saved by your sagacity and unremitting labour; indeed, your services were so great that it is hard to make the world believe it. That all this great work should be brought about by a woman is inconceivable to vulgar minds. You cannot be deprived of the honour of having done greater and more efficient services for the country in time of her greatest peril than any other person in the Republic, and a knowledge of this cannot be long repressed.

Col. Thomas A. Scott, Assistant Secretary of War, to whom her plans were submitted, informs her in 1862 that "the adoption of her plan has saved the country millions of money."

Hon. L. D. Evans, justice of the supreme court of Texas, in a pamphlet entitled *The Material Bearing of the Tennessee Campaign in 1862 upon the Destinies of our Civil War*, shows that no military plan could have saved the country except this, and that this was unthought of and unknown until suggested by Miss Carroll, who alone had the genius to grasp the situation.

How clearly the Confederate leaders recognised the fatal effects of this Tennessee campaign is indicated by a letter found among the papers captured by General Mitchell at Huntsville, written by General Beauregard to General Samuel Cooper, Richmond, Va.:

> Corinth, April 9, 1862.
>
> Can we not be reinforced by Pemberton's army?
>
> If defeated here, we lose the Mississippi Valley and probably our cause, whereas we could even afford to lose Charleston and Savannah for the purpose of defeating Buell's army, which would not only insure us the valley of the Mississippi, but our independence.

The feeling of the Confederate Army is curiously indicated by the following letter received by Miss Carroll as the struggle drew towards its close and filed by Mr. Stanton among his papers:

> Fort Delaware, March 1, 1865.
>
> Miss Carroll, Baltimore, Md.:
>
> Madam: It is rumoured in the Southern Army that you furnished the plan or information that caused the United States Government to abandon the expedition designed to descend the Mississippi River, and transferred the armies up the Tennessee River in 1862. We wish to know if this is true. If it is, you are the veriest of traitors to your section, and we warn you that you stand upon a volcano.
>
> Confederates.

Miss Carroll's patriotic labours continued to the end. She contributed papers on emancipation and on reconstruction, and wrote articles for the leading journals in support of the government.

While her pen was tireless in the cause of loyalty, her sympathy and interest extended themselves toward the prisons, the battlefields, and the hospitals, and many were the individual cases of suffering and want that she relieved. She was especially successful with procuring discharges for Union prisoners, and where such were in need her own means were most generously used to give adequate help.

Although the agreement with the government was that she should be remunerated for her services and the employment of her private resources, it was not until sometime after the close of the war that she endeavoured, by the advice of her friends and prominent members of the War Committee, to make a public claim and establish so important a fact in the history of the war.

Miss Carroll's own feeling was a desire to make her services a free gift to her country, and her aged father, who felt the proudest satisfaction in his daughter's patriotic career, was of the same disinterested opinion.—Abbie M. Gannet, in the Boston *Sunday Herald*, February, 1890.

The same high and chivalrous feeling that led him to sacrifice his ancestral home to liquidate the debts incurred by others made him unwilling that his daughter should press even for the payment of the debt due for the publication of her pamphlets and campaign documents, though published at the request of the War Department on the understanding that she was to be repaid. His loftiness of feeling and unbounded generosity continued even under adverse fortunes.

But as time went on, her father no longer living, Miss Carroll noted how honours and emoluments were allotted to her fellow-labourers, and that her own work, owing to the peculiar circumstances that at first surrounded it and the untimely deaths of Mr. Lincoln and others who would gladly have proclaimed it, was wholly sinking into obscurity. A sense of the injustice of the case took possession of her and the conviction that history itself would be falsified if her silence continued.— Abbie M. Gannet, in the *Boston Sunday Herald*)

Thomas A. Scott and Mr. Wade, chairman of the Committee on the Conduct of the War, and others well acquainted with her work were still living, able and desirous to establish her claim. By their advice and with their enthusiastic endorsement she made a statement of her case in 1870 and presented it before Congress, asking for recognition and a due award.

Every lover of history, every true patriot, and, above all, every patriotic woman will be glad that she so decided.—Mrs. Abbie M. Gannet.

It was not fitting that such achievements should be allowed to sink into oblivion.

Accordingly, she made her claim, supported by the strongest and clearest testimony from the very men who were most competent to speak with absolute authority, Mr. Wade, Mr. Scott, and others of the War Department testifying again and again to the facts of the case.

It immediately became evident that a most determined effort was to be made to crush her claims. The honours of war were not to be allowed to rest on the head that had so ably won them. Personal and political interests were too strongly involved. If it had been a little matter it might have passed; but this was a case of such magnitude and importance, a case that must greatly change existing estimates.

To defeat the testimony was impossible. Other means must be used. Chicanery of every kind was resorted to.

Twice Miss Carroll's whole file of papers were stolen from the Military Committee, who were considering her claims.

Fortunately, Miss Carroll possessed the original drafts of these letters. She speedily reproduced them, and the Military Committee and Mr. Hunt, the keeper of the records, having already examined the letters, accepted the new file and ordered them to be printed, thus giving them their guarantee; so that, to all intents and purposes, they became the same as the originals.

Judge Wade advises Miss Carroll:

I want you to set forth to these gentlemen, in your private letters, the facts about the abstracting of these papers. It has never been properly done. It is exceedingly important as evidence of the truth of your claim. Tell them how your papers were abstracted from the files twice. Send a letter to General Banning. Tell Judge Evans to ask the general to appoint a sub-committee to investigate it, so as to submit it to the general committee. Tell them all, and remind them that when one report was made in the Senate Committee by Mr. Howard the papers were abstracted from the files, as the Secretary of the Committee, Rev. Samuel Hunt, will testify.

I hope the report will be a very emphatic and explicit one in setting forth your plan as you took it to Colonel Scott. It makes the strongest foundation to commence upon in the sub-committee. There will undoubtedly be a minority of Republicans, and it will be so much the better for that, because they can find no evidence to invalidate the report of the majority, and I would like to see them make the attempt. Being at the head of the War Committee, I had most to do with it. The committee not half the time were present. Nobody knows the difficulty the War Committee had to get the army moved. We had almost to fight for that campaign.

Mr. Hunt writes from Natick, Mass.:

March 7, 1876.

My Dear Miss Carroll:

I remember well your failure to recover twice all the papers you intrusted to the charge of the Military Committee and our inability to account for their loss.

Hoping you will have better success now, I remain as ever,

Very truly yours,

S. Hunt,

Late Secretary of Senate Military Committee.

Senator Howard tells Miss Carroll she has a right to feel disappointed that her claims should be neglected, but he says, "you know the great power of the *military*, who don't want you to have the recognition."

"Senator Howard," she replies, "there is something in moral integrity. I understand you, but just tell the *truth*. I ask only to be sustained by truth, and am not afraid of this power."

"Miss Carroll," he says with emphasis, "you have done more for the country than them all. You told and showed where to fight and how to strike the rebellion upon its head. No one comprehends the magnitude of that service more than I."

Judge Wade's remarks to Senator Wilson last of May, 1862 (as taken down by a reporter):—

Judge Wade said he talked just right to Wilson for the delay in Miss Carroll's matter before his committee; that Wilson said he was no more against the claim than Wade. Wade told him it would *kill* him politically if he didn't act soon; that it ought to kill any party who knew the truths of the great civil war and conspired to conceal them for their own purposes; that it would be a great feather in a man's cap and a great help to his own cause to bring the matter before the country *right*, no matter *who* it offended, and he only regretted he was not in the Senate then on this very account, and would always be sorry he had not induced Miss Carroll to come out and make claim for her rights while the rejoicing was going on at the final surrender. Wilson said it was a big thing, and he agreed that the American people would cheerfully pay for it, if it had been so done, by contribution boxes at the cross-roads and post-offices of the country.

Mr. Tucker writes from Philadelphia in 1870:—

I saw Colonel Scott yesterday and placed your papers in his hands. He remarked that he should stand by all he had said or written in the matter, and he presumed that was all you would want.

1872

Judge Wade says: "I went to Morton, in the Senate, and told him that it was infamous that the Military Committee did not report at once. He said, for himself he was ready to endorse your claim fully, and had done so when Howard reported. I went on to tell him more, but he said, I could not be more strongly convinced of the justice of that claim. Your own statement satisfied me without anything more. If Wilson will send down for the report I will sign my name to it right now. I then went over to Wilson and told him what Morton had said, and told him he had better send down for it. Wilson said he didn't think that was the best way of doing it, but that he would call a special meeting of the Committee and have it done. I then saw Cameron. He said he was ready and always had been."

1873

Judge Wade tells her: "Howe said your claim had been sent to his committee—on Claims—but that it did not properly belong there; but that he had examined the papers; that your claim was entirely just and ought to be paid."

And again: "That he had spoken to Wadleigh, a member of the Military Committee, about her claim. He said he had no question that it was clearly proved, and no doubt she would be ultimately paid by the Government."

Judge Wade says: "I asked Logan what he was going to do about

Miss Carroll's claim." He said "he didn't know what to say." "I told him it ought to be paid at once; that it was clearly established."

Logan said, "Yes; but she claims so much."

Wade replies, "She claims to have furnished the information that led to the military movements that decided the war."

Logan didn't say any more, or what he would do.

Judge Wade asked Merrill what he was going to do; that this claim had been before Congress long enough. Morrill said your claim was clearly established; "that were you applying for a title for a new patent of discovery nothing could defeat you, but that it was indispensable to have the Military Committee act again."

Wade says "he feels embarrassed in appearing as an advocate, being a witness, but that he will go before the committee anyhow and insist upon action."

Jefferson, Ohio, October 3, 1876.

My Dear Miss Carroll:

I do assure you that the manner in which your most noble services and sacrifices have been treated by your country has given me more pain and anxiety than anything that ever happened to me personally; that such merit should go so long unrewarded is deeply disgraceful to the country, or rather to the agencies of the government who have had the matter in charge. I hope and trust it will not always be so. The truth is, your services were so great they cannot be comprehended by the ordinary capacity of our public men; and then, again, your services were of such a character that they threw a shadow over the reputations of some of our would-be great men. No doubt great pains have been taken in the business of trying to defeat you, but it has always been an article of faith with me that truth and justice must ultimately triumph.

Ever yours truly,

B. F. Wade.

Jefferson, Ohio, April 10, 1877

My Dear Miss Carroll:

There is nothing in my power I would not most gladly do for you, for none have ever done so much for the country as you, and none have had so little for it. I cannot but believe justice will be done you yet for the immense services you rendered the country in the civil war. But when I reflect what mighty work you have done for the country and how you have been treated it keeps me awake nights and fills my soul with bitterness.

Truly yours ever,

B. F. Wade.

Jefferson, Ohio, September 4,

My Dear Miss Carroll:

.... I know you are right and I will never fail to do all I can to aid you in attaining it. Your only trouble is you have the whole army to fight, who seem better skilled in opposing you than they were in finding out the best method of fighting the enemy. I hope your health holds out and continues good, for what you have done and what you have to do would break down any weaker intellect and physical constitution.

Mrs. Wade joins me in wishing you all success.

Truly yours,

B. F. Wade.

Governor Corwin writes her:—

Washington, Jan. 13, 1878.

Dear Friend:

I thank you for the address of your good governor of the third instant. I believe you will succeed in saving Maryland, but there is nothing to be done with this Congress, and your counsel to your friends is wise. Art, finesse, and trick are in this age worth the wisdom of Solomon, the faith of Abraham, and the fidelity of Moses.

Truly yours,

Tom Corwin.

(Thomas Corwin was Secretary of the Treasury under Fillmore, U.S. Senator, a noted lawyer and wit, and a man of letters).

Soon after the close of the war Miss Carroll inquires of Mr. Stanton if he could not furnish what was termed "a transportation and subsistence" for a southern tour. Many people were present. He remarks he had rather pay her millions of dollars than to say no to any request she could make of him. "You," he says, "who have done such in comparable services for the country with so much modesty and so little pretension," etc.

Miss Carroll does not like so much in the line of compliment and says to General Hardie as she passes out, "Mr. Stanton said too much and attracted the attention of all in the room."

Hardie says, "Don't take it in that light. Mr. Stanton is not the man to say what he don't mean, and, I venture to say, never said so much to any one besides during the war."

Miss Carroll relates this to Judge Wade.

"Why," says he, "Stanton has said the same of you to me, and often in the same vein; he said your course was the most remarkable in the war; that you found yourself, got no pay, and did the great work that made others famous."

For these reports and conversations see—

45th Congress, 2nd Session, House of Representatives. pp. 30, 31, 32, 33. Miss. Doc. No. 58.

Vol. 6, Miscellaneous Documents, Document Room of the Senate.

CHAPTER 7

Miss Carroll's Pamphlets in Aid of the Administration

In July of 1862 Miss Carroll presented her very modest bill for the pamphlets that had been accepted at the War Department, which included the expenses paid by herself of printing and circulating.

Of the Breckenridge pamphlet, she printed and circulated 50,000, which went off, as Hon. James Tilghman (president of the Union Association in Baltimore in 1860) testifies, "like hot cakes."

In the library of the State Department specimens of two large editions of the War Powers may be seen side by side in the volumes of bound manuscripts.

It is over 23 closely printed pages in length, and was circulated east and west with admirable results, all expenses borne by Miss Carroll personally.

The Power of the President to Suspend the Writ of *Habeas Corpus*, The Relation of the Revolted Citizens to the United States, and other able papers followed.

The Secretary of War suggested the presentation of Miss Carroll's bill, advising her to obtain the opinion of one or more competent judges as to the reasonableness of her charges and a statement of the understanding upon which they were written.

The bill is as follows, and the testimonials are as reported in the Miss. Doc. 58 (House), 45th Congress, 2nd session:

SECRET-SERVICE FUND OF THE WAR DEPARTMENT TO ANNA ELLA CARROLL, DR., AS PER AGREEMENT WITH HON. THOMAS A. SCOTT, ASSISTANT SECRETARY OF WAR.

Sept. 25.	To circulating the Breckenridge reply . .	$1,250
Dec. 24.	To writing, publishing, and circulating the "War Powers," etc.	3,000
1862.		
May —.	Writing, publishing, and circulating the relations of the National Government to the rebelled citizens	2,000
		$6,250
Credit, October 2, 1861 :		
By cash		1,250
		$5,000

Philadelphia, January 2, 1863.
I believe Miss Carroll has earned fairly, and should be paid, the compensation she has charged above.

Thos. A. Scott.

Philadelphia, January 28, 1863.
All my interviews with Miss Carroll were in my official capacity as Assistant Secretary of War, and in that capacity, I would have allowed, and believed she should be paid, the amount of her bill within, which is certified as being reasonable by many of the leading men of the country.

Thos. A. Scott.

Philadelphia, January 28, 1863
The pamphlets published by Miss Carroll were published upon a general understanding made by me with her as Assistant Secretary of War, under no special authority in the premises, but under a general authority then exercised by me in the discharge of public duties as Assistant Secretary of War. I then thought them of value to the service, and still believe they were of great value to the government. I brought the matter generally to the knowledge of General Cameron, then Secretary of War, without his having special knowledge of the whole matter; he made no objections thereto. No price was fixed, but it was understood that the government would treat her with sufficient liberality to compensate her for any service she might render, and I believe she acted upon the expectation that she would be paid by the government.

Thomas A. Scott.

New York, October 10, 1862.
Without intending to express any assent or dissent to the positions therein asserted, but merely with a view of forming a judgment in respect to their merits as argumentative compositions, I have carefully perused Miss Carroll's pamphlets mentioned in the within account. The propositions are clearly stated, the authorities relied on are judiciously selected, and the reasoning is natural, direct, and well sustained, and framed in a manner extremely well adapted to win the reader's assent, and thus to obtain the object in view. I consider the charges quite moderate.

Charles O'Conor.

Washington, September 19, 1862.
Without having seen the writings mentioned in the within account I have heard them so favourably spoken of by the most competent judges that the charges of the account seem to be most reasonable.

Reverdy Johnson.

706 Walnut St., Philadelphia, Oct. 11, 1862.
Having been requested to give my opinion of the pamphlets described in the within list, I have in a cursory way looked over them. As I have just returned from Europe from a long absence and am at present with many unsettled matters of my own, I cannot undertake therefore to study them. From the examination, I have given them I cheerfully say they appear to be learned and able productions and the work of a well-stored mind. They are written in a clear style and must be read with interest and advantage, and certainly cannot fail to be of service to the cause they uphold.
Much labour must have been given to these productions. Their actual value in money I cannot determine, but I think they are well worthy of a high and liberal compensation.

Benjamin H. Brewster.

(Benjamin H. Brewster was a noted lawyer of Philadelphia and a member of Arthur's Cabinet).

Washington, September 23, 1862.
I have read several of the productions of Miss Carroll, and, among others, two of the within mentioned. The learning,

ability, and force of reasoning they exhibit have astonished me. Without concurring in all the conclusions of the writer, I think that the writer is fully entitled, not only to the amount charged, but to the thanks and high consideration of the government and the nation.

Richard S. Coxe.

Washington, September 10, 1862.
Having read with care the several pamphlets mentioned within, and comparing them with professional arguments in causes of any considerable importance, and considering the vast learning and the ability with which it is handled, I have to say that in my judgment the charges are not only very reasonable, but will, in the estimation of all men of learning who will carefully examine the documents, be deemed *too small.*

L. D. Evans.

Washington, D. C., September 23, 1862.
I have read the pamphlets mentioned within, together with others on similar subjects written by Miss Carroll, and I fully concur in the opinion above expressed, believing that said pamphlets have been of essential service to the cause of the Union.

S. T. Williams.

September 8, 1862.
I have carefully perused, some time since, the papers referred to within, and without entering into any question of concurrence or non-concurrence of views I deem the documents of great value to the government, and that the estimate of the account is reasonable.

Robert J. Walker.

Washington, October, 1862.
Miss Carroll:
While I never put my name to any paper, I would very cheerfully state at the department that I consider the charges for your publications *too small,* but I do not think it can be necessary. What more could anyone want than such an endorsement as you have from Mr. O'Conor and other eminent men?

Very respectfully,

Edwards Pierrepont.

(Edwards Pierrepont was Minister to England under Grant).

Later developments showed that the $1,250 that Miss Carroll had credited to the secret-service fund had come out of Thomas A. Scott's own pocket as his private contribution to the national cause and to help on the circulation of such important documents.

Mr. Scott sent the following letter, to be found in Miss. Doc. 167:—

> Philadelphia, January 16, 1863.
> Hon. John Tucker, Assistant Secretary of War:
> I believe Miss Carroll has fairly earned and ought to be paid the amount of her bill ($6,750), and if you will pay her I will certify to such form as you may think necessary as a voucher.
> Thomas A. Scott.

Mr. Tucker not having the settlement of the account, and the matter being referred to Assistant Secretary Watson, Miss Carroll submitted the account endorsed by many eminent men as reasonable, and also endorsed with Hon. Thomas A. Scott's recollection of the agreement upon which they were produced.

An agent tendered but $750, *with a receipt in full*.

On objecting, he said her redress was with Congress, and, upon being informed by Mr. Reverdy Johnson that the receipts would not bar her claim, she accepted it. The original account, with endorsements, etc., it is stated, is "on file in the War Department." The Senate Military Committee of the 41st Congress, 3rd session, Report 339, referring to these publications, said:—

> Miss Carroll preferred a claim to reimburse her for expenses incurred in their publication which ought to have been paid.

Miss Carroll having also credited the $750 to the secret-service fund, Mr. Thomas A. Scott wrote her that she should not have done so; that it came out of his own pocket in his indignation at finding the agreement made by himself in his capacity of Assistant Secretary of War disregarded by his successor. For thirty years, this account has been presented in vain. In 1885 it was retransmitted from the Court of Claims on some judicial grounds, though accompanied by the "moral assent" of the court.

Miss Carroll had written the great and influential pamphlets of the day which ought to have made her a minister of state. She had devised the military movements that ought to have given her a very high military rank. Under our arrangements for securing a male aristocracy no services, however brilliant, could secure to a woman any post whatever. She must remain an unrecognised member, and being an *unrecognised* member for her there was no pay—not even her traveling expenses. Any help towards the circulation of her invaluable pamphlets had to come out of the private means of Thomas A. Scott. From first to last, for all her intense and unremitting labours through all the years of the civil war, she has, it would appear, received from the government, in any department whatever, not one cent. To her personally, through the generous and unhesitating use of her own private means, the result has been a long martyrdom of poverty and suffering.

That is how America has treated her noblest daughter.

That is the result of belonging to a disfranchised class.

CHAPTER 8

Miss Carroll before Congress

Miss Carroll's first memorial was brought before Congress March 31, 1870. It was simple and short, with a copy of the plan of campaign appended.

A Military Committee, with General Jacob M. Howard as chairman, was appointed to consider it. Thomas A. Scott wrote twice to the Military Committee endorsing the claim. Mr. Wade, Judge Evans, etc., made their statements on affidavit.

The evidence being thorough and incontrovertible, Mr. Howard reported accordingly on February 2, 1871. He recapitulates the letters and evidence received; gives Mr. Wade's testimony; states that a copy of Miss Carroll's paper was shown him immediately after the success of the campaign, by the late Hon. Elisha Whittlesey, of Ohio (Mr. Whittlesey had asked Miss Carroll for a copy that he might leave it in his family as an heirloom); notes Miss Carroll's statement that no military man had ever controverted her claim to having originated the campaign, and concludes:

From the high social position of this lady and her established ability as a writer and thinker, she was prepared at the inception of the rebellion to exercise a strong influence in behalf of liberty and the Union; that it was felt and respected in Maryland during the darkest hours in that State's history, there can be no question. Her publications throughout the struggle were eloquently and ably written and widely circulated, and did much to arouse and invigorate the sentiment of loyalty in Maryland and other border States. It is not too much to say that they were among the very ablest publications of the time and exerted a powerful influence upon the hearts of the people. Some of these publications were prepared under the auspices of the War Department, and for these Miss Carroll preferred a claim to reimburse her for the expenses incurred in their publication, which ought to have been paid; and, as evidence of this, we subjoin the following statement from the Assistant Secretary of War:

Philadelphia, January 28, 1863.

All my interviews with Miss Carroll were in my official capacity as Assistant Secretary of War. The pamphlets published were, to a certain extent, under a general authority then exercised by me in the discharge of public duties as Assistant Secretary of War. No price was fixed, but it was understood that the government would treat her with sufficient liberality to compensate her for any service she might render.

Elisha Whittlesey was Comptroller of the Treasury at the time of his death, a very distinguished lawyer in Ohio, and for many terms a Representative in Congress.

On the fifteenth of June, 1870, Hon. Thomas A. Scott addressed a letter to Hon. J. M. Howard, U. S. Senate, in which he says:—

I learn from Miss Carroll that she has a claim before Congress for services rendered in the year 1861 in aid of the government. I believe now that the government ought to reward her liberally for the efforts she made in its behalf to rouse the people against the rebellious action of the South. I hope you will pass some measure that will give Miss Carroll what she is certainly entitled to.

Thos. A. Scott.

In view, therefore, of the highly meritorious services of Miss Carroll during the whole period of our National troubles, and especially at that epoch of the war to which her memorial makes reference, and in consideration of the further fact that all the expenses incident to this service were borne by herself, the committee believe her claim to be just, and that it ought to be recognised by Congress, and consequently report a bill for her relief.

An accompanying bill was sent in, leaving the amount of compensation blank for Congress to determine, but the committee agreeing that the bill ought to be passed in some manner that should recognise the remarkable and invaluable nature of the services rendered.

Congress having thus received the report made by their own Military Committee appointed for the purpose, for reasons plainly given by Mr. Wade and others, at once ignored it, tossing it over to the Court of Claims, who would have nothing to do with it, and so that Congress adjourned.

Then followed that singular and disheartening feature of congressional committees.

Action having been taken, a Military Committee appointed, and a conclusive report made, Congress could utterly neglect it, and at the following Congress the previous action would count for nothing, and the whole wearisome proceeding of a new memorial, a new effort to procure attention, a new examination of evidence, a new report, a new bill, and again utter neglect. But the brave woman continued. She was really fighting alone and at terrible odds another Tennessee campaign for the rightful recognition of woman's work.

Accordingly, the following year another memorial was sent in, another committee appointed, renewed testimony given by Scott, Wade, Evans, and others. Mr. Wilson testified that the claim was "incontestably established," referred to the evidence given in Miss Carroll's own memorial, but for want of time made no regular report, apparently, except this:—

Report.

Mr. Wilson, on behalf of the Committee on Military Affairs, laid before the Senate the memorial of Anna Ella Carroll, of Maryland, setting forth certain valuable military information given to the government by her during the war and asking compensation therefor, which was ordered to be printed, together with a bill rewarding her for military and literary services"—twice read in United States Senate—amount left $—, to be filled by this body. Then Congress again quietly dropped a recognition that might interfere with party plans, and so *that* Congress adjourned.

And so, the weary work went on of presenting new memorials and meeting with the same neglect, Congress never denying the claim and none of the military commanders making any claim or denying the facts.

Miss Carroll gave extracts from every known historical work showing the surmises made, endeavouring to attribute the plan to one and another, and no evidence found to establish such surmises.

Miss Carroll wrote to Hon. J. T. Headley, the distinguished historian of the Civil War, and received the following letter:

Newburgh, N.Y., February 6, 1873.

My Dear Madam:

I am much obliged for the pamphlet you sent me. I never knew before with whom the plan of the campaign up the Tennessee River originated. There seemed to be a mystery attached to it that I could not solve. Though General Buell sent me an immense amount of documents relating to this campaign I could find no reference to the origin of the change of plan. Afterwards I saw it attributed to Halleck, which I knew to be false, and I noticed that he never corroborated it. It is strange that after all my research it has rested with you to enlighten me. Money cannot pay for the plan of that campaign. I doubt not Congress will show not liberality but some justice in the matter. Yours very sincerely,

J. T. Headley.

So, matters went on. New memorials presented for the most part met with "leave to withdraw." Then Miss Carroll gathered herself up for a supreme effort, presented fresh testimony, and in 1878 sent in a memorial that is a mine of wealth and the most interesting memorial she has ever presented. It is labelled

45TH CONGRESS, 2ND SESSION, HOUSE OF REPRESENTATIVES.
MISC. DOC. NO. 58.

Being a document of the first importance and containing some singular evidence, it has been systematically excluded from every Congressional index, though published by order of Congress and included in the bound volumes.

Miss Carroll having made in 1878 this very notable memorial, on February 18, 1879

45TH CONGRESS, 3RD SESSION, SENATE, REPORT NO. 775.

Mr Cockrell made a report entered on the Congressional lists as *adverse*, but really an additional evidence of the in controvertible nature of the facts and the testimony of the. case, the report being only adverse as to compensation. The report admits the services, both literary and military, and even concedes the proposition that "*the transfer of the national armies from the banks of*

the Ohio up the Tennessee River to the decisive position in Mississippi
was the greatest military event in the interest of the human race known
to modern ages, and will ever rank among the very few strategic move-
ments in the world's history that have decided the fate of empires and
peoples" and that *"no true history can be written that does not assign*
to the memorialist the credit of the conception."

The report thereupon proceeds to state the opinion of the committee, that with all the evidence before them every subsequent Congress having failed to make an award they must have had some unknown reasons for the omission, and that the claim, having been so long neglected, may as well be indefinitely postponed—a surprising mode of reasoning and manner of disposition of a claim.

The report supposes the neglect was due to the fact that the services were rendered to the Secret Service Commission and inclines to think that the two thousand dollars received was considered a sufficient remuneration for the literary work.

> The committee have not been able to find a precedent for payment of claims of this character. . . . . . But it would destroy much of the poetry and grandeur of noble deeds were a price demanded for kindred services, and achievements of this nature huckstered in the market as commodities of barter. (*And that is all a report intended to be adverse can say against the claim*).

One might remark that it is not wholly unprecedented for honourable gentlemen to receive remuneration from the government for services rendered, or even to ask for their traveling expenses. But this looks somewhat like a sneer.

Was it directed against the noble invalid who had devoted her life and strength, her great ability, and her private fortune to the service of her country for years, with such lavish prodigality and such brilliant success, and had left a fitting award wholly to the determination of Congress, asking only that it should be made in some way that should mark the unusual and distinctive nature of the services rendered?

No; surely it must have been directed against the government agent who wanted Miss Carroll, for the consideration of $750, to give a receipt in full for a bill of $5,000 remaining—a bill certified by the highest authorities to be sufficiently low or altogether *too* low for the literary work performed. (No wonder if *such* huckstering moved Mr. Cockrell's righteous soul.) His remarks also were exceedingly applicable to a liberal-minded person who shortly after sent in a bill recommending that after all these years Congress would kindly allow Miss Carroll a pension of $50 *a month* for "the important military services rendered the country by her during the late civil war." If any more $50 miseries are proposed, we would commend to the committees Mr. Cockrell on "huckstering."

The true description of such a report would be "admission of the incontestable nature of the services rendered."

Then followed the report of the Military Committee of 1881— the last report, so far as I have been able to ascertain, "printed by order of Congress."

It is as follows, *verbatim*:

46TH CONGRESS, 3RD SESSION, HOUSE OF REPRESENTATIVES. REPORT. NO. 386.

ANNA ELLA CARROLL.

MARCH 3, 1881.—COMMITTED TO THE COMMITTEE OF THE WHOLE HOUSE AND ORDERED TO BE PRINTED.

E. S. BRAGG, FROM THE COMMITTEE ON MILITARY AFFAIRS, SUBMITTED THE FOLLOWING

REPORT.

(TO ACCOMPANY BILL H. R. 7256.)

The Committee on Military Affairs, to whom the memorial of Anna Ella Carroll was referred, asking national recognition and reward for services rendered the United States during the war between the States, after careful consideration of the same, submit the following:

In the autumn of 1861 the great question as to whether the Union could be saved, or whether it was hopelessly subverted, depended on the ability of the government to open the Mississippi and deliver a fatal blow upon the resources of the Confederate power.

The original plan was to reduce the formidable fortifications by descending this river aided by the gunboat fleet then in preparation for that object.

President Lincoln had reserved to himself the special direction of this expedition, but before it was prepared to move he became convinced that the obstacles to be encountered were too grave and serious for the success which the exigencies of the crisis demanded, and the plan was then abandoned and the armies diverted up the Tennessee River and thence southward to the centre of the Confederate power.

The evidence before this committee completely establishes that Miss Anna Ella Carroll was the author of this change of plan, which involved a transfer of the national forces to their new base in north Mississippi and Alabama, in command of the Memphis and Charleston railroad. That she devoted time and money in the autumn of 1861 to the investigation of its feasibility is established by the sworn testimony of L. D. Evans, chief justice of the supreme court of Texas, to the Military Committee of the United States Senate in the 42nd Congress (see pp. 40, 41 of the memorial); that after that investigation she submitted her plan in writing to the War Department at Washington, placing it in the hands of Col. Thomas A. Scott, Assistant Secretary of War, as is confirmed by his statement (see p. 38 of the memorial); also confirmed by the statement of Hon. B. F. Wade, chairman of the Committee on the Conduct the War, made to the same committee (see p. 38), and of President Lincoln and Secretary Stanton (see p. 39 of memorial); also by Hon. O. H. Browning, of Illinois, Senator during the war, in confidential relations with President Lincoln and Secretary Stanton (see p. 39 of memorial); also that of Hon. Elisha Whittlesey, Comptroller of the Treasury (see p 41 of memorial); also by Hon. Thomas H. Hicks, Governor of Maryland, and by Hon. Frederick Feckey's affidavit, Comptroller of the Public Works of Maryland (see p. 127 of memorial); by Hon. Reverdy Johnson (see pp. 26 and 41 of memorial); Hon. George Vickers, United States Senator from Maryland (see p. 41 of memorial); again by Hon B F Wade (see p. 41 of memorial); Hon. J. T. Headley (see p. 43 of memorial); Rev. Dr. R. J. Breckenridge on services (see p. 47 of memorial); Prof. Joseph Henry, Rev. Dr. Hodge, of theological seminary at Princeton (see p. 30 of memorial); remarkable interviews and correspondence of Judge B. F. Wade (see pp. 23–26 of memorial).

That this campaign prevented the recognition of Southern independence by its fatal effects on the Confederate States is shown by letters from Hon. C. M. Clay (see pp. 40, 43 of memorial), and by his letters from St. Petersburg; also, those of Mr. Adams and Mr. Dayton from London and Paris (see pp. 100–102 of memorial).

That the campaign defeated national bankruptcy, then imminent, and opened the way for a system of finance to defend the Federal cause is shown by the debates of the period in both Houses of Congress; by the utterances of Mr. Spalding, Mr. Diven, Mr. Thaddeus Stevens, Mr. Roscoe Conkling, Mr. John Sherman, Mr. Henry Wilson, Mr. Fessenden, Mr. Trumbull, Mr. Foster, Mr. Garrett Davis, Mr. John

C. Crittenden, &c., found for convenient reference in appendix to memorial, page 59; also therein the opinion of the English press as to why the Union could not be restored.

The condition of the struggle can best be realized as depicted by the leading statesmen in Congress previous to the execution of these military movements (see synopsis of debates from *Congressional Globe*, pp. 21, 22 of memorial).

The effect of this campaign upon the country and the anxiety to find out and reward the author are evinced by the resolution of Mr. Roscoe Conkling in the House of Representatives, 24th of February, 1862 (see debates on the origin of the campaign, pp. 39-63 of memorial). But it was deemed prudent to make no public claim as to authorship while the war lasted (see Colonel Scott's view, p. 32 of memorial).

The wisdom of the plan was proven, not only by the absolute advantages which resulted, giving the mastery of the conflict to the national arms and ever more assuring their success even against the powers of all Europe should they have combined, but it was likewise proven by the failures to open the Mississippi or win any decided success on the plan first devised by the government.

It is further conclusively shown that no plan, order, letter, telegram, or suggestion of the Tennessee River as the line of invasion has ever been produced except in the paper submitted by Miss Carroll on the 30th of November, 1861, and her subsequent letters to the government as the campaign progressed.

It is further shown to this committee that the able and patriotic publications of the memorialist in pamphlets and newspapers, with her high social influence, not only largely contributed to the cause of the Union in her own State, Maryland (see Governor Hicks letters, p. 27 of memorial), but exerted a wide and salutary influence on all the border States (see Howard's Report, p. 33, and p. 75 of memorial). These publications were used by the government as war measures, and the debate in Congress shows that she was the first writer on the war powers of the Government (see p. 45 of memorial). Leading statesmen and jurists bore testimony to their value, including President Lincoln, Secretaries Chase, Stanton, Seward, Welles, Smith, Attorney General Bates, Senators Browning, Doolittle, Collamer, Cowan, Reverdy Johnson, and Hicks, Hon. Horace Binney, Hon. Benjamin H. Brewster, Hon. William M. Meredith, Hon. Robert J. Walker, Hon. Charles O Connor, Hon. Edwards Pierrepont, Hon. Edward Everett,

Hon. Thomas Corwin, Hon. Francis Thomas, of Maryland, and many others, found in memorial.

The Military Committee, through General Howard, in the Forty-First Congress, 3rd session, Document No. 337, unanimously reported that Miss Carroll did cause the change of the military expedition from the Mississippi to the Tennessee, &c.; and the aforesaid act of the 42d Congress, 2nd session, Document No. 167, as found in memorial, reported through Hon. Henry Wilson the evidence and bill in support of this claim. Again, in the Forty-Fourth Congress, the Military Committee of the House favourably considered this claim, and Gen. A. S. Williams was prepared to report, and, being prevented by want of time, placed on record that this claim is incontestably established, and that the country owes to Miss Carroll a large and honest compensation, both in money and in honours, for her services in the national crises.

In view of all these facts, this committee believes that the thanks of the nation are due Miss Carroll, and that they are fully justified in recommending that she be placed on the pension rolls of the government as a partial measure of recognition for her public service, and report here with a bill for such purpose and recommend its passage.

Hon. E. M. Stanton came into the War Department in 1862 pledged to execute the Tennessee campaign.

Statement from Hon. B. F. Wade, chairman of the Committee on the Conduct of the War, April 4, 1876. (This is the long letter from Mr. Wade, which we have already given, and we need not repeat it.)

★★★★★★

General Bragg prepared and suggested the following bill to accompany the report, (I copied this from a printed account some years ago, conversing lately with a friend of General Bragg, I was assured that this was the first bill prepared):—

> *Be it enacted,* That the same sum and emoluments given by the government to the major generals of the United States Army be paid to Anna Ella Carroll from the date of her services to the country, in November, 1861, to the time of the passage of this act; and the further payment of the same amount as the pay and emoluments of a major general of the United States Army be paid to her in quarterly instalments to the end of her life, as a partial measure of recognition of her services to the nation, (and recommend its passage).

To suggest a bill that should rightfully mark the pre-eminently military nature of the services rendered without giving offense to the class accustomed to monopolise the sounding titles and to wear the glittering plumes was a wonderfully difficult thing to do. Here at least was a brave and honest effort to accomplish what no previous committee had even attempted. The other committees had left the award a blank, to be filled in by a puzzled and unwilling Congress, who preferred to do nothing at all.

In England, probably there would not have been the same insuperable difficulty, a sovereign lady holding high military office as a matter of course; but we have thrown aside some noble traditions, and America never has a sovereign lady.

There was something noble and fitting in this recommendation of award by General Bragg. Considering how great public services have been formerly rewarded, it was certainly not extreme.

To go back to English history:—

The Duke of Marlborough, who commanded the allied armies of England, Austria, and Germany, received the most flattering testimonials in all forms. A principality was voted to him in Germany, while the English Government settled upon him the manor of Woodstock, long a royal residence, and erected thereon a magnificent palace as an expression of a nation's gratitude. On the Duke of Wellington honours, offices, and rewards were showered from every quarter. The crown exhausted its stores of titles, and in addition to former grants the sum of £200,000 was voted in 1815 for the purchase of a mansion and estate, etc. The rank of field marshal in four of the greatest armies in the world was bestowed by the leading governments of Europe.

"In England it has for a long time been the custom to reward and honour those illustrious in the realms of science and literature as well as of military success. Though with less demonstration and expenditure of wealth, our own country has not overlooked signal services in its behalf. The government of Pennsylvania in the days of the Revolution voted £2,500 for the political writings of Thomas Paine, and New York a farm of 300 acres in a high state or cultivation, with elegant and spacious buildings. Washington himself gave a woman a sergeant's commission in the army, who stood at the gun by which her husband had fallen, and on his recommendation, she was placed on the pay-roll for life.

Congress, in pursuance of this feeling, has not been un mind-ful of Anderson's heroic defence of Fort Sumter, of Farragut's capture of New Orleans, of Rawlins, etc., of Stanton, and of Lincoln, in conferring tokens of recognition for their services upon the families who survived them. Many instances might be cited where public-spirited women have been rewarded for services rendered in individual cases during the late struggle and in other forms since.

And was it not fitting that the author of such influential pamphlets and the designer of the remarkable plan of the Tennessee campaign should be honourably recognised and rewarded?

Miss Carroll was in her 66th year at the time of General Bragg's recommendation. Her father was no longer living, her family was scattered, her health was failing, and her time, strength, and fortune had been wholly expended in the service of her country with noble generosity and the most brilliant results. Surely she deserved to spend the remaining years of her life in honourable independence, distin-guished and beloved by the nation to whom she had rendered incal-culable service.

Now it seemed as if, after such an unqualified indorsement of her work by three successive military committees appointed for the pur-pose, and a suitable bill prepared, that surely her cause was won. Miss Carroll had been informed of the report and of the bill that had been prepared. But the Military Committee, having made this excellent summary of evidence, indorsed Miss Carroll's claim in the strongest manner, and prepared a noble and fitting bill, became greatly alarmed at what they had done. Leaving their report unchanged, at the last moment they hastily withdrew the dignified and fitting bill and sub-stituted in its place the following surprising performance:—

Be it enacted by the Senate and House of Representatives of the Unit-ed States of America in Congress assembled, That the Secretary of the Interior be, and he is hereby, authorised and directed to place upon the pension-rolls of the United States the name of Anna Ella Carroll, and to pay to her a pension of fifty dollars per month from and after the passage of this act, during her life, for the important military service rendered the country by her during the late civil war.

Such a report and *such* a bill side by side stand an anomaly unparalleled.

Truly the life of the nation was rated as a cheap thing.

Of course, the bill died immediately of its own glaring and ineffable meanness.

One can hardly say whether it would have been the more unworthy thing to pass such a bill or to pass none at all; but the last, being the most timorous course, had been adopted for ten successive years, as it has also been resorted to in the ten succeeding ones.

The Military Committee of 1881, having accomplished this astonishing feat, threw away their arms and ignominiously fled—and Congress followed in the rear, indefinitely postponing action on an unwelcome claim, that always *would* turn up "incontestably proven."

CHAPTER 9

A Wounded Veteran Retires from the Field

Miss Carroll, urged on by the friends of justice and historical verity, had made great efforts rightly to present her case and to get together a wonderful mass of indubitable testimony.

She had been informed of the thorough endorsement of her claim made by the Military Committee and reported by General Bragg, and of the noble and fitting bill which he had prepared. Then came that pitiful little bill and the adjournment of Congress without taking further action upon the claim.

She perhaps did not realise, in the presence of what seemed immediate defeat, that she had performed a great and lasting historical work in putting the whole matter on immovable record; but she certainly realised that, though an angel should come from heaven to testify, it would be useless to expect national recognition. A reaction of discouragement followed, and she was suddenly stricken down by paralysis, which threatened at once to terminate her noble life. For three years, she hovered between life and death, no hope being entertained of her recovery.

Then the natural vigour of her constitution reasserted itself, and she slowly regained a very considerable portion of health; but any subsequent efforts with regard to her claim, though receiving her assent, had to be made without her personal co-operation, as mental fatigue was imperatively forbidden. She had ceased to hope for any benefit to herself personally from the prosecution of her claim; but, rejoicing in the sense of the great work that she had been providentially called upon to accomplish, she rested in the serene conviction that with the incontestable evidence that had been presented the facts could not be forever buried out of sight, and that ultimately the truths of history would be secure.

When Miss Carroll, who had hitherto been as a tower of strength to her family, was suddenly stricken down, fortune seemed to be at its lowest ebb; but again, the Carroll energy and ability came to the rescue. An unmarried sister, with noble devotion, sustained the nation's benefactress. She obtained work in teaching in Baltimore and by hard daily toil provided for her support. But those were very dark days that followed. Then this same brave sister, through the influence of an eminent lady at the White House, obtained a clerkship at the Treasury, at Washington, brought her sister from Baltimore and established her in a little unpretending family home, which she has sustained to this day, (1894).

★★★★★★

Note.—Owing to the confusion attendant upon Miss Carroll's well-nigh fatal illness and her subsequent removal to Baltimore, a trunk and box marked A. E. C. were left behind at the Tremont House, in Washington.

After the severe three years' prostration ended, Miss Carroll inquired for this trunk and box, and learned that the Tremont House had gone into other hands after the death of Mr. Hill; that all its contents had been sold off, and to this day she has sought in vain to learn what has become of that box and trunk. They contained a great number of letters, a completed history of Maryland, and her materials for several projected works.

Thus, through the cruel neglect she had experienced, the world has lost the benefit of works which, from her exceptional ability and her exceptional opportunities, would have been of inestimable value to our future literature.

If anyone knows of the fate of that trunk and box they are requested to send word to Miss Carroll or to the present writer, and if ever that history of Maryland comes to light it will be claimed for Miss Carroll, as there are internal evidences which would establish its identity.

Governor Hicks a few days before his death committed to Miss Carroll all his papers with a request that she would write the history of Maryland in connection with the civil war, and the part performed by him in the maintenance of the Union.

Cassius M. Clay also sent to her his letters and papers desiring that she should write his biography.

During Miss Carroll's long and apparently hopeless illness Mr. Clay's letters were sent for and returned to him.

★★★★★★

Another ray of light, too, had come to cheer the invalid. A new power was rising upon the horizon in the growing thoughtfulness and development of women, now banding together in clubs, societies, and confederations, with their own journals, newspapers, and publications, and with the avowed determination of never resting until women, as an integral half of the people, had obtained all the rights and privileges proclaimed in the Declaration of Independence, the granting of which alone could make of our country a sound and true Republic and secure the ultimate triumph of the moral and humane considerations and measures upon which its welfare must depend.

Naturally, when this growing party came to know of Miss Carroll's remarkable work they were not disposed to let it fall into oblivion. It seemed as if the Lord himself had declared for their cause in giving to a woman, at the crisis of the national peril, the remarkable illumination that, so far as human knowledge can judge, had turned the scale of war in favour of our National Union, and had thus pledged the country for all future time to the just recognition of the equal rights of women as an integral half of the people, and of equal importance with their brethren to the welfare of the State. Every effort may be made to ignore and hide the remarkable fact, but the work of the Lord remains steadfast, immovable, and incapable of lasting defeat.

The moving finger writes,
And, having writ,
Moves on.

A notice of Miss Carroll and her brilliant achievements had been written by Mrs. Matilda Joselyn Gage and incorporated in the history of Woman Suffrage, a considerable work, giving a sketch of the career of many eminent women. Mrs. Gage also wrote and circulated a pamphlet calling attention to the case, and Miss Phoebe Couzzins made great exertions in her behalf. One and another began to inquire what had become of the woman who had done such wondrous work for the national cause and had been treated with such deep ingratitude. Mrs. Cornelia C. Hussey, daughter of a high-principled New York family of friends, sought her out, visited her at Baltimore, cheered her with her sympathy, and, interesting others in her behalf, she was enabled to strengthen the hands of the devoted sister. She induced the

North American Review, of April, 1886, to publish an account furnished by Miss Carroll, and she procured the publication of a series of letters in the *Woman's Journal*, of Boston, that increased the knowledge and interest beginning to be felt for Miss Carroll's work.

Petitions began to pour in asking Congress to take action in the case. In 1885 it was taken up by the Court of Claims, and in case 93 may be seen the result. The evidence presented, though remarkable, was by no means as complete as it should have been, owing to Miss Carroll's illness and to the difficulty of now procuring copies of her pamphlets. Consequently, though the judgment rendered makes notable admissions and the *moral assent* runs all through, the court was enabled, through some legal defects, to retransmit the case to Congress for its consideration; and having once made its decision, the case cannot again come before that court without a direct order from Congress to take it up and try it again.

Looking over the brief at the Court of Claims, made by the late Colonel Warden, I noted this significant passage, (Brief of claimant in Congressional case 93):—

It may not be amiss here to submit that the two and only drawbacks or obstacles that we have met to the immediate, prompt, and unanimous passage of an act of Congress in recognition of and adequate compensation for the patriotic services and successful military strategy of Miss Carroll in the late civil war are found first in an obstruction which President Lincoln encountered and which he referred to when he explained to Senator Wade that the Tennessee plan was devised by Miss Carroll, and military men were exceedingly jealous of all outside interference. (House Miss. Doc. 58). The second obstacle which has stayed us is founded in a (to some men) seemingly insuperable objection, often demonstrated in words and acts by our legislators—a misfortune or disability (if it be one) over which Miss Carroll had no control whatever, namely, in the fact that she is a woman.

It would appear that the decision of the Court of Claims retransmitting the claim to Congress was considered by Miss Carroll's friends to be in her favour.

Erastus Brooks writes her at this time:—

Dear Miss Carroll:

Your *Reminiscences of Lincoln* (a work suggested by Mrs. Hussey) should, as far as possible, bring out the words and own thoughts of the man. The subject, the man, and the occasion are the points to be treated, and in this order, perhaps.

Again, my old and dear friend, I am very glad and hope the award will meet all your expectations—mental, pecuniary, and of every kind. The hope of the award to yourself and friends must be as satisfactory as the judgment of the court.

Yours,

Erastus Brooks.

Miss Carroll showed this letter to Mrs. Hussey, who copied and immediately published it.

Miss Carroll, who had always been on friendly terms with General Grant, spoke to him of her claim. They conversed together concerning her work. He assured her that he had not been aware of its extent, and advised her by all means to continue to push her claim. I have seen the draft of a letter, written by Miss Carroll at this time, to General Grant in which she alludes to the advice he had given her to push her claim before Congress. The letter is written in the friendliest spirit and in a tone of touching modesty. It should be here noted that there never was any antagonism between these two who had done such great work for the salvation of their country.

Cassius M. Clay wrote to the editor of the New York *Sun* the following letter, as published in that journal:

White Hall, Kentucky, March 3, 1886.
In 1861, as soon as I could get General Scott apart from his staff of rebel sympathizers, I advised him to reach the Southern forces by all the waterways, as the shortest and most practical lines of attack. This advice was hardly necessary as every tyro in the Union Army would probably have done the same. But it belonged to Miss Anna Ella Carroll to project and force upon the bewildered army officers—Halleck, Grant, and others—the cutting in two of the Confederacy by way of the Tennessee River by means of the gunboats, and of our facilities of thus concentrating troops and supplies. It was the great strategical coup of the war.

I call the attention of the American nation to Miss Carroll's article in the April number of the *North American Review* of 1886. It appears that the splendid conception of this project called for the immediate reward of a grateful Congress as the representative of the whole people. But when it was found that it was neither Grant, nor Halleck, nor Buell, but a woman, who showed more genius and patriotism than all the army of military men, the resolution was suppressed and the combined effort of many of the ablest men of the Republican party could never resurrect it. Miss Carroll merely states her case. There is no event in history better backed up with impregnable evidence.

Cassius M. Clay.

Mr. Clay also wrote to Mrs. Hussey the following letter, which she sends me for publication:—

April 12, 1886.

C. C. Hussey.

Dear Madame: Your letter and circular of the 8th inst. are received. I was a long time a correspondent of Miss C., never having seen her, but holding a letter of introduction from Vice-President Henry Wilson. I have no stand point in politics of influence now. . . . . .Miss Carroll's case shows the infinite baseness of human nature—how few worship truth and justice. I am already assailed for speaking a word in her cause, and shall have all the old feuds against me revived; but I am not dependent upon the American people for subsistence and am not a petitioner for money or office, so I speak my mind.

Very truly yours,

C. M. Clay.

Miss Katharine Mason, Miss Anna C. Waite, Miss Phoebe Couzzins, Mrs. H. J. Boutelle, Mrs. Louisa D. Southworth, Mrs. Esther Herrman, and a host of other prominent ladies in succession took up the cause, publishing articles east and west, and speaking upon the subject or contributing in some way to the cause. Petitions to Congress continued asking attention to Miss Carroll's case, and that due recognition and award should be accorded to her. High-principled Senators and Representatives would take up these petitions and present them with their own endorsement of the case.

But ten righteous men count for little among a mass of Senators and Representatives wildly pushing their own individual and party measures. Every human being with a ballot might be worthy of their attention, but a disfranchised class must go to the wall. With every extension of the ballot such a class sinks deeper and deeper in the scale, and the disregard and contempt for women and their claims becomes inborn for law is an educator.

In the spring of 1890 Mr. and Mrs. Root spent weeks in Washington verifying, step by step, the incontrovertible facts of Miss Carroll's work. The *Woman's Tribune,* of Washington, generously published a large edition of their report, enclosed advanced sheets, with a personal letter, to every Senator and Representative, and laid them upon their desks, with the invariable result of continued neglect.

Mrs. Abby Gannett Wells, of a highly cultivated Boston family, took up the cause with enthusiasm, made a tour among the army relief posts, and created among soldiers and soldiers' wives a lively interest in the work of their great coadjutor. Tokens of recognition were sent to Miss Carroll, and many a retired veteran, beside his evening fire, put down his name to petitions for her just recognition. Then this brave lady made another effort. She published in the Boston *Sunday Herald,* of February, 1890, an account, from which we give the following extract, having already given extracts from the earlier portion:

> In the last year so many women throughout the country had come to take an interest in this case, petitions to Congress asking for Miss Carroll's suitable recognition and remuneration were sent in considerable numbers, some being presented in the Senate by Mr. Hoar and some in the House by Mr. Lodge. In September last, at an interview with these gentlemen in Boston, I learned it to be their opinion that if I made a plea in Miss Carroll's behalf before the two Congressional Committees on Military Affairs an interest might be aroused to lead to successful results. I therefore promised to visit Washington, and went to the city in the second week in February of the present year. The bill calling for an appropriation from Congress for Miss Carroll's services during the civil war, such services consisting of the preparation of papers used as war measures and the furnishing of the military plan for our western armies, known as the plan of the Tennessee campaign, had already been presented in the Senate by General Manderson, of Nebraska, and in the House by Mr. Lodge, of Massachusetts.
>
> As Mr. Hoar was ill when I arrived in Washington, he wrote a letter to Mr. Manderson, asking for an early hearing for me, and then sent his private secretary to conduct me to that gentleman in person. I write particulars of the obtaining of these hearings simply to show that even a case demanding urgent action

like this finds unexpected obstacles that threaten to retard it in definitely.

Mr. Manderson met me kindly, but stated that the committee had such a pressure of business on hand it seemed impossible to take time for Miss Carroll's case, greatly as some of the members had it at heart. But on my replying that I represented the wishes of many women, and we could appeal nowhere else in order for this injustice to be righted, he said if I would come to the committee-room on the morning of the 5th I should be given what time was possible.

On that morning, General Hawley, the chairman, received me pleasantly, but stated, as he introduced me to the members, that it was unusual to give such a hearing, and he trusted that I would occupy only a little time; but I am glad to add that the committee's courtesy quite exceeded what might be expected of these busy workers. I had over half an hour of their most earnest attention, and if the expressions upon their faces were a criterion to judge by, Miss Carroll's story was not without its effect upon their sympathy and sense of right. I was particularly glad to see such evidences, because among their members were ex-Confederates, Gen. Wade Hampton being one.

When Mr. Lodge presented me to General Cutcheon, chairman of the House committee, I heard again the plea of overmuch business; yet the concession was made—I might come on the morning of the 7th and occupy a "few minutes." Promptly at the hour I was at the committee-room, and since the time was to be so short I had put aside my notes and was telling of Miss Carroll's work, and growing sure of the interest of my listeners, when the chairman interrupted, saying that it now occurred to him that a bill asking for an appropriation belonged with the Committee on War Claims.

A book was consulted, and it became the opinion of the committee that this bill did belong with the War Claims Committee. As, in order for me to appear before that committee, the bill would have to go back to the House and be remanded there, and there might be some delay about it, the Military Committee passed a unanimous vote asking the Committee on War Claims to hear my plea at their next meeting, in view of the bill not appearing until later.

This was discouraging, and the matter grew more so when,

on meeting General Thomas, of the War Claims Committee, I was assured that the bill could not possibly belong there. By good fortune I met General Cutcheon at one of the doors of the ladies' gallery of the House, and I told him the dilemma. He generously went to the Speaker and got his decision, which was that either committee could decide as to the merits of the bill. Being given my choice, I decided to appear again before the Military Committee.

That brought the hearing round to the 11th, the limit of my possible stay in the city. When a quorum had assembled General Cutcheon stated the case, and I was about to begin, when a member objected. He was sure that the bill belonged with the Committee on War Claims. A second member expressed himself as decidedly. A short discussion took place, the vote was put, it was against me and I was dismissed.

I turned away, having never had in my life a greater sense of disappointment. Had I not known that the objection was so purely technical I could have borne the situation better; but to lose the opportunity for this, return home with my mission unaccomplished, see Miss Carroll herself, and tell her that the effort had been nipped in the bud, it seemed impossible to submit to it.

Mr. Wise of Virginia, the gentleman who had first objected, now appeared to have a second thought.

Since the lady has come so far, and in behalf of another person, it seems to me we hardly ought to dismiss her so summarily.

I hastened to say that the bill had had a similar fate before, had passed and repassed from Military and War Claims Committees until action was wholly prevented.

Mr. Wise thereupon asked for a reconsideration of the motion. The final result was that a unanimous vote allowed me to present my appeal.

After this generous action I found the presentation of the case a pleasure rather than a duty. It was rather a conversation with liberal-minded gentlemen. When they learned that President Lincoln, his Secretaries, and Senators and Representatives whose names are famous vouched for Miss Carroll's work, the integrity of her claim more surely revealed itself to them.

The case was ordered to Mr. Wise for special consideration, which he cordially promised to give.

As I left the committee-room I could not help congratulating myself over the ill-omened beginning, since it had resulted toward a relation of the work far more complete than had otherwise been the case.

That day I saw the aged invalid for the first time. She is a most remarkable woman still. I heard from her own lips the story I knew so well, but rendered more thrilling than ever as thus repeated; and I had the happiness of telling her that I believed her case was now in safe hands.

Not long after, through the unseating of Mr. Wise, of Virginia, Hon. Francis W. Rockwell, of this State, received the case as sub-committee. In view of this we ought to be even more hopeful, since his colleagues, Messrs. Hoar and Lodge, have put forth so many efforts in its furtherance.—*Boston Sunday Herald*, February., 1890.

Abby M. Gannett.

The *Century* magazine, which had been publishing an exhaustive account of "the men who fought and planned our battles," was appealed to in the name of historical verity to give an account of Miss Carroll's work. Having had the matter under consideration for more than a year and having convinced themselves of the truth of the claim, they published, in August of 1890, an open letter bringing the case to the attention of their readers. A public-spirited lady of Washington purchased copies and laid the marked article on the desks of Senators and Representatives, with the same invariable result. But though Congress disregarded the matter, not so the reading public, and inquiries began to be made for further information, which it was difficult to furnish for want of an easily attainable printed account. It was therefore determined to meet this demand, and the present relation is the result.

In consequence of the petitions continually received, friendly Senators and Representatives have again and again brought in bills asking for $10,000, or even $5,000, for Miss Carroll's relief (invariably neglected).

Such bills, though very kindly meant, seem to me a mistake. It is—not a question of $5,000 or $500,000. It is it always has been—a question of *recognition*.

Granted that this wonderful woman by the intense labour of heart and brain, by her whole-souled devotion of life and fortune, has saved the national cause for the thousands upon thousands of precious lives laid down would have been of no avail had the plan adopted at the crisis of fate been an unwise one—this granted, a noble bill might be acted upon by Congress, but an *ignoble* one—never. Whatever may be our faults, we are at heart a proud and self-respecting people, and no paltry bill would be endured, and no bill which did not award military honour for pre-eminent military services could meet the case with justice and with dignity.

Although weighed down with an immense mass of obsolete law and custom, shall we say that England leads the van in integrity of principle and devotion to human rights? Although the doctrine of divine right was exploded long ago, England loyally holds to her queen.

As long as it pleases the English people to maintain a royal line, it makes no difference to them whether its representative be a man or a woman. England never had a Salic law. But America—when a grand woman comes to her for her deliverance at the crisis of her fate, crowned with heaven's own prerogative of genius, what America does for her in return for her accepted services is to stamp her under foot and bury her out of sight, that her well-earned glory may fall by default upon the ruling class.

Can America continue to be so unjust to women? Can it continue to hold them down as a disfranchised class?

Owing to continued petitions, Military Committees were appointed during this last Congress to investigate Miss Carroll's claim.

I have not heard the result, but again Congress has adjourned without taking action. About March 27 I had the opportunity of looking over the file which had just comeback from the Senate Committee. First of all, came a surprising number of petitions sent in during this past year; then the documents in evidence of the claim. They were a meagre lot compared to what they should have been. In a case of this importance one would suppose that a copy of every memorial and of every report should have been on the file. Not at all. Quite early in the history of the case "supply exhausted" was the answer given to every request for these documents, and Miss Carroll herself was unable to obtain them.

The reprint of a few of the earlier ones by no means represents them, and owing to the universal exclusion from the Congressional indexes of the later and more important ones, especially the memorial of 1878 and Bragg's report thereon, much important evidence was wanting. Still considering that all that has been printed by "order of Congress" is guaranteed, I should have thought that the evidence given before the Military Committee of 1871 would have been sufficient. Certain I am that if a woman had been on that committee the matter would have assumed more prominence, and there would have been a research for the additional documents that have been omitted. It is the old, old story that every intelligent woman is coming to understand, that you cannot leave to others the interests of a disfranchised class.

In looking over the file at the War Department I noted that there had been inquiries from committees asking if there was a letter of Miss Carroll's there of November 30, 1861, and others mentioned, and the answer returned was "no." It would be in place here to call attention to the fact that they had once been on file there, and the reason that they are there no longer is given in the memorial of 1878, on the evidence of Wade, Hunt, and others.

On April 16, 1891, at the file-room of the House, I saw the file that had come back from the House Committee of this past Congress, whose attention also had been called to the subject in consequence of the many petitions received by the House as well as by the Senate. I counted twenty-five petitions with numerous signatures, as well as some detached letters. An interesting petition was from one of the Army Posts, signed by soldiers and by officers, asking for award to their great coadjutor. I noted a statement in one of them that the widow of one of the generals employed in carrying out the Tennessee campaign had been in receipt, ever since her husband's death, of a pension of $5,000 a year, while the great projector of the campaign had been left neglected.

Asking if there was anything more, another bundle of petitions was handed to me, each package containing a paper, with extracts from the memorials and reports, neatly arranged, giving some of the remarkable letters of Scott, Wade, and Evans, and the decisions of the Military Committees fully endorsing the claim. It would seem that the committees were appointed to receive the petitions, not to consider evidence, as the documentary evidence was not here on the file. And why should they consider it, when the case had been at the first examined carefully, tried, and a unanimous vote had endorsed the claim, and succeeding reports, including the one mistakenly marked as "adverse," all bore witness to the incontestable nature of the evidence. To go on trying a case so established over and over for twenty years would be a manifest absurdity.

And thus, the case stands.

In reading these records a sorrowful thought must come into every woman's soul as she recognises how deep must have been the feeling against women to prevent Congress, in all these years, from coming to a fair and square acknowledgment of the truth.

But a different spirit is coming over the world: A spirit of justice, a spirit of brotherly kindness towards women, shown in innumerable ways and recognised by them with gratitude and joy.

The active men of today, (1894), were children when the Union was saved. Helpless children, when Miss Carroll, in the prime of her life and fullness of her powers, with clearness of perception, with firmness of character, with the light of genius upon her brow, devoted her time, her strength, her fortune, and her great social influence to the national cause that the men of today might have a country, proud, prosperous, and peaceful, to rejoice in themselves and to hand down in unbroken unity to their children.

It should be not only a duty but a blessed privilege—still possible—to see that all that earth can give to brighten the latter days of our great benefactress shall be given her. That she shall be crowned with the undying love and gratitude of a great and a united nation.

And let us remember, too, what it would have been for our country if the noble daughter of Governor Carroll had thought it her duty to keep out of politics while her country was perishing, and to regard the military movements, upon which its life depended, as something outside of a woman's province.

The nation belongs to its women as surely as it belongs to its men. All that concerns its welfare concerns them also, and nature has gifted them with especial attributes of heart and intellect to aid in its guidance and to aid in its salvation.

Life and Writings

Contents

Civil War Papers

41ST CONGRESS, 3RD SESSION. SENATE. REPORT NO. 339.

IN THE SENATE OF THE UNITED STATES.

★★★★★★

FEBRUARY 2, 1871.—ORDERED TO BE PRINTED.

★★★★★★

MR. HOWARD MADE THE FOLLOWING

REPORT:

(TO ACCOMPANY BILL S. NO. 1293.)

The Committee on Military Affairs and the Militia, to whom were referred the memorial and papers of Miss Carroll, of Maryland, claiming to have furnished the government with the information which caused the change in the military expedition which was preparing in 1861 to descend the Mississippi River front that river to the Tennessee River, submit the following report:

Miss Carroll placed in the hands of Hon. Thomas A. Scott, Assistant Secretary of War, on the 30th of November, 1861, the following paper:

The civil and military authorities seem to be labouring under a great mistake in regard to the true key of the war in the Southwest. It is not the Mississippi, but the Tennessee River. It is well known that the eastern part or farming interests of Tennessee and Kentucky are generally loyal, while the middle and western parts, or what are called the planting districts, are in sympathy with the traitors, but, except in the extreme western parts, the Union sentiment still lives. Now all the military preparations made in the West indicate that the Mississippi River is the point to which the authorities are directing their attention. On that

147

river, many battles must be fought and heavy risks incurred before any impression can be made on the enemy, all of which could be avoided by using the Tennessee River.

This river is navigable for medium-class boats to the foot of the Muscle shoals in Alabama, and is open to navigation all the year, while the distance is but two hundred and fifty miles by the river from Paducah, on the Ohio. The Tennessee offers many advantages over the Mississippi. We should avoid the almost impregnable batteries of the enemy, which cannot be taken without great danger and great risk of life to our forces, from the fact that our boats, if crippled, would fall a prey to the enemy by being swept by the current to hills and away from the relief of our friends. But even should we succeed, still we will only have begun the year. for we shall then have to fight to the country front whence the enemy derives his supplies.

Now, an advance up the Tennessee River would avoid this danger, for, if our boats were crippled, they would drop back with the current and escape capture.

But a still greater advantage would be its tendency to cut the enemy's lines in two, by reaching the Memphis and Charleston railroad, threatening Memphis, which lies one hundred miles due west, and no defensible point between; also, Nashville, only ninety miles northeast, and Florence and Tuscumbia, in north Alabama, forty miles east. A movement in this direction would do more to relieve our friends in Kentucky and inspire the loyal hearts in east Tennessee than the possession of the whole of the Mississippi River. If well executed, it would cause the evacuation of all those formidable fortifications on which the rebels ground their hopes of success; and, in the event of our fleet attacking Mobile, the presence of our troops in the northern part of Alabama would be material aid to the fleet.

Again, the aid our forces would receive from the loyal men in Tennessee would enable them soon to crush the last traitor in that region, and the separation of the two extremes would do more than one hundred battles for the Union cause.

The Tennessee River is crossed by the Memphis and Louisville railroad and the Memphis and Nashville railroad. At Hamburg the river makes the big bend on the east, touching the northeast corner of Mississippi, entering the northwest corner of Alabama, forming an arc to the south, entering the State of

Tennessee at the northeast corner of Alabama, and if it does not touch the northwest corner of Georgia, comes very near it. It is but eight miles from Hamburg to the Memphis and Charleston railroad, which goes through Tuscumbia, only two miles from the river, which it crosses at Decatur, thirty miles above, intersecting with the Nashville and Chattanooga road at Stephenson. The Tennessee River has never less than three feet to Hamburg on the "shoalest" bar, and, during the fall, winter, and spring mouths, there is always water for the largest boats that are used on the Mississippi River. It follows from the above facts that in making the Mississippi the key to the war in the West, or rather in overlooking the Tennessee River, the subject is not understood by the superiors in command.

That this plan as suggested was adopted, we submit the following letter from Hon. Thomas A. Scott, then Assistant Secretary of War:

Hon. Jacob M. Howard, United States Senate:
On or about the 30th of November, 1861, Miss Carroll, as stated in her memorial, called on me as Assistant Secretary of War, and suggested the propriety of abandoning the expedition which was then preparing to descend the Mississippi River, and to adopt instead the Tennessee River, and handed to me the plan of campaign, as appended to her memorial, which plan I submitted to the Secretary of War, and its general ideas were adopted. On my return from the Southwest, in 1862, I informed Miss Carroll, as she states in her memorial, that through the adoption of this plan the country had been saved millions, and that it entitled her to the kind consideration of Congress.

Thos. A. Scott.
Philadelphia, June 24, 1870.

The affidavit of Hon. Lemuel D. Evans, of Marshall, Texas, at present chief justice of that State, shows that he was intrusted by our government with a confidential mission to the Mexican border on the Lower Rio Grande, and in the autumn of 1861 proceeded to St. Louis, the then headquarters of the Army of the Southwest, and as the success of his mission depended on the movements of the army in that military department, it became his business to obtain accurate information, and with that object in view he remained in St. Louis until sometime in November. This deponent states that Miss Carroll was in St. Louis in October and November, seeking information, as she claimed and as he believes, in aid of the union; that he held many conversations with her on the military and political situation; that there was boarding in the same hotel with Miss Carroll a Mrs. Scott, a lady who seemed well informed as to what was going on, and whose husband was then a pilot on the steamer *Memphis*, one of the transports in the expedition designed to descend the Mississippi.

A few days after the Battle of Belmont this gentleman, Mr. Scott, came to the hotel, when Miss Carroll sought and obtained an interview through his wife, and becoming impressed with the value of his special knowledge, she requested deponent to join in the interview and to interrogate Mr. Scott, which he did at great length, in regard to the Mississippi, the Tennessee, and Cumberland Rivers; and in reply he stated that it was his opinion, in which all the pilots connected with the expedition concurred, that it would be next to impossible to open the Mississippi with the gunboats.

He mentioned one pilot who had been familiar with these waters for forty years. He stated that it was entirely practicable for the gunboats to ascend, at favourable stages of water, the Cumberland to Nashville, and, at all stages, the Tennessee to the foot of the Muscle shoals. Miss Carroll requested Mr. Scott to write down for her the principal facts she had elicited, and also requested him to communicate to her his observations during his connection with the expedition, to do which he at first declined, on the ground of defective education, as he alleged, but finally he consented. On Miss Carroll's return from the West, she prepared and submitted to deponent for his opinion the plan of the Tennessee River expedition as set forth in her memorial. Being a native and resident of that section, and intimately acquainted with its geography, and particularly with the Tennessee River, deponent was convinced of the military importance of her paper, and advised her to lose no time in laying the same before the War Department, which she did on or about the 30th of November, 1861.

On the 5th of January, 1862, Miss Carroll addressed the following letter to Hon. T. A. Scott:—

Some weeks since, on my return from the West, I gave you my views of the Tennessee River, as being the true strategical key to overcome the rebels in the Southwest. That river is never obstructed by ice at any period of the coldest winter, while every year the Mississippi and Cumberland Rivers sometimes are. Then the gunboats are not well fitted to retreat against the current of the western waters, and as their principal guns are placed forward, they cannot be so efficient against an enemy below them. They must fight with their two stern guns, or else lose all advantage of motion by anchoring by the stern, which will prevent the enemy feeling their range. The gunboats anchored would be at the mercy of the enemy.

The Tennessee River, beginning at Paducah, fifty miles above Cairo, after leaving the Ohio, runs south-southeast, *across* rather than through Kentucky and Tennessee, until it reaches the Mississippi line, directly west of Florence and Tuscumbia, which are fifty miles east, and Memphis, one hundred and twenty-five miles west, with the Charleston and Memphis railroad eight miles from the river. There is no difficulty in reaching this point throughout the year; as I have said before to you, the water is at all times deeper at this point than the Ohio. Again, it is but ninety miles from Nashville, northeast from this. You can see by the map in what condition Buckner would be placed if we could make a strong advance up the Tennessee River He would be compelled to retreat from Kentucky, or if he did not, our forces could take Nashville in his rear, and compel him to lay down his arms.

Hon. B. F. Wade, ex-United States Senator and chairman of the Committee on the Conduct of the War, states that—

He had always understood that it was the information Miss Carroll gave that caused the change in the expedition that was to be sent down the Mississippi River, *from* that river *to* the Tennessee; that a copy of Miss Carroll's paper was shown him immediately after the success of the campaign, by the late Hon. Elisha Whittlesey, of Ohio; that he knows how highly the information and services of this lady were appreciated by President Lincoln and Secretary Stanton, and has heard them both say that she ought to be liberally rewarded; that Hon. Thos. A. Scott, then Assistant Secretary of War, will, no doubt, corroborate what he states, as well as many others; that he is glad to hear her claim is before Congress, and as her services were most beneficial to the government, it is just, and he hopes will be liberally rewarded.

In preferring her claim, Miss Carroll says:—

My claim to having originated this movement receives strong confirmation in the fact that no military man has ever controverted it. It is not to be doubted that no educated gentleman could have been ignorant of the fact that the Tennessee was a navigable river, and run from the very centre of the rebellion north through the States of Tennessee and Kentucky, but the significance of this knowledge had not awakened the attention of any one, and my special claim to merit is that I was the first to point out to the government how this knowledge could be made available. In preferring my claim to this, I cannot, by any possibility, detract from our brave and heroic commanders, to whom the country owes so much, and, so far from opposing me, I believe that, as a class, they would be gratified to see me or anyone properly rewarded according to the part performed in this mighty drama.

From the high social position of this lady and established ability as a writer and thinker, she was prepared at the inception of the rebellion to exercise a strong influence in behalf of liberty and Union. That it was felt and respected in Maryland during the darkest hours in that State's history there can be no question. Her publications throughout the struggle were eloquently and ably written and widely circulated, and did much to arouse and invigorate the sentiment of loyalty in Maryland and other border States. It is not too much to say that they were among the very ablest publications of the time, and exerted a powerful influence upon the hearts of the people.

Some of these publications were prepared under the auspices of the War Department, and for these Miss Carroll preferred a claim to reimburse her for the expenses incurred in their publication, which ought to have been paid; and as evidence of this we subjoin the following statement from the Assistant Secretary of War:—

Philadelphia, January 28, 1863.
All my interviews with Miss Carroll were in my official capacity as Assistant Secretary of War. The pamphlets published were, to a certain extent, under a general authority then exercised by me in the discharge of public duties as Assistant Secretary of War. No price was fixed, but it was understood that the government would treat her with sufficient liberality to compensate her for any service she might render.

On the 15th of June, 1870, Hon. Thomas A. Scott addressed a letter to Hon. J. M. Howard, U. S. Senate, in which he says:—

I learn from Miss Carroll that she has a claim before Congress for services rendered in the year 1861 in aid of the government. I believe, now, that the government ought to reward her liberally for the efforts she made in its behalf to rouse the people against the rebellious action of the South. I hope you will be able to pass some measure that will give Miss Carroll what she is certainly entitled to.

Thos. A. Scott.

In view, therefore, of the highly meritorious services of Miss Carroll during the whole period of our national troubles, and especially at that epoch of the war to which her memorial makes reference, and in consideration of the further fact that all the expenses incident to this service were borne by herself, the committee believe her claim to be just, and that it ought to be recognised by Congress, and consequently report a bill for her relief.

46TH CONGRESS. 3RD SESSION, HOUSE OF REPRESENTATIVES. REPORT NO. 386.

ANNA ELLA CARROLL.

★★★★★★

MARCH 3, 1881.—COMMITTED TO THE COMMITTEE OF THE WHOLE HOUSE AND ORDERED TO BE PRINTED.

★★★★★★

E. S. BRAGG, FROM THE COMMITTEE ON MILITARY AFFAIRS, SUBMITTED THE FOLLOWING

REPORT:

(TO ACCOMPANY BILL H. R. 7256.)

The Committee on Military Affairs, to whom the memorial of Anna Ella Carroll was referred, asking national recognition and reward for services rendered the United States during the war between the States, after careful consideration of the same, submit the following:

In the autumn of 1861 the great question as to whether the Union could be saved, or whether it was hopelessly subverted, depended on the ability of the government to open the Mississippi and deliver a fatal blow upon the resources of the Confederate power. The original plan was to reduce the formidable fortifications by descending this river, aided by the gunboat fleet, then in preparation for that object.

President Lincoln had reserved to himself the special direction of this expedition, but before it was prepared to move he became convinced that the obstacles to be encountered were too grave and serious for the success which the exigencies of the crisis demanded, and the plan was then abandoned, and the armies diverted up the Tennessee River, and thence southward to the centre of the Confederate power.

The evidence before this committee completely establishes that Miss Anna Ella Carroll was the author of this change of plan, which involved a transfer of the national forces to their new base in North Mississippi and Alabama, in command of the Memphis and Charleston railroad; that she devoted time and money in the autumn of 1861 to the investigation of its feasibility is established by the sworn testimony of L. D. Evans, chief justice of the supreme court of Texas, to the Military Committee of the United States Senate in the Forty-Second Congress (see pp. 40, 41 of memorial); that after that investigation she submitted her plan in writing to the War Department at Washington, placing it in the hands of Col. Thomas A. Scott, Assistant Secretary of War, as is confirmed by his statement (see p. 38 of memorial); also confirmed by the statement of Hon. B. F. Wade, chairman of the Committee on the Conduct of the War, made to the same committee (see p. 38), and of President Lincoln and Secretary Stanton (see p. 39 of memorial); also by Hon. O. H. Browning, of Illinois, Senator during the war, in confidential relations with President Lincoln and Secretary Stanton (see p. 39, memorial); also that of Hon. Elisha Whittlesey, Comptroller of the Treasury (see p. 41, memorial); also by Hon. Thomas H. Hicks, governor of Maryland, and by Hon. Frederick Feckey's affidavit, comptroller of the public works of Maryland (see p. 127 of memorial); by Hon. Reverdy Johnson (see pp. 26 and 41, memorial), Hon. George Vickers, United States Senator from Maryland (see p. 41, memorial), again by Hon. B. F. Wade (see p. 41, memorial), Hon. J. T. Headley (see p. 43, memorial), Rev. Dr. R. J. Breckinridge on services (see p. 47, memorial), Professor Joseph Henry, Rev. Dr. Hodge, of Theological Seminary at Princeton (see p. 30, memorial); remarkable interviews and correspondence of Judge B. F. Wade (see pp. 23—26 of memorial).

That this campaign prevented the recognition of Southern independence by its fatal effects on the Confederate States is shown by letters from Hon. C. M. Clay (see pp. 40, 43 of memorial), and by his letters from St. Petersburg; also, those of Mr. Adams and Mr. Dayton from London and Paris (see pp. 100-102 of memorial).

That the campaign defeated national bankruptcy, then imminent, and opened the way for the system of finance to defend the Federal cause is shown by the debates of the period in both houses of Congress; by the utterances of Mr. Spalding, Mr. Diven, Mr. Thaddeus Stevens, Mr. Roscoe Conkling, Mr. John Sherman, Mr. Henry Wilson, Mr. Fessenden, Mr. Trumbull, Mr. Foster, Mr. Garrett Davis, Mr. John J. Crittenden, &c., found for convenient reference in appendix to memorial, page 59. Also therein the opinion of the English press as to why the Union could not be restored.

The condition of the struggle can best be realized as depicted by the leading statesmen in Congress previous to the execution of these military movements (see synopsis of debates from Congressional Globe, pp. 21, 22 of memorial).

The effect of this campaign upon the country and the anxiety to find out and reward the author are evidenced by the resolution of Mr. Roscoe Conkling in the House of Representatives 24th of February, 1862 (see debates on the origin of the campaign, pp. 39-63 of memorial). But it was deemed prudent to make no public claim as to authorship while the war lasted (see Colonel Scott's view, p. 32 of memorial).

The wisdom of the plan was proven, not only by the absolute advantages which resulted, giving the mastery of the conflict to the national arms and ever more assuring their success, even against the powers of all Europe, should they have combined, but it was likewise proven by the failures to open the Mississippi or win any decided success on the plan first devised by the government.

It is further conclusively shown that no plan, order, letter, telegram, or suggestion of the Tennessee river as the line of invasion has ever been produced except in the paper submitted by Miss Carroll on the 30th of November, 1861, and her subsequent letters to the government as the campaign progressed.

It is further shown to this committee that the able and patriotic publications of memorialist in pamphlets and newspapers, with her high social influence, not only largely contributed to the cause of the Union in her own State, Maryland (see Governor Hicks's letters, p. 27, memorial), but exerted a wide and salutary influence on all the border States (see Howard's report, p. 33 and p. 75 of memorial).

These publications were used by the government as war measures, and the debate in Congress shows that she was the first writer on the war powers of the government (see p. 45 of memorial). Leading statesmen and jurists bore testimony to their value, including President Lincoln, Secretaries Chase, Stanton, Seward, Welles, Smith, Attorney General Bates, Senators Browning, Doolittle, Collamer, Cowan, Reverdy Johnson, and Hicks; Hon. Horace Binney, Hon. Benjamin H. Brewster, Hon. William M. Meredith, Hon. Robert J. Walker, Hon. Charles O'Conor, Hon. Edwards Pierrepont, Hon. Edward Everett, Hon. Thomas Corwin, Hon. Francis Thomas, of Maryland, and many others found in memorial.

The Military Committee, through Senator Howard, in the Forty-First Congress, third session, document No. 337, unanimously reported that Miss Carroll did cause the change of the military expedition from the Mississippi to the Tennessee River, etc.; and the aforesaid committee of the Forty-Second Congress, second session, document No. 167, as found in memorial, reported, through the Hon. Henry Wilson, the evidence and bill in support of this claim.

Again, in the Forty-Fourth Congress, the Military Committee of the House favourably considered this claim, and General A. S. Williams was prepared to report, and being prevented by want of time, placed on record that this claim is incontestably established, and that the country owes to Miss Carroll a large and honest compensation, both in money and in honours, for her services in the national crisis.

In view of all the facts, this committee believe that the thanks of the nation are due Miss Carroll, and that they are fully justified in recommending that she be placed on the pension-rolls of the government, as a partial measure of recognition for her public service, and report herewith a bill for such purpose and recommend its passage.

Hon. E. Stanton came into the War Department, in 1862, pledged to execute the Tennessee campaign.

Statement from Hon. B. F. Wade. chairman of the Committee on me Conduct of the War, April 4, 1876.

> Dear Miss Carroll: I had no part in getting up the committee; the first intimation to me was that I had been made the head of it. But I never shirked a public duty, and at once went to work to do all that was possible save the country. We went fully into the examination of the several plans for military operations then known to the government; and we saw plainly enough that the time it must take to execute any of them would make it fatal to the Union.

We were in the deepest despair, until just at this time Colonel Scott informed me that there was a plan already devised that, if executed with secrecy, would open the Mississippi and save the national cause. I went immediately to Mr. Lincoln and talked the whole matter over. He said he did not himself doubt that the plan was feasible, but said there was one difficulty in the way; that no military or naval man had any idea of such a movement, it being the work of a *civilian*, and none of them would believe it safe to make such an advance upon only a navigable river with no protection but a gunboat fleet, and they would not want to take the risk. He said it was devised by Miss Carroll, and military men were extremely jealous of all outside interference.

I plead earnestly with him, for I found there were influences in his cabinet then averse to his taking the responsibility, and wanted everything done in deference to the views of McClellan and Halleck. I said to Mr. Lincoln:

"You know we are now in the last extremity, and you have to choose between adopting and at once executing a plan that you believe to be the right one and save the country or defer to the opinions of military men in command and lose the country."

He finally decided he would take the initiative; but there was Mr. Bates, who had suggested the gunboat fleet, and wanted to advance down the Mississippi as originally designed, but after a little he came to see no result could be achieved on that mode of attack, and he united with us in favour of the change of expedition as you recommended.

After repeated talks with Mr. Stanton I was entirely convinced that if placed at the head of the War Department he would have your plan executed victoriously, as he fully believed it was the only means of safety, as I did.

Mr. Lincoln, on my suggesting Stanton, asked me how the leading Republicans would take it; that Stanton was so fresh from the Buchanan cabinet and so many things said of him. I insisted he was our man withal, and brought him and Lincoln into communication, and Lincoln was entirely satisfied; but so soon as it got out the doubters came to the front, Senators and members called on me. I sent them to Stanton and told them to decide for themselves. The gunboats were then nearly ready for the Mississippi expedition, and Mr. Lincoln agreed, soon as they were, to start the Tennessee movement. It was determined that soon as Mr. Stanton came in the department that Colonel Scott should go out to the western armies and make ready for the campaign in pursuance of your plan, as he has testified before committees.

It was a great work to get the matter started; you have no idea of it. We almost fought for it. If ever there was a righteous claim on earth, you have one. I have often been sorry that, knowing all this, as I did then, I had not publicly declared you as the author. But we were fully alive to the importance of absolute secrecy. I trusted but very few of our people, but to pacify the country I announced from the Senate that the armies were about to move and inaction was no longer to be tolerated, and Mr. Fessenden, head of the Finance Committee, who had been told of the proposed advance, also stated in the Senate that what would be achieved in a few more days would satisfy the country and astound the world.

As the expedition advanced Mr. Lincoln, Mr. Stanton, and myself frequently alluded to your extraordinary sagacity and unselfish patriotism, but all agreed that you should be recognised for your most noble services, and properly rewarded for the same. The last time I saw Mr. Stanton he was on his deathbed; he was then most earnest in his desire to have you come before Congress, as I told you soon after, and said if he lived he would see that justice was awarded you. This I have told you often since, and I believe the truth in this matter will finally prevail.

B. F. Wade.

Preface to the Second Volume of Miss Carroll's Biography

The first volume of the biography was written and published in the winter of 1890-'91.

It was undertaken at the desire of many friends, that work so remarkable in aid of the Union cause during the Civil War should be put upon permanent record.

In carrying out that project Miss Mary Henry Carroll gave valuable aid by furnishing at our request facts of personal history.

At first we feared to make our work known to Miss Anna Ella Carroll, owing to her invalid condition and the danger of causing her excitement, but on receiving the advanced sheets we concluded to submit them to her inspection that we might be satisfied as to their entire accuracy.

As the relation progressed we felt that the papers written under Government auspices should be given in full. They were difficult to obtain as, owing to Miss Carroll's long illness and subsequent removals, the copies had not been preserved. After considerable inquiry, it was ascertained that Charles Sumner had included Miss Carroll's pamphlets in the collection donated by him to the Law School of Harvard College.

Two editions of the War Powers were also found side by side in the library of the State Department at Washington. The librarian kindly allowed them to be copied by Miss Isabel Howland, who gave her valuable assistance out of love for the cause. The short article on the suspension of the writ of *habeas corpus* was from one of Miss Carroll's memorials published by order of Congress. The *Reply to Breckinridge* and the *Relation of the Revolted Citizens* were copied at the Harvard Library by order of the librarian.

On receiving the papers, it was suggested to Miss Carroll that it would add to their interest if she would write a short note for each one, stating under what circumstances it was written. It was an agreeable surprise to receive from her a few days after the graphic short notes now prefacing each article. The bill for writing the pamphlets was presented by Miss Carroll in 1862. It was accompanied by letters from the most distinguished lawyers of the day, certifying that the charge was not only moderate but altogether "too small" for the work accomplished. Yet it remained unpaid, and when the case finally came before the Court of Claims, in 1885, during Miss Carroll's severe illness, the payment was again postponed on the ground that the papers should have been produced, that they might have been valued by the court.

As they were not then at hand, the case was remitted to Congress for its consideration—a consideration which has never yet been accorded or the bill paid. This fact seemed to make it all the more desirable that the papers should be collected and republished They form also a valuable addition to the records of the war and as such we commend them to the attention of the future historian.

S. Ellen Blackwell,

December, 1894.   1708 F St., Washington, D. C.

Note Written by Miss Carroll to Accompany the Republication of Her "Reply to Breckinridge"

(In the spring of 1891 in her seventy-sixth year)

The Hon. John C. Breckinridge was a warm personal friend. I saw much of him during his term as Vice-President and felt an unaccountable interest in him, possibly in a degree augmented by my friendship for his uncle, the Rev. Dr. Robert J. Breckinridge, my former pastor. I regarded him as a Union man, and this impression was well fixed in my mind from the repeated conversations with him in 1860. He was elected to the U. S. Senate almost immediately, if I remember aright, after he retired from the Vice-Presidency. I was present when he took the oath of office. It was on the 4th of March, when Abraham Lincoln became President of the United States. Mr. Breckinridge looked up and saw me as he was sworn in, and I smiled approval of the act, which I then thought equivalent to an open declaration for the Union.

My surprise was therefore unmeasured when, a few days after, he made the finished speech in which he declared himself an uncompromising advocate of secession. I could scarcely realise this sad and solemn fact, in face of the past. His speech was mainly addressed to the border States, and especially to Maryland, where he had many friends and admirers. I at once perceived its baneful influence in my own State, and, without a moment's hesitation, determined to reply to it, and did so to the best of my ability, as will be seen by the following pamphlet, which seemed to have some effect in thwarting the wishes and designs of the Secession party.

A. E. Carroll.

Reply to the Speech of Hon. J. C Breckinridge

Delivered in the United States Senate July 16th, 1861.
By Anna Ella Carroll, of Maryland.
Washington:
Printed Henry Polkinhorn,
1861

Note.—This article was written some weeks since, and was designed for the newspaper press. Its length made it "too voluminous" for that source of publication, and at the solicitation of many distinguished friends it now appears in the present form. Maryland, September 9th, 1861.

★★★★★★

REPLY

I had read with pain the speech of the Hon. John C. Breckinridge, delivered recently in the United States Senate, and with still deeper pain I now see him descending from his high position as a Senator and come to Maryland, to use the fallacies of that speech, for the purpose of stimulating and strengthening the Confederate rebellion. I see him addressing the passions of the crowd, as they cheer "Davis and Beauregard," and evidently his purpose is to excite the military uprising of the people in this State against the government, in aid of Southern treason, and to prepare them for action whenever the leaders shall give the signal.

I have in the spirit of friendship repeatedly repelled by my pen the charge of disunion heretofore made against him. I could not bring myself to believe that one belonging to a family so illustrious in our annals as his own could now be willing to alienate our blessed political heritage. When I also witness the devoted patriotism of his great and gifted uncle (Rev. Dr. R. J. Breckinridge) in the present struggle for constitutional liberty, I cannot but feel sorrow that one who has enjoyed under this government every degree of elevation but the Presidency, and to whom so large a portion of the American people have hitherto looked with confidence and hope, should at last prove himself recreant to the Union's cause.

In his Senatorial speech, to which he refers so vauntingly, he charges that:

> The President, in violation of the Constitution, made war on the Southern States for subjugation and conquest, has increased the army and navy, called forth the militia, blockaded the Southern ports, suspended the writ of *habeas corpus*, and without warrant arrested private persons, searched private houses, seized private papers and effects, &c.

And now, in his Baltimore speech, he asserts that the State of Maryland is abolished, and that her people are "under the shadow of a broad-spreading military despotism." With splenetic acerbity and the skill of the demagogue, he reiterates the charge of arrest without warrant of citizens in this State.

These are grave charges, and if true the President should be made to suffer the extreme penalty of the law.

I shall not refer to the "small band," including Messrs. Powell, Polk, Kennedy, *id genus omne*, whom he says "*would* be heard in the Senate on the personal and political rights of the people," but confine my remarks to Mr. Breckinridge himself.

The argument turns wholly on the question of *fact*, whether the overt act of treason which the Constitution defines to be levying war against the United States has been committed; whether the Confederate States of the South commenced the war.

But, granting his main proposition, that the President has been guilty of making the war (the sad realities of which are before us), it is not less the duty of every American citizen to stand by his country and sustain the government until the war is terminated by an honourable peace.

There can be no equivocal position in this crisis; and he who is not with the government is against it and an enemy to his country. But the major premise of the Senator, namely, that the President made the war upon the South, is *untrue*, and I proceed to show that no one in America knows this better than that gentleman. So far, then, as his

163

position as a Senator of the United States can serve, he has assumed the awful responsibility of conspiring for the overthrow of *his* government, defending accomplices in their labours to dissolve it, and proclaiming the President a usurper for his efforts to preserve it.

Secret but powerful efforts to dissolve this Union have been made in the cotton States since 1831; but, on the 7th of May, 1849, under the instigation of Calhoun, then the chief conspirator, a meeting was held at Jackson, Mississippi, when the secession party formally organised to form a *Southern Confederacy* upon the first act of the General Government on which they could base a pretext. They there laid down their programme, which the conspirators of '60 and '61 have faithfully acted out.

After the death of Calhoun, in 1850, Senator Davis and his confederates in both branches of Congress agreed upon a provisional government and sketched a constitution for a Southern Confederacy! He managed by intrigue to have himself named as its president! This document and the proceedings of the conspirators found its way into the hands of Mr. Clay, but under such circumstances as forbade any public use of it.

In the running debate in the United States Senate, Mr. Clay made frequent pointed and personal allusions to Mr. Davis, in order to draw forth some remark would justify its public use; but Davis, undoubtedly suspecting the motive, studiously avoided giving him the opportunity. That constitution was similar to the one the traitors have now adopted, except that it specially provided for the acquisition of Cuba, Mexico, and all Tropical America.

General Quitman, however, was the recognised leader of the disunion party, and his correspondence as Governor of Mississippi with the prominent conspirators, especially in South Carolina, fully illustrates that programme and develops the treason movement of this day.

Writing to Governor Seabrook the 29th of September of that year, he said:—

Without having fully digested a programme of measures which I shall recommend to the Legislature, it may be of service to you to know that I propose to call a regular convention to take into consideration our Federal relations, with *full powers to annul the Federal compact, establish relations with other States, and adapt our organic to such new relations.* Having no hope of an effectual remedy for existing and prospective evils but in separation from the

Northern States, my view of State action will look to *secession*.

On the 28th of September, Governor McRae, of Mississippi:

> I have not acted without first looking at the ground before me, and I take the privilege of communicating to you in confidence thus early a hasty programme of our future movements. First, then, I believe there is no effective remedy for the evils before us but *secession*.
>
> My idea is that the Legislature should call a convention of delegates, elected by the people, fully empowered to take into consideration our Federal relations and to change or annul them, to adapt our organic law to such new relations as they might establish, to provide for making compacts with other States, and that in the meanwhile an effective *military system* be established and patrol duties most rigidly enforced. In the meantime, every patriot should leave no point untouched where his influence can be exerted. Cheer on the faithful, strengthen the weak, disarm the submissionists, send a fiery cross through the land, and send every gallant son of Mississippi to the rescue.

Governor Seabrook to Quitman, 23rd October, 1850:

> Let me, however, reiterate the assurance that South Carolina is prepared to second Mississippi or any other State in any and every effort to arrest the career of a corrupt and despotic majority. She is ready and anxious for an immediate separation from a Union whose aim is the prostration of our political energies. May I hope Mississippi will begin the patriotic work and allow the *Palmetto* banner the privilege of a place in the ranks.

On December 17, 1850, Governor Seabrook to Quitman:

> I candidly confess to you that I am advocating the immediate action of the Legislature in order to suggest the first Monday in December next for the time and Montgomery, Alabama, as the place of the meeting of Congress. I am rejoiced that the house resolved to suggest to our Southern sister States the propriety of meeting in Congress at Montgomery on the 2nd of January, 1852.
>
> For arming the State $350,000 has been put at the disposal of the governor. I shall be happy to know that the time and place of the proposed Congress will be agreeable to Mississippi.

If our movement be seconded by her I have good reason for the belief that Alabama, Florida, and Arkansas will soon follow the *patriotic* example.

Quitman to Colonel John S. Preston, of South Carolina, March 29, 1851:

The plan proposed by the address of the central committee, which I have forwarded to you, is that the committee *demand redress* for past aggressions and guarantees against future assaults upon our rights, and in the meantime to provide for meeting our sympathizing sister States in a Southern Congress. the proposed redress is:

1. A repeal of the law suppressing the slave trade in the Federal District.

2. Opening of the Territories to the admission of States.

3 Concessions of California south of 36° 30'.

The guarantees to be amendments to the Constitution explicitly to protect slavery from hostile interference by Congress or States, and to restore equal taxation, direct and indirect.

In case the address and guarantees be refused, the States to make formal propositions to their Southern sisters for a *separate* Confederacy, and to unite with any number of them sufficient to secure *national independence*. There are many of us who believe— indeed, are *well assured*—that neither the majority in Congress nor in the non-slaveholding States will assent to either of these just propositions unless demanded by the Southern States with a unanimity not to be expected; but still we think the propositions are due to our confederates *before we part with them*.

I concur with you in the opinion that the political equality of the slaveholding States is incompatible with the present Confederation, as construed and acted on by the *majority*, and that the *present Union and slavery cannot coexist*.

There's no hope whatever of united action beyond the cotton States! For my part I have long ceased to look beyond the cotton *States* for any united action. Indeed, I fear that the frontier States—I mean those bordering on the free States—will never abandon the present Union, however great its oppressions, unless rudely driven from it the North or *forced to choose between a Southern and a Northern Confederacy!*

There is even danger in case of the assembling of a Southern Congress that Virginia, uniting with the other slaveholding States now disposed to submit, will attempt to force upon us some new 'compromise' to preserve the shadow of the Union when the substance is gone.

If, therefore, the people of South Carolina have made up their minds to withdraw from the Union at all events, whether joined by other States or not, my advice would be to do so *without waiting for the action of any ether State,* as I believe there would be more probability of favourable action on the part of the Southern States *after* her secession than before. So long as the several aggrieved States wait for one another, their action will be overcautious and timid. Great political movements, to be successful, must be *bold* and must meet practical and simple issues.

There is, therefore, in my opinion, greater probability of the dissatisfied *States uniting with a seceded State* than of their union for the purpose of secession; The secession of a Southern State would startle the whole South, and *force* the other States to meet the issue plainly. It would present *practical* issues and exhibit everywhere wider-spread discontent than the politicians have imagined. In less than two years all the States south would unite their destiny with *yours.* Should the Federal Government attempt to employ force, an active and cordial union of the whole South would instantly be effected and a complete 'Southern Confederacy' organised.

Governor Means, of South Carolina, to General Quitman, May 15, 1851:—

There is not now the slightest doubt that the next Legislature will call the convention together at a period during the ensuing year, and when *that* convention meets the State will *secede.* We are anxious for co-operation, and also desire that some other State should take the lead, but from recent developments we are satisfied that *South Carolina is the only State* in which sufficient unanimity exists to commence the movement. We will therefore *lead off,* even if we are to stand alone, but trust that our sister States will unite with us.

On the 15th of May, 1851, Colonel Maxy Gregg, of South Carolina, to General Quitman:—

Let them contend manfully for secession, and if beaten in the election they will form a minority so powerful in moral influence that when South Caroline secedes the *first drop of blood that is shed* will cause an irresistible popular impulse in their favour, and the *submissionists* will be *crushed*. Let the example be set in Mississippi, and it will be followed in Alabama and Georgia. Imparting and receiving courage from each other's efforts, the Southern rights men will be ready to carry everything before them in all the three States the moment the *first blow is struck in South Carolina.*

General Quitman to Governor Means, May 25, 1851:—

Experience has fully demonstrated that united action cannot be had. The frontier slave States are even now indicating a disposition to cling to the Union at the hazard of their slave institution. They will not, in my opinion, unite in any effective remedy unless *forced choose between a Northern and Southern Confederacy.*

Governor Seabrook to General Quitman, June 9, 1851:—

The course of the convention will depend somewhat on our sister Southern States. If they affirm the right of secession and the *non-existence of a power to prevent a State from exercising it,* should South Carolina strike a decisive blow, may she confidently rely on the undivided support of her present friends in your State?

Governor Seabrook to Quitman, July 15, 1851:—

I speak advisedly when I say that *volunteers by thousands* are signifying their wish *to be received into our ranks.* Our final course will depend much on Mississippi. If she demands of the Central Government indemnity for the past and security for the future, South Carolina will undoubtedly second the movement.
"If this scheme fail, what then? Let the State proclaim to the world that at a time to be designated, say six months, she will withdraw from the Union, If Mississippi be not prepared to follow her example, a simple annunciation on her part that *any hostile attempt, direct or indirect, by Congress to prevent her* (South Carolina) *from exercising the tights of an independent nation, or to keep her in the Confederacy, would be considered by your Commonwealth a subversion of the fundamental principles on which the States*

confederated, and consequently a full release for her obligations in the Union.

Here we have every idea on which the conspirators are now acting—the calling of conventions; the withdrawal of South Carolina to *force the issue*; the assembling of the cotton States at Montgomery, Alabama; the organisation of a Southern Confederacy; the forcing the border slave States to choose between a Northern and Southern Confederacy; the proposition even of the Crittenden compromise; the arming of the Southern States; the firing on Fort Sumter, with the hope of *drawing blood to cement the Southern States.*

Unfortunately, through Mr. Breckinridge, the original programme of tendering a compromise to the Northern States "before parting with them" was incorporated into the Crittenden compromise. Abusing the confidence reposed in him by Mr. Crittenden, he being in the entire interest of the traitors, artfully introduced into it the very platform on which the Secessionists had supported him for the Presidency. This was done to make its passage through Congress an impossible thing.

This was an audacious insult to every party but the supporters of Mr. Breckinridge, *per se,* because each of these parties had expressly repudiated the doctrine by an overwhelming vote of the American people at the presidential election. But the *people* were clamorous for the salvation of the Union, and without reference to this objectionable feature they at once committed themselves to the proposition, and when it was rejected thousands at the South went over to secession. Men who in voting for Bell or Douglas had planted themselves defiantly against that doctrine were unwittingly cheated and captured by the dastardly secession *manoeuvre.*

An illustration of the use made of the Crittenden compromise may be proper. The State of Georgia passed an ordinance of secession in convention, but agreed to refer it to the people. During the canvass, it became apparent that the people would *defeat* it, and the Secessionists resorted to the strategy of *agreeing to abide by the Crittenden compromise* in order to commit the Union party to the measure, and Toombs returned to the Senate for the purpose of *defeating* that compromise while ostensibly favouring it.

"There was a majority in the Senate committee of thirteen in favour of its passage had *the Secessionists voted for it.* They went into that committee with the express design (as they afterward boasted) of entrapping the opposition into a vote rejecting the proposition. They assumed in committee that as the compromise was a tender to the South, the North should make the terms, and thereby declined to vote with such a supercilious bearing as to constrain Northern men to reject it *in toto*. One of the conspirators then Jesuitically suggested that they had better adopt the "Chicago platform," when some of the Republicans most unwisely assented; whereupon the Secessionists hurried off telegrams to all parts of Georgia that "*all hope of compromise is gone. The Crittenden Proposition has been rejected and the Chicago Platform adopted as the ultimatum.*" The people were thus deceived by these lying dispatches and the Union party was silenced and subdued.

The doctrine found in Seabrook's letter is the doctrine of the conspirators today, (1894), that *the Government cannot use force against a State*; and, if so, it is an act of war. This fatal idea was introduced by Buchanan in his message in December, and, whether by his own treachery or by the traitorous advisers who controlled his administration, it thrust a knife into the ribs of the Constitution, which is now pouring out its life's blood. Had he been true to his oath and exercised his constitutional authority he would have sent a military force to South Carolina, as General Jackson did in 1833, to suppress the rebellion, and enabled men to rally to the flag of the Union throughout the South.

It was on this heretical idea, that the General Government cannot use force in a State to execute *its* laws, that Virginia, Tennessee, North Carolina, and Arkansas seceded. Mr. Breckinridge, in connection with Magoffin, used the doctrine in his State; Jackson did so in Missouri, and the Secession party in Maryland.

The Southern people in 1851 would not sustain the leaders in sufficient strength to enable them to carry out their treasonable designs at that period. These men, therefore, went into the Democratic party to expedite their ambitious and wicked designs against the Union. They were in the Baltimore convention in 1852, and forced the Virginia and Kentucky resolutions into the Democratic platform in order to commit the party stealthily to the doctrine of secession. They then secured the nomination of Franklin Pierce, and thereby controlled his administration. The same party procured the nomination of Buchanan, and took the stand that they never would surrender the power.

They openly proclaimed that if Frémont was elected they would dissolve the Union. That opportunity having been lost, it is not necessary to say here how the administration of Buchanan was improved to their advantage. It is also a matter of too recent occurrence to adduce the proof that the delegations from the cotton States were instructed to go into the Charleston convention to plant their right to the protection of slave property in the Territories, and, failing in that, to secede and nominate a candidate representing their peculiar views. *They failed* and adjourned to Richmond; but, finding only the delegates of the cotton States in attendance, they feared to risk a nomination, and adjourned temporarily, sending a portion of their members to Baltimore under the Jesuitical pretence of harmonising the Democratic party. Their real purpose was to draw recruits from the border slave States, which being accomplished, they again seceded and nominated Mr. Breckinridge; then, returning with his name to Richmond, they *renominated* him, and he thus became the disunion candidate *per se,* formally accepting the same.

The object of that nomination was, if they should fail in the election, *to prevent by armed force* the inauguration of a Republican President. They had planned to inaugurate Breckinridge. I have the avowal of one of the conspirators, who, when asked if Breckinridge assented, replied, "We have not asked him, but he accepted our nomination and of course will carry out our views."

In fact, they addressed to the ambition of the Vice-President the exciting language of Maxy Gregg to General Quitman in 1851:—

> In this great struggle the South wants a great leader, with the mind and the name to impel and guide revolution. *Be that leader*, and your place in history will remain conspicuous for the admiration of all ages to come.

The chiefs of the conspirators went to Washington after the election and assumed the direction of the entire treason movement, and proceeded to organise a military force for the purpose of seizing the government, expelling Lincoln, and inaugurating Breckinridge; but failing to secure Maryland and Virginia by ordinances of secession, they fell back in January upon their original programme, and they directed the seceded States to assemble in convention at Montgomery, Alabama, on the 4th of February, for the purpose of installing the provisional government organised at Washington, with Senator Davis at its head. They resolved to seize the entire property belonging to the General Government in the Southern States, and to retain in their seats a sufficient number of Senators from the seceded States to embarrass any legislation of Congress which might be inimical to their movements, and to act as spies upon the government. They improvised armies and continued to exercise all the functions of the provisional government until its formal installation at Montgomery on the 4th of February.

I have it upon the authority of a Senator who was present that Mr. Breckinridge united with the conspirators in their consultations and gave to them the influence and sanction of his high position. It is a phenomenon in the history of governments without a parallel, and will be an everlasting disgrace upon our civilization, that cabinet ministers, the Vice-President, Senators, and members of Congress should for weeks and months, by the apparent sanction of the President of the United States, have wielded the powers of an organised rebellion for the overthrow of the Constitution and Government they had sworn to support!

Our fathers never could have anticipated this catastrophe. They never dreamed of this parricidal assault upon the Constitution! They wisely provided for the alteration, change, or amendment of our government whenever a majority of the people in the whole United States willed it, or that two-thirds of the States demanded it; but they never foresaw that a few atrociously corrupt men would rise, without regard to the will of the majorities in their several States, and perpetrate the crime of double treachery against their State and Federal Governments!

After the formal meeting of the Confederate Government and the inauguration of Mr. Davis at its head, they continued the augmentation of the army by recruits from all the Southern States, including Maryland and the District of Columbia. They invested Fort Pickens, stormed Fort Sumter, and put in motion a formidable army for the capture of Washington and the overthrow of the government.

In the sight of these astounding facts, the President issues his proclamation appealing to the patriotism of the nation for the salvation of the Union, and Mr. Breckinridge grossly insults the intelligence of the country by charging that the President made war against the South! The facts adduced establish beyond controversy that the President *did not* make the war, as charged, but that the traitors made the war which now threatens the subversion of the government and endangers our national existence.

Under this fearful exigency, I proceed to inquire, what are the duties imposed upon the President by the Constitution?

I maintain that the Government of the United States is a government of limited powers; that the President of the United States can exert no power that is not granted in express terms or clearly implied as necessary to carry into effect the powers which are expressed. I should be the last person to defend any usurpation of power or unconstitutional act of anyone in authority, much less a President of the United States. The Constitution is written thus:—

Art. 2, Section 1. The executive power shall be vested in the President of the United States of America.

By another clause of the same section he is required to swear:—

I will faithfully execute the office of President of the United States and will, to the best of my ability, preserve, protect, and defend the Constitution of the United States.

Article 2. The President shall be Commander-in-Chief of the Army and Navy of the United States and of the militia of the several States when called into the actual service of the United States.

Section 3. He shall take care that the laws be faithfully executed.

Article 4. The Constitution and the laws of the United States made in pursuance thereof . . . . is the supreme law of the land, ... anything in the constitution or laws of any State to the contrary notwithstanding.

This supreme law is administered in our *duplex* system by various authorities, each in its appropriate department acting in harmony with the general whole.

"The executive power is vested in the President," and he is required "to take care" that each government, State and Federal, and the several authorities are maintained in their respective spheres.

In the event of the rebellion or insurrection assuming such proportions as to overthrow the "*republican form of government guaranteed to every State in the Union*," so that the officers can no longer execute the supreme law, the President is required by his oath of office to "preserve, protect, and defend" this supreme law. For this purpose, the sword, by the Constitution, is placed in his hands. He is the Commander-in-Chief of the Army and Navy and of the militia of the several States when called into the service of the United States." He needs, therefore, no statute law to enable him, in the absence of Congress, to defend the assault on the nation's life, because his right rests on the supreme or universal law of self-defence, common to nations as individuals—that everything that has life, every being that has existence, bas the right to resist and slay the assailant when an attack is made upon that life.

Our fathers presumed not to foresee all the dangers which in time might beset the Constitution, or to prescribe the mode of its defence, but in making the President its defender it was wisely left to him to resist the sword raised against the nation's heart by the sword. The express grant of the *war-conducting power* conferred upon the President carries with it the implied power to use every belligerent right known to the law of war.

Now an atrociously wicked war is waged against the government and its formidable armies have overwhelmed every civil right from the Potomac to the Rio Grande, and threaten the annihilation of the government and the nation itself. By virtue of the express and implied powers of the Constitution just indicated it is impossible to question the duty of the President to use every belligerent right, every instrument known to the law of war, to annoy, to weaken, to destroy the enemy, until its armies are overthrown and the civil authority is re-established. If there was no statute law, or no act of Congress authorising an army and navy, and even if the act of 1795 did not apply to this exigency, still the act of the President in improvising an army for the defence of the government was strictly in accordance with the principles of the Constitution, and if Congress had failed to perform its duties it was still the right and duty of every American citizen to rally under the flag in its defence.

It is a maxim at common law:

> When a known felony is about to be committed upon anyone, not only the party assaulted may repel force by force, but his *servant attending him, or any other person present*, may interpose to prevent the mischief, and if *death* ensue, the party so interposing *will be justified*.

Upon this principle of common law, which justifies a servant or bystander in slaying a felon who attempts the life of a friend, *a fortiori*, is a citizen of the United States justified who rises at the call of the President and slays the enemy endeavouring to kill, not one man only or a generation of men, but the nation itself?

According to Rutherford:

> No action can be unlawful if it is not possible for a man to have done otherwise. Whatever is unavoidable is not unlawful. An

act done from compulsion or necessity is not a crime, is not unlawful. To this proposition the law makes no exception.

Mr. Breckinridge cites the authority of Webster and Douglas against the blockade of the Southern ports. Their opinions have no application whatever to a state of war. Blockade is a *belligerent* right, and can be exercised only by the President, as Commander-in-Chief, in time of war and against the enemy.

The following authority from the Father of his Country is of greater weight and much more applicable to the extraordinary exigence under which the President is placed. April 17, 1776, General Washington wrote to the Committee of Safety in New York:—

> If in the prosecution of such measures as shall appear to me to have a manifest tendency to promote the interest of the great American cause, I *shall encounter the local convenience of individuals, or even a whole colony*, I beg it may be believed that I shall do it with reluctance and pain; but in the present important contest the least of two evils must be preferred. . . . . We are to consider ourselves *either in a state of peace or war* with Great Britain. If the former, *why are our ports shut up, our trade destroyed, our property seized, our towns burnt, and our wealthy and valuable citizens led into captivity and suffering the most cruel hardships?*
>
> It is indeed so glaring to permit intercourse with the enemy's ships-of-war that even the *enemy themselves must despise us for suffering it to be continued*; for besides their obtaining supplies of every kind, by which they are enabled to continue in your harbours, it also opens a regular channel of intelligence, by. which they are from time to time made acquainted with the number and extent of our works, our strength, and all our movements, by which they are enabled to regulate their own plans, to our great disadvantage and injury.
>
> Relying on your zeal in the cause of American liberty, I ask your assistance in putting a stop to this evil—either to prevent any future correspondence with the enemy or in bringing to condign punishment such persons as may be hardy and wicked enough to carry it on otherwise than by a prescribed mode, if any can possibly require it.

Now, the Senator himself cannot deny that the enemy had repudiated the Constitution of the United States, organised a hostile government, seized all the Southern ports, filled them with privateers, and blockaded them against the commerce of the United States.

Under these circumstances, it became the manifest duty of the President to close these ports against the enemy as a constitutional war measure. Had the President not done so, he would have subjected our government to the contempt of the civilized world, and, in the language of Washington, whose letter I have just cited, it would have been "so glaring to permit intercourse with the enemy's ships .... that even the *enemy* itself must *despise* us for suffering it to be continued."

The Senator assumes that the power to suspend the writ of *habeas corpus* is vested only in Congress. He concedes that there is nothing in the language of the great Washington which so restricts it; but, following Chief Justice Taney, he rests his argument simply on the fact that it is found classified under the grant of legislative powers.

But that argument has no value whatever, because there is in the tenth section, under the same article, an enumeration of powers *denied* to the States which Congress even cannot exercise.

Judge Taney, in using his mandate to liberate the man who had been imprisoned upon the charge of complicity with the enemy by General Butler, was as guilty as any private person who should have attempted to free him by force. The opinion of the Chief Justice adds nothing whatever to the argument. His extreme age and his known and cherished sympathies with the secession heresy (of which the Dred Scott decision furnished mournful evidence) prepared the public mind for that given in the present case.

The Senator asserts that "George Washington conducted the Revolution of the thirteen colonies without martial law." He may have stated this ignorantly, but every student of American history should have known that there was really nothing but martial law during that war.

Washington wrote to the secret committee of the convention of the State of New York July 13, 1776:—

I have mentioned the necessity of the body falling on some measure to remove from this city and environs persons of known disaffection and enmity to the American cause. The safety of the army, the success of every enterprise, and the security of all depend on adopting the most speedy and effectual steps for this purpose; .... and I do most earnestly entreat you to adopt some plan for this purpose; .... so as to remove those disquieting and discouraging apprehensions which pervade the whole army on this subject. . . . I foresee very dangerous consequences in many respects if a remedy for the evil is not soon and efficaciously applied. The removal of Tory prisoners confined in this city is a matter to which I would solicit your attention. In every view, it is dangerous and alarming. In case of attack or alarm there is doubt what part they would take and none can tell what influence they might have, etc.

This letter from Washington caused the thirteen Tory prisoners who had been most obnoxious for their principles and conduct to be removed, by order of the convention, to *the jail at Litchfield, Connecticut.* The crimes alleged against them were *disaffection to the rights and liberties of the American States; . . . . corresponding with the enemy or engaging in treasonable conspiracies.* The *mayor* of the city of New York was among the number.

June 30, 1776, General Washington wrote to the committee of Essex County, New Jersey, in regard to Governor Franklin, of that colony:

. . . . .that he had evinced a most unfriendly disposition to our cause, and the colony convention having ordered him to Connecticut, ... I am of opinion that your committee should interfere in the matter and give immediate orders to the officer of the guard to proceed with him in the execution of the duty wherewith he is charged. . . . . If there is the *least danger of his rescue* or the guard appointed being remiss in their duty your committee should appoint a strong escort for the purpose, ... *and conduct him securely to the place fixed for him.*

The New Jersey convention had declared Governor Franklin an enemy to his country, and the Continental Congress ordered him to be sent *under guard to Governor Trumbull, of Connecticut, with a request to treat him as other prisoners* if he refused to give his parole. Washington's letter settled the matter.

June 7, 1776, Washington referred to the case of Sir John Johnson in his communication to Congress. This man Johnson was possessed of large wealth and lived about forty miles west of Albany, New York. He had several hundred Highlanders as tenants, and these, with many Indians under him, he incited against the American cause.

General Schuyler ascertained that Johnson had virtually broken his parole, and likely to produce much mischief; but he fled under an apprehended arrest. Sir John's papers were searched in his house, and *his wife was removed to Albany as a kind of hostage for the peaceful conduct of her husband.* Lady Johnson wrote to General Washington asking his interference for her release, but he *declined* to take the matter out of the authority of Schuyler and the Albany committee.

Dr. Benjamin Church, of Massachusetts, an active member of the Provincial Congress, was sent on a special mission to the Continental Congress, and was appointed by that body Surgeon General of the Army. He was recommended to Washington by the Massachusetts delegation as worthy of special confidence. He was detected October 1, 1775, in correspondence with a Mr. Fleming, in Boston, who adhered to the enemy. The discovery of his treason was somewhat remarkable. The letter was sent by a woman who was betrayed in her efforts to deliver it.

The letter was shown to the Commander-in-Chief by General Greene. It was written in cypher. He was tried before the General Court of Massachusetts and expelled from the House; then by the Continental Congress, as laid before them by General Washington, and they decided that:—

> Dr. Church should be confined *in jail in Connecticut, without the use of pen, ink, or paper, and that he should not be allowed to converse with any person, except in the hearing of a magistrate of the town or the sheriff of the county.*

He was accordingly imprisoned at Norwich.

The case of the arrest of the Pennsylvania *Friends* is another instance. Twenty of these persons were arrested and imprisoned by the authorities of Pennsylvania, who refused to surrender these prisoners to the civil power or allow them a hearing. It was on the ground that these parties were believed to be in complicity with the enemy and against the American cause. Congress was in session at the time, in Philadelphia, and approved the suspension of the writ. These Pennsylvania prisoners were first sent to Staunton, Virginia, and afterwards to Winchester, where they were kept in partial confinement for eight months without any provision having been made for their support. The only allusion to this is a resolution passed the 8th of April, 1778, requiring the expenses of arrest, the journey from Pennsylvania to Virginia, and all incidental charges to be *paid by said prisoners*, two of whom had died in the meantime from privation and suffering.

I might cite instances where Tories were shot and hung and their property confiscated without the form of law during the American

Revolution. In fact, martial law transcended all civil authority while our ancestors were struggling to establish our national existence.

Mr. Breckinridge was careful to refrain from referring to the authority of General Jackson. The suspension of the writ of *habeas corpus* in 1815 and the imprisonment of the judge, as well as the arrest and execution of Arbuthnot and Ambrister without trial, have received the unanimous sanction of the American people.

Mr. Jefferson, to whom the Senator refers as authority, said in his letter to J. B. Colvin, December, 1810, that—

> A strict observance of the written law is doubtless one of the highest duties of a good citizen, but it is not *the highest*. The laws of necessity, of self-preservation, of saving our country when in danger, are of higher obligation. To lose our country by a scrupulous adherence to written law would be to lose the law itself, with life, liberty, property, and all those who are enjoying them with us, thus absurdly sacrificing the end to the means. When in the Battle of Germantown General Washington's army was annoyed from Chew's house he did not hesitate to plant his cannon against it, though the property of a private citizen.
>
> When he besieged Yorktown, he levelled the suburbs, feeling that the laws of property must be postponed for the safety of the nation. While the army was before Yorktown the Governor of Virginia took horses; carriages, provisions, and even men, by force to enable the army to stay together till it could master the public enemy, and he was justified. In all these cases the unwritten law of necessity, of self-preservation, and of public safety control the written law of *meum and teum*.

If there had been no express grant in the Constitution to suspend the writ of *habeas corpus*, still the power to suspend all civil authority when necessary to maintain our national existence would have been complete. It stands upon "*the unwritten laws of necessity, of self-preservation, and of the public safety.*"

The Senator charges that the blood-bought rights of the people secured by the fourth article of the Constitution have been wantonly violated by the President. This has no foundation in fact. On the contrary, the enemy, which commands all the sympathies of the distinguished Senator, are themselves the violators of these sacred rights.

The fourth article of the Constitution, which secures the right of the people to their persons. houses, papers, and effects against searches or seizures without warrant of law, does not apply to the public enemy in time of war. This article does not conflict with or control the constitutional principles which have been adduced, but strictly harmonizes with them. Should a spy be found within the American camp or the chances of war throw Davis or Beauregard in the hands of our army, no one would think their arrest and imprisonment unconstitutional or doubt the duty of the commander to disregard any writ of *habeas corpus* issued for their liberation. Should a commander capture a cargo of provisions or a wagon-load of Enfield rifles *in transitu* to the enemy, no one could pretend to believe that he had violated this article of the Constitution!

The Senator complains that this article of the Constitution has been infracted in Maryland and Missouri by the arrest of private persons and the seizure of private property. He assumes that the parties in Baltimore were innocent. They may have been so, but yet their arrest and imprisonment was justifiable under the maxim of the common law:—

> If the circumstances were such as to furnish reasonable ground for apprehending a design to commit felony, etc., and there is also a reasonable ground for believing the danger imminent that such design will be accomplished, although it may afterwards turn out that the appearances were false and there was in fact no such design nor any danger that it would be accomplished.

The letter of Mr. Jefferson, already quoted, referring to the conspiracy of Burr, says of General Wilkinson:—

> In judging this case we are bound to consider the state of the information, correct and incorrect, which he then possessed. He expected Burr had a band from above, a British fleet from below, and he knew there was a formidable conspiracy within the city. Under these circumstances was he justifiable, first, in seizing notorious conspirators? On this there can be but two opinions—one of *the guilty and their accomplices*; the other that of all *honest men*. Second, in sending them to the seat of government when the written law gave them a right to a trial in the territory? The danger of their rescue, of their continuing their machinations, the tardiness and weakness of the law, apathy of the judges, active patronage of the whole tribe of lawyers, unknown disposition of the juries, an hourly expectation of the enemy, *salvation of the city* and of the *Union itself*, which would

have been convulsed to its centre had the conspiracy succeeded. All these constituted a law of necessity and self-preservation, and rendered the *salus populi* supreme over the written law. The officer who is called to act on this superior ground does indeed risk himself on the justice of the *controlling powers of the Constitution*, and his station makes it his duty to incur that risk; but those controlling powers and his fellow-citizens generally are bound to judge according to the circumstances under which he acted. They are not to transfer the information of this place or moment to the time and place of his action, but to put themselves in his situation. We know now that there never was danger of a British fleet from below, and that Burr's band was crushed before it reached Mississippi; but General Wilkinson's information was very different and *he could act on no other.*

Our military commanders in Maryland and Missouri are fully justified upon the precise principle upon which Mr. Jefferson exonerated General Wilkinson.

Finally, Mr. Breckinridge charges that the Constitution was violated by the suppression of a St. Louis press! This is a grave charge. The freedom of speech and the press are especially guarded by constitutional provisions. I hold the right as inalienable to citizen and Christian. It has a priceless value to our civil liberty, and as an independent member of the press I will never consent to see its power trammelled or its freedom abridged by President or ruler.

It is unquestionably true that the press seized in St. Louis was in the service of the Southern rebellion and engaged: in the destruction of *these very rights* and of the entire Constitution and Government. Upon the principles of the Constitution which I have heretofore cited in this article it necessarily follows that anyone who is aiding the rebellion by treasonable utterances, whether spoken or written, is as amenable to martial law as though enrolled in the Confederate Army, and by the same authority it is as much the duty of the commander-in-chief to arrest and hold subject to martial law anyone found aiding the rebellion by treasonable utterances, spoken or written, as it is his duty to arrest anyone found sending to the enemy's camp intelligence, provisions, or arms.

In the progress of events the rebellion may assume such formidable proportions as to override both the judicial and legislative powers, leaving the military as the only visible power in the land. It would then be the clear duty of the President, as Commander-in-Chief, to maintain the military authority over every foot of territory of the United States until the judicial and legislative power could be restored. In such an exigency, it may be his duty to call several millions of men into the service. It may be necessary to arrest traitorous Senators and members of Congress, judges of courts, etc., who are in complicity with the rebellion, and treat them as public enemies. Instead of suppressing one press, extend it to all presses engaged in exciting and stimulating the treason. Instead of arresting a few traitors he may arrest all traitors and deprive them of the means of warring on the government.

This government relies on individual duty and obligation. It has the power to tax *individuals* in any mode and to any extent to maintain it, and to call out citizens as individuals for military service to defend it.

In this supreme struggle for its existence men of all sections adhere to it. They should not only sustain it, but, if necessary meet death to preserve it, until the roar of the final fire and the judgment of the quick and dead.

Better that Washington had perished like Hampden; that Jefferson had never drafted the Declaration of Independence; that Lee, Hancock, Adams, Franklin, Sherman, Livingston, etc., had died like Sydney and Russell upon the block, than that this Union, created to be the *daylight* to break the night of ages, should finally collapse, and *traitors* be permitted to write the epitaph "It lived and died."

Anna Ella Carroll.

Maryland, August 8, 1861.

In the first volume of the biography will be found some of the numerous letters testifying to the great influence on the border States of this able and timely reply.

Edward Bates, Attorney General of Lincoln's cabinet, writes her that he is requested by President Lincoln to thank her most cordially for her able support.

Governor Hicks, of Maryland, writes for a supply and tells the Union Committee of Baltimore that if they expect to carry the election they go to work and send Miss Carroll's documents over the entire State. Mr. Mayer and Mr. Fickey, of the committee, make application for all that she can spare. The committee sends them broadcast over the entire State, and writes that to their surprise and the relief of their treasury Miss Carroll makes no charge.

Mr. James Tilghman writes her from Baltimore that he placed his son at the door of his house on Camden street, with paper and pencil, and five hundred men called for the pamphlet in one day, and that these are the bone and sinew of the city, wanting to know which army they ought to enter, and he begs her to send more—all she can—as they go like hot cakes.

Miss Carroll's own private means are supplied for the publication. The War Department takes up the pamphlet and circulates a large edition with admirable effect, and the department then requests Miss Carroll to continue to write in support of the administration, and suggests the War Powers of the government as her next subject.

Miss Carroll's, pamphlets together with the great influence that she exercised over Governor Hicks, of Maryland, to hold him to the Union cause, were largely instrumental in keeping Maryland within the Union and thus ensuring the safety of the National Capital.

CHAPTER 2

Note Written by Miss Carroll to Accompany the Republication of "The War Powers of the Government"

(In the spring of 1891)

Having made an agreement with Honourable Thomas A. Scott, Assistant Secretary of War, to write in aid of the Union, it was determined that I should produce a document on *The War Powers of the Government*, as none had then been written and such a pamphlet was essentially demanded by the exigency of the crisis. While in St. Louis, in the autumn of 1861, I gave every spare moment to the preparation of this work and visited the Mercantile library in that city almost daily in quest of books bearing on the subject.

Mr. Johnston, brother of Albert Sydney Johnston in supreme command of the Confederate forces west, was the librarian. Soon a controversy between him and myself arose and was most earnestly continued. He ridiculed the idea of the Northern army being successful and said the matter was even then accomplished, and before spring the South would have her independence assured and Price's army would have the whole of Missouri.

I derived much information from him. As the brother of Albert Sydney Johnston, he was fully acquainted with the Confederate prospects in that section. He said he was astonished to meet one of my family on the wrong side, as he had long lived in my section of the country. This quickened my activity to finish my book and do all I could to serve the Union cause.

I hastened to Washington city, wrote the following document, which was fully approved at the War Department and by President Lincoln, and as soon as published sent it to the Capitol, where it was generally read, early in December, 1861.

A. E. Carroll.

UNITED STATES CIVIL WAR.

★★★★★★

PAMPHLETS.

★★★★★★

II.

★★★★★★

1862.

(SEAL OF DEPARTMENT OF STATE.)

★★★★★★

THE WAR POWERS

OF

THE GENERAL GOVERNMENT.

WHO MADE THE WAR—THE STATUS OF THE CITIZENS OF THE SECEDED STATES DEFINED—CONGRESS HAS NO POWER TO CONFISCATE SLAVES OR OTHER PRIVATE PROPERTY—THE OPINIONS OF JOHN QUINCY ADAMS AND CHARLES SUMNER REFUTED—THE RIGHT TO CAPTURE ALL PROPERTY USED FOR INSURRECTIONARY PURPOSES—THE RIGHT TO SUSPEND THE WRIT OF HABEAS CORPUS AND ARREST THE ENEMY IN EVERY PART OF THE NATIONAL TERRITORY—THE DUTY OF ALLEGIANCE AND PROTECTION.

★★★★★★

BY ANNA ELLA CARROLL, OF MARYLAND.

★★★★★★

WASHINGTON:

PRINTED BY HENRY POLKINHORN.

1861 (1862).

THE WAR POWERS OF THE GENERAL GOVERNMENT.

The purpose of the following pages is to offer some considera-tion in respect to the powers and duties of the General Government in its endeavours to suppress the present insurrection, but to treat this subject intelligently it is requisite to recur briefly to the peculiar origin and characteristics of the insurrectionary movement, and the first remark to be made is that this rebellion differs from most others in the singular fact that it did not proceed so much from the people of the States which nominally seceded as from the governments of those States.

At the outset, it was, for the most part, a conspiracy of official persons, and to render the enormity greater these very traitors, using the Democratic party as a means, had sought and obtained office only for the purpose of employing the power it gave them to strike down the government of the nation. This was the condition of things throughout the Southern States. The conspirators held every position of public influence—executive, legislative, and judicial—while as cabinet ministers or members of Congress they controlled the administration at Washington.

At length, when the opportunity, so ardently longed for, arrived, they raised the standard of revolt, and then the loyal men of the South found themselves wholly without the means of effectual opposition to a treason which held in its hands every State authority, and seemed at the same time to have even the countenance of the General Government. What could these patriots do?

The adversaries of the nation bore the ensign of State sovereignty, and thus appeared to be clothed with all the colours of political legitimacy, while they possessed, in fact, the most energetic agencies of power—the purse, the sword, and the public press.

In addition to all this, the General Government, with apparent unconcern, beheld its banner trailing in the dust, yet moved not, either to avert the fact or avenge the indignity. Can it then be a matter of surprise that fidelity itself should falter, thus left without its natural protection and in the presence of a power for the time irresistible?

To hasty thinkers it may, indeed, seem strange that a sufficient number of the Southern people could be induced to acquiesce in the rebellion so as to give it the appearance of a popularity to which it could lay no just claim; and this political enigma can only be explained by a proper appreciation of the different theories which have prevailed most widely in regard to the nature of the complex Federal system under which we live, and more especially by an accurate estimate of that peculiar theory which has always been a favourite with the South.

As is well known, at the time of framing the Constitution American statesmen were divided into two great schools of opinion in relation to the character of the government which they were about to organise.

One school, aware of the necessity of strength, as well to prevent anarchy as to preserve independence, was led to advocate such a powerful national government as could make itself felt at home and feared abroad.

The other school, knowing the inherent tendency of all power to usurpation, proposed to strengthen the States as a counterpoise to the authority of the General Government.

But as it was impossible for two schools entertaining such opposite views to agree, and yet, since both felt the necessity to be absolute for some new system, the result was a compromise, and that compromise was the present Constitution.

The great difficulty experienced by its authors was to trace the dividing line between the powers to be granted to the National Government and those to be reserved to the States and the people. They succeeded, nevertheless, in the accomplishment of the perplexing task in a manner which must excite the admiration of all posterity. But there was one case for which they did not provide which might seem to be more important than any other. They prescribed clearly enough the bounds of Federal and State authority, but they omitted to appoint any judge of boundaries.

They constituted no umpire to determine questions arising from a conflict of jurisdictions; and yet this was no oversight. They constituted no judge between the General and State governments, because the exercise of any judicial functions in the case proved an impossibility. If the General Government were the exclusive judge as to the line between its own powers and those of the States, it might push that line to any extent whatever. It would thus have the ability to absorb at pleasure the entire jurisdiction reserved to the States. On the other hand, if the States were made the exclusive judges of the case they could usurp in like manner all the powers of the General Government, for whoever is judge in his own case will never fail to judge in his own favour, being sure to take for himself whatever is in controversy.

Again, to have provided some third power as arbiter in cases where the Federal Government and the States could not agree would have rendered such power the common sovereign over both, so as to enable it to usurp every other authority.

Hence our fathers designated no common judge between the States and the Nation, because the very idea of such a judge implies a contradiction. They therefore merely provided in the Federal compact for the division and distribution of the sovereign powers between the General Government and the States, trusting to the wisdom and prudence of each to remain content with its own share.

It has sometimes been made a question as to what is the nature of this Federal compact and who are the parties to it, but a very simple rule would seem to furnish a clear and decisive answer. It is a principle alike of national law and common sense that all are parties to a contract who are intended to be bound by it and assent to its terms. Hence by this rule the Constitution is a compact to which all the States and all the people, as well as the General Government, are parties, because all these are mentioned in it and all assented to it at the same time or in succession.

But far different from this clear and precise view of the Federal compact have been the opinions of most politicians, and they have differed not less widely among themselves, for as soon as the new government was fairly in operation the two schools revived their old war, transferring the field of battle to the question of construction.

The advocates of strong government asserted the Constitution to be a compact between all the people of the United States in the mass, and therefore inferred it to be indissoluble unless by their consent.

On the other hand, those who dreaded the power of the National Government as being dangerous to the liberties of the States assumed that the latter were in their corporate capacity the real parties to the Federal compact, and hence argued that any State might treat such compact as null whenever broken either by the other States or by the General Government, and for this doctrine as to the power of any party to avoid a social compact in the case of a breach of its terms by the other side the school of State rights could always adduce the powerful support of the great writers upon natural law.

Rutherforth expresses it in his own inimitable style as follows:—

In these States, where the Constitution has divided the supreme power between the king and people, Grotius allows that the people have a right to resist the king by force when he invades their part of the power.

Now that part of the sovereign power which the monarch has was granted to him at first by the compact which settled the Constitution and is holden by him afterwards by the same compact. As long, therefore, as the obligation of the compact continues he has a right to his part of the supreme power, and the people have no right to take it from him, either by war or by any other means, without his consent; but by wilfully and notoriously invading the other part he breaks the constitutional compact.

And this compact is so far like all other compacts that a violation of it on his side will leave the people at liberty to choose whether they will abide by it or not.

A compact which is violated by one of the parties may be made void at the discretion of the other party.

However, it is sufficient for our present purpose that when the compact by which the people gave their civil government a part of the supreme power is broken on his side, the obligation of it is voidable or may be set aside at the discretion of the people.

It follows from the point of view presented by Rutherforth, that in case of the alleged breach of the Federal compact or in any question of jurisdictional power arising between a State and a General Government, each must have the independent right to determine the matter for itself, because the Constitution has appointed no umpire between them, and it is plain that if those who have no common judge will persistently assert their claim to the same thing the force of the strongest must necessarily take it.

Hence the feeble, when associated with the strong, would seem to have no other resource left in a case of final difference than to withdraw from the unequal association, and the right to withdraw would also seem as clear in a case where the other party might employ the prerogative of mere strength to put aside any material article in the agreement by which the association was originally constituted. Hence by this apparently fair mode of reasoning a State would have the privilege of secession in a case where the National Government should invade its reserved powers and thus violate the compact upon which the Union is alone founded.

Now, it was this theory of the Federal system which always predominated in the Southern States, and naturally so, too, because it was the doctrine most favourable to the weaker section of the Union, and weakness, by the law of interest, as well as that of reason, never fails to look with affection upon any means which may be employed to give it equality in a contest with power. Hence this theory was taught and accepted in one form or another almost universally for years in all the States where the rebellion is now in the ascendant.

The demagogues used it as the most reliable instrument to raise themselves to official place, and at length the conspirators seized upon it as the only possible lever which could move their States out of the Union. Other circumstances, however, contributed to the same end. The ever-increasing numerical majority of the North excited uneasy apprehensions in the Southern mind, and, instead of labouring to tranquilise such fears, many Northern politicians were incessantly making utterances which necessarily tended to agitate them still more. At last all these causes operating jointly resulted in the great insurrection.

But it is useless to consume more time in tracing the action of causes. The period for controversy bas passed, and that for penning impartial history has not yet come. In the meanwhile, the urgent realities of the present demand undivided attention and action as prompt as it should be powerful.

What, then, are the rights and duties of the General Government in its treatment of the insurrection?

This is the momentous question of the day, and the dreadful crisis seems to call for a more careful answer than it has yet received; for it must now be apparent to all that this is no petty strife, but one of those great contests of arms which make eras in the war-cycle of history.

There are now seen standing face to face more than a million of men, armed for murderous combat, and, as it were, pausing for the sound of the trumpet to signal them to mutual death! Yet to these is committed the question of civilization on the continent.

It therefore behoves us first of all to inquire, What is the object of this mighty war? because it is the object alone which can justify the horrors of any war to a correct national conscience or before the Judge of the Universe. Now, on the side of the old flag, the instinctive answer of every lover of its stars is that "we are fighting to preserve the Constitution and restore the Union."

Let us, then, accept this answer as the first and most general criterion of the power to carry on the war, because it is self-evident that the powers employed must never be subversive of the very purpose which they are only intended to accomplish. Therefore, since the government is using all the sinews of the public force to restore the authority of the Constitution over others, it is obliged by every principle of justice and prudence to keep that Constitution inviolable on its own part. It cannot act, without becoming a thing of shame among the nations of the earth, upon the insidious maxim that the end justifies the means. It cannot adopt the flagitious doctrines of a Jacobinic delusion and break the Constitution in order to save it. Hence the special and avowed object of the war imposes upon its conduct this one general rule——that it can be carried on alone under the direction of constitutional powers.

Now, the first question of power which naturally suggests itself to every mind is: By what authority granted in the Constitution does the government assume to wage such a war as this at all?

By what colour of authority does it muster and march such powerful armies across the borders of the States, there to encounter other hosts equally powerful and assuming to battle by the authority of those States?

By what sanction of authority does it strew the fields of Virginia with slain and wounded, taking thousands of prisoners, and exercising, and according to the adverse force, all the usual rights of a belligerent in a great war?

The spectacle is as painful as it is unparalleled, and the inquiry cannot but be relevant, where is the warrant in the Federal compact for this?

And yet we need not go far to find an answer. The scenes of the dread array themselves present the answer. They proclaim it to be a case of war. And yonder flies a flag that gives another answer, and yet the same. It is not the old flag of the nation; it has neither the stripes nor the stars which were wont to float in triumph over the old fields of our glory. That flag says *it is a foreign war*, and the fact is true as far as the strength of rebel prowess can make it so. Is not this, then, an answer to the question of power? Here is war; here are colours hostile to the nation.

And has not every government power to wage battle against a force bearing such a banner on its own territory? The case is plain. The Federal Government is moving its soldiery under the warrant of the war power; but no one will pretend to deny the power of the National Government to engage in a war. The right to make war is the self-defence of nations, and the Constitution expressly grants, as well as implicitly recognises, this power. By one clause it confers on Congress the right "to declare war;" and it is manifest that no declaration is needed when the war has been commenced against the government by others.

There are, however, two cases of war: that of war with a foreign power, and that against an insurrection or rebellion; and the Constitution, in the clearest manner, makes provision for the latter case. It gives to Congress the authority "to provide for calling forth the militia to execute the laws of the Union, suppress insurrections, and repel invasion." Here foreign war and internal war are both mentioned. By another clause power is granted "to suspend the privilege of the writ of *habeas corpus* when in cases of rebellion or invasion the public safety may require it."

Here the power to suppress rebellion is necessarily conferred in terms. By another clause the President is made Commander-in-Chief of the Army and Navy of the United States, and of the militia of the several States when called into the actual service of the United States."

In this connection, it should be especially remarked that these clauses of the Constitution place the two cases of war—the one being internal and the other external—in the same predicament as to power. Thus Congress is to call forth the militia "to suppress insurrections and repel invasions; thus the writ of *habeas corpus* is to be suspended only in cases of rebellion or invasion," and thus the President only becomes Commander-in-Chief of the militia of the several States when called into the actual service of the United States."

But the actual service of militia means war alone. Hence as Congress can only call forth the militia to suppress insurrections and repel invasions, and the President can only command the militia when so called forth, it is plain that the two cases of insurrection and invasion are both located by the Constitution in the common category of war, and the classification is perfectly accurate in a scientific point of view, because insurrection and invasion are both alike cases of resistance to the sovereignty of the nation—the one being the resistance of an internal force, the other that of a foreign and independent power, while each in precisely the same manner tends to impede the execution of the laws and to assail the supremacy of the government.

Hence, if it be possible for the powers of war to be vested by human language, they have been granted to the government by the Constitution. That instrument makes provision for war in the only three cases where it can be imagined to arise—the war by "declaration," when the government may choose to assail the territories of a foreign power; the war from "invasion," when a foreign power assails our own territories, and the war of "rebellion," when subjects of the nation organise a force in opposition to its authority.

Secessionists, however, urge that the government cannot march its armies into the territory of a State against its expressed will. The objection is futile, for how could the government otherwise either repel an invasion or suppress an insurrection?

The universal rule of law and reason is, that when a power is granted all the means are granted at the same time which may be necessary to render such power effectual. Nor can the action of the government be regarded in any sense as war against a State, according to the meaning of the term "State" in the Constitution, which signifies only one of the local political bodies having a prescribed place in the Federal system—that is to say, one of the "United States."

But these new insurrectionary powers do not even pretend to have such a character; they deny it in arms; they resist the imputation unto death; they proclaim to all the world that they are no longer members of the "United States." Hence these cannot be considered "States," but only rebellious powers which have displaced at once the authority of the States and that of the General Government. They are not so much evil stars that have wandered from their orbits as comets of revolution which have dashed away for a time the true stars of the system from their spheres.

Hence this is a civil war, and therefore the government may employ all the constitutional powers at its command for the subjugation of the insurrectionary forces in the field but while it is enabled to employ all the powers, it is obliged to observe at the same time all the established usages of war, for the same enlightened maxims of prudence and humanity are as obviously applicable to a civil war as to any other.

According to Vattel:

When a party is formed in a state who no longer obey the sovereign and are possessed of sufficient strength to oppose him, or when, in a republic, the nation is divided into two opposite factions and both sides take up arms, this is called 'civil war.'
Custom appropriates the term civil war to every war between the members of one and the same political society. If it be between a part of the citizens on the one side and the sovereign with those who continue in obedience to him on the other, provided the malcontents have any reason for taking up arms, nothing further is required to entitle such disturbance to the

name of 'civil war,' and not that of rebellion.

This latter term is applied to such an insurrection against lawful authority as is void of all appearance of justice.

The sovereign, indeed, never fails to bestow the appellation of rebels on all such of his subjects as openly resist him, but when the latter have acquired sufficient strength to give him effectual opposition and to oblige him to carry on the war against them according to established rule, he must necessarily submit to the use of the term *civil war*.

A civil war breaks the bonds of society and government, or at least suspends their force and effect. It produces in the nation two independent parties, who consider each other as enemies and acknowledge no common judge. These two parties, therefore, must necessarily be considered as thenceforward constituting, at least for a time, two separate bodies, two distinct societies. Though one of the parties may have been to blame in breaking the unity of the state and resisting the lawful authority, they are not the less divided in fact. Besides, who shall judge them? Who shall pronounce on which side the right or wrong lies? On earth, they have no common superior. They stand, therefore, in precisely the same predicament as two nations who engage in a contest, and, being unable to come to an agreement, have recourse to arms.

This being the case, it is very evident that the common laws of war—those maxims of humanity, moderation and honour— ought to be observed by both parties in every civil war.

Whenever, therefore, a numerous body of men think they have a right to resist the sovereign and feel themselves in a condition to appeal to the sword, the war ought to be carried on by the contending parties in the same manner as by two different nations, and they ought to leave open the same means for preventing its being carried to outrageous extremes and for the restoration of peace.

Hence we perceive that the general power of the government to direct the operations of the war is subjected to the necessary limitation that it shall be conducted in accordance with the public law of all civilized warfare.

There is, however, one essential difference between the case of civil strife and that of foreign war, which imposes a further qualification on the power of the government.

One of the peculiar characteristics of foreign war is that it not only places the opposing sovereignties in a state of neutral hostility, but also at the same time it imprints the condition of belligerents upon all their subjects individually without their acquiescence or even against their will.

In reference to a case of conflict with any foreign power, a nation cannot be at war and a single one of its citizens at peace, or, in the words of Chancellor Kent:

> When war is duly declared it is not merely a war between this and the adverse government in their political character. Every man is, in judgment of law, a party to the acts of his own government, and a war between the governments of two nations is a war between all the individuals of the one and all the individuals of which the other nation is composed.

But the rule in cases of civil war is different, and for obvious reasons, because no man should be implicated in the guilt of insurrection unless he actually rebels.

No man becomes a part of the 'insurrectionary force unless he actually joins it. One cannot be considered criminal unless in both fact and intention he has committed a crime.

No citizen is held responsible on account of the locality of his domicile, and none can be hung for treason by mere fiction of law.

Hence the rule of reciprocal hostility between all the subjects of two sovereigns at war can find no sort of application in the case of a civil war.

In the case of a rebellion no one is an enemy to the government unless he *voluntarily* casts off its authority nor can the people of the Southern States be regarded as criminal, whether legally or morally, merely from the fact of their temporary submission to an irresistible force. The people of any city or district are always justified in doing so, alike in cases of invasion and rebellion. By the laws of God and man, the *vis major, irresistible force*, excuses everything.

It follows clearly, therefore, that in carrying on the present war its operations can only be aimed against the insurrectionary force which resists the authority of the government, because this is the only public enemy, and not the people of any State or district.

Another question may be proposed as to what is the precise nature of the power to be employed in overcoming the resistance to rebellion. Is the instrument to be used the civil force or the military force of the nation? If it be the former, it will be put in motion as subsidiary to judicial process; but if the latter, it must necessarily be moved by the President, as Commander-in-Chief of the Army.

This question, however, may be considered as having been virtually answered already, for when a given case is pronounced to be one of war it necessarily results that it cannot possibly be dealt with by any other than the military force; for, as defined by Demosthenes, war is made against those who cannot be restrained in a judicial view; and Grotius, citing the passage, adds:—

> Judicial proceedings are of force against those who are sensible of their inability to oppose them; but against those who make or think themselves of equal strength wars are undertaken.

Hence the war power springs into sudden activity the moment when the functions of the judicial power are rendered impracticable.

The general power of directing all the movements of any war is vested in the President of the United States, under the constitutional clause which makes him "Commander-in-Chief of the Army and Navy and of the militia of the several States when called into actual service." Hence the President, by virtue of this chief command, must necessarily direct every operation intended to overcome the resistance of an adverse force, whether it may be that of rebellion or invasion. He is thus invested by the Constitution with the exclusive authority to wield the whole military power of the United States in its three great divisions—the army, the navy, and the militia of the several States when called into actual service. He is the sole power of the government, having the competency to give any order in the application of martial law.

It is true that Congress alone has the power "to declare war;" but, as we have seen, war may come without declaration on our part by the hostile action of others, namely, by "invasion" or by "insurrection." To Congress also is delegated the power to provide for calling forth the militia to suppress insurrections and repel invasions but although Congress may provide for calling forth the militia, Congress cannot command them when in actual service. Congress may declare war, yet cannot direct such operations of the army and navy as can alone render the war itself effectual.

The Constitution has appointed the President to the chief command, and there is no authority in our system to displace him; nor does the President thereby become a part of the military force, though he obtains, by virtue of his office, the exclusive title to control it, and hence when a case of war occurs, whether from invasion or insurrection, it is then his right and duty to interpose all the military power of the nation for the purpose of overcoming the hostile force in arms against its authority. It is the fact of war which calls this constitutional right into action, and not any vagrant power supposed to come forth from chaos at the invocation of the plea of necessity—a plea which justifies nothing because it justifies everything.

It surely cannot be pretended that the constitutional clause imposing upon the President the duty to take care that the laws be faithfully executed would authorise him to interpose in every case where the laws may be broken or even resisted, and thus to supersede the ordinary functions of the judiciary by those of a tyrant's discretion. Such a power would enable him to displace judicial action in every instance where its exercise is possible—not merely in a state of war, but in time of peace.

But the question of the greatest difficulty is not that which relates to the mere existence of the power of war to subjugate the forces of the rebellion, but that which concerns the incidents and extent of the power.

Some wild theorists even allege that the power to wage this civil war against the insurrection carries with it the transcendent power of general confiscation over all the property situated in the States where the insurrection rages, as well as to strike down whatever State institution the government may deem even indirectly opposed to the success of its arms.

Now, we have already shown that the war must be waged to restore the Constitution, and hence the war power itself must not trample that instrument in the dust; but the adoption of any such policy as that recommended would be as flagrant an invasion of the rights reserved to the States and to the people as it would be an outrage against the usages of modern warfare.

The Constitution expressly forbids the taking of private property for public use without just compensation."

The terms of the clause imply two restrictions: *First*, that whenever private property is taken by the government the act must be accompanied with "compensation;" and, *secondly*, that such property can only be taken for "public use," and consequently not for "private use," or for any other whatsoever.

Therefore, without annulling that clause of the Constitution, it is clearly impossible to confiscate the property of even the rebels themselves, unless when it is in actual use as an instrument of war; but in the latter predicament the property is no longer private in the constitutional sense. It has passed into the species of public property belonging to an enemy, and thus become liable to capture under the laws of war.

The proposed general emancipation of slaves is repugnant to the second prohibition implied in the clause quoted, as well as to the first, because the proposition here is not to take the slaves and convert them to "public use" at all, but to liberate them from subjection as property.

I know it has been contended by a statesman of great name that war gives to the military commander the power to abolish slavery whenever the powers of war entitle him to set aside the civil authority, and he adduces two examples of the exercise of such a power in the war of the Colombian revolution——one by the Spanish general, Murillo, and the other by the revolutionary general, Bolivar.

It is surprising that a mind so acute did not perceive the utter impertinence of the precedents cited in their application to the case of the Southern people. In the first instance, the Spanish general was bound by no constitution, since Spain acknowledged none—at least in regard to the American colonies. In the second instance, Bolivar, heading an independent force, did not for the time recognise any other powers than those of the sword, and did not pretend to employ any other.

While both examples are from the half barbarous and bloody annals of a cruel race, infamous in every age for its violations of the laws of war, it is true a Senator, also of high reputation, by a more thorough research of universal history, has recently been able to discover another precedent evincing the competence of war to break the chains of the slave; but he had to accept this third example from the horrors of the most frightful civil war that ever desolated the earth and at the hands of its greatest monster, the insatiably revengeful Marius.

However, a bare statement of the argument propounded by Mr. Adams is enough to demonstrate its fallacy. It is concisely this: Since military power, within the sphere of its operations, takes the place of all civil authority, it thereby necessarily acquires the right to decree the general emancipation of slaves. Now, the sophistry of this logic consists in its tacitly assuming that the military power not only suspends the local civil authorities, but also, at the same time, the general and supreme authority of the Constitution.

But will anyone say that this is so? Can war be waged at all, especially in the Territories of the Union, but under the warrant of the Constitution? And can anyone who acts by the authority of the Constitution pretend to have the privilege of breaking it? Is not, then, the assertion that any power known to our system, whether civil or military, State or Federal, can supersede the Constitution in any particular a revolutionary doctrine as rebellious in character as secession itself? There is a single constitutional right which may be suspended for a time, and that is the "privilege of the writ of *habeas corpus*." But such suspension, being provided for by the Constitution, is itself constitutional, and therefore not repugnant to it. This subject, however, will be considered more fully in the sequel.

If the confiscation of private property suggested would thus be a clear infraction of the Federal compact, it would be not less an enormity against the practice of civilized nations.

Chancellor Kent says:—

> The general usage of war is not to touch private property upon land without making compensation, unless in special cases dictated by the necessary operations of war, or when captured in places carried by storm, and which have repelled all the overtures of a capitulation, and, according to Vattel, for the same reasons which render the observance of those maxims a matter of obligation between state and state, it becomes equally and even more necessary in the unhappy circumstance of two incensed parties lacerating their common country.

Nevertheless, I am sensible that to every argument of reason and consideration of justice and humanity the same objection of political delusion will be urged, that the Southern people have forfeited all their rights under the Constitution by their treason against it.

This objection, however, has been fully answered, since it has been clearly shown that no one can be arraigned for the crime of treason who has not voluntarily participated in rebellion against the government; and it is perfectly apparent that since the war is intended not to destroy the Constitution but to preserve it, the government can gain no new powers by putting down the rebellion other than those it possessed before.

Rutherforth says:—

> The act of the people, however injurious it may be, will not

increase the power of the sovereign or will not give him a right to any more power than the Constitution has given him.

For the sovereign power was originally vested in the collective body of the society, *called the people.* The sovereign cannot of right claim any greater part of it than the people have granted to him by compact in forming the Constitution.

When the people violated the compact on their side it is voidable at the sovereign's discretion.

If he chooses to abide by it he has no right to any other power than he derives from it, and if he chooses to make it void instead of gaining a greater part of the supreme power he will lose what he has and it will, as in the other case, revert to the people.

Thus the people may claim to change the Constitution when the sovereign invades their part of the power, whereas *he can only claim to continue the Constitution* though the people should carelessly and wrongfully invade his part.

This is the whole of his right, and no event whatsoever can give him a more extensive right without the consent of the people. If the struggle between him and them should end in civil war and victory should declare itself on his side, yet conquest will not of right increase his power, however strongly we may put the case in his favour by supposing the breach of the Constitution to have begun from the people and the whole blame of the war rests upon them.

For the use of force, though it should be superior to the force opposed to it, only serves to support a right which might otherwise have been hindered from taking effect; It does not produce a right where there was none before.

The proposed general confiscation of Southern property is as repugnant to the rules of expediency as it is to that of constitutional power. It is simply a proposal to convert every Southern man into an enemy and to perpetuate the hostility through all future generations. It is a proposal to make the Southern States forever what Ireland is to England, what Italy has been to Austria, what Poland has been to Russia.

It is a proposal to treat all Southern territory as a conquered province, in order to rule it at the expense of a standing army of half a million of bayonets. Such a policy can never hope to restore the Union, while it would be sheer suicide to the Constitution. Such a policy might create unity, which is a very different thing from union, but it would be the unity of a frightful despotism over both the South and the North.

Besides, this extreme policy would insure the defeat of the very object which its advocates have chiefly in their view, namely, the emancipation of the slave. Its immediate effect would be to array the whole South as one man in the most deadly hostility to the government, and thus render all hopes of reconciliation utterly impossible for all time to come. Disunion would then be a fact already accomplished; but this would leave the Confederate States forever free from all restraint, whether physical or moral, to pursue their favourite schemes for the extension and perpetuation of slavery, while the gates of the ocean would be thrown open for fresh importations from Africa; a military despotism of great strength would be so firmly seated in the South as to prevent all attempts of servile insurrection. It is thus that the only hope of emancipation for the slave is connected with the preservation of the Union, and with that silent progress of intelligence and virtue which the Union alone can guarantee.

A distinction must be taken between the powers which the government may wield so long as the insurrectionary force is capable of affording it effectual resistance and those which are to be employed so soon as that force shall be subjugated. While the war continues, the President must conduct it by the instrumentality of the military force, but when the war ceases, upon having accomplished its end, then *ipso facto* the functions of the war power cease and those of the judiciary are replaced in complete authority.

Because, although the President has the lawful power to conquer any organised force which resists the exercise of Federal jurisdiction in any part of the national territory, yet he has no power or pretence of authority to punish any offenses other than those against the laws of war. The President cannot punish treason any more than he can punish ordinary homicide or larceny. He can only conquer traitors and then turn them over to the courts.

The principle just announced stands upon that article of the Constitution which prescribes that:—

> No person shall be held to answer for a capital or otherwise infamous crime unless on a presentment or indictment of a grand jury, except in cases arising in the land or naval forces

or in the militia when in actual service in the time of war or public danger.

Here the power to punish is unquestionably denied to any other authority than the judiciary except in the case of strictly military persons, and the prohibition extends in terms to "time of war or public danger." Therefore, it matters not how fearful may be the war or how pressing the necessity of the public danger, though every institution in land should tremble on the verge of national ruin, still no non-military person can be capitally punished or punished for any infamous crime but by a judicial sentence.

However, it does not follow that a military tribunal cannot punish spies and others offending against the known rules of war, because spies, by assuming the fictitious character of friends and by pretending to act in aid of the military force, subject themselves voluntarily to the laws governing such force, and by their own conduct are thus estopped from disputing a fact which they have thus solemnly asserted for so base a purpose.

It follows also that the President has no power to punish even the insurgents taken in battle; they maybe slain if they will not submit. In the same manner, the marshal may slay one who resists to the death the execution of civil process; but should the agent of military power go beyond this and assume to punish capitally the prisoners who have surrendered themselves the act is in a civil sense murder, and in a military one a monstrous outrage against the laws of war.

It results from the same course of reasoning that whenever the contest shall be terminated by the triumph of the Federal arms, whatever prisoners the government may think fit to hold responsible for treason must be tried by the courts, under the direction of legal and constitutional forms. Only the question as to what persons shall be arraigned is still left to the discretion of the government, which will be required to take care that in making the selection it does not transcend the necessities of a proper example and the laws of humanity and mercy.

Vattel says:—

When the sovereign has subdued the opposite party and reduced them to submit and sue for peace, he may except from the amnesty the authors of the disturbance, the heads of the party; he may bring them to a legal trial, and punish them, if they be found guilty. He may act in this manner particularly on occasion of these disturbances in which the interests of the people are not so much the object in view as the private aims of some powerful individuals, and which rather deserve the appellation of *revolt* than *civil war.*

In the case of our government the power to punish for treason is under the limitation of that clause of the Constitution which provides that:—

Congress shall have power to declare the punishment of treason; but no attainder of treason shall work corruption of blood or forfeiture except during the life of the person attainted.

Here, then, the sweeping power of confiscation for treason so vehemently urged by our zealous yet revolutionary friends cannot possibly be exercised without overturning the Constitution.

With such wonderful foresight did the wisdom of a better age provide for the protection of all the rights of life, liberty, and property that no ruthless hand, whether of fanaticism or revenge, can strike one of them down without first shattering into fragments the shield of the blessed Constitution which guards them all alike.

But if the government cannot confiscate the *private* property of the rebels which is situated in the seceded States, neither can it claim the right to do so as to that which may be found within the limits of the loyal States, because the same constitutional guaran tees are always operative to protect the property of citizens, whatever may be its locality. It is no answer to this reasoning to say that the rebel government has assumed the power to confiscate all the property situated in the seceded States belonging to persons domiciled or doing business in the loyal States, because the rebel government may perform in perfect logical accordance with its political theory many acts which the Federal Government cannot do without the utter subversion of its Own theory of the war.

The rebel government assumes that the Constitution as to it has become null, and under the pretension of its independence it treats the subjects of all other powers as aliens, and especially the citizens of the United States as alien enemies; but the theory of the Federal Government is as different as day from darkness. It affirms as a prime postulate of all its arguments, whether of the pen or the sword, that the Constitution is in as vigorous force as ever. Consequently, should our government claim the right to treat the people of the so-called seceded States as aliens the assumption would be logically a self-contradiction, because the war is waged upon the sole hypothesis of their being citizens.

The government has clearly the power to forbid the passage of men or munitions of war into the States where the insurrection predominates, if intended to be used in aid of it, because the power to overcome the rebellious force at all necessarily implies the power to take away from it all the means of resistance; but it is plain that the government can do this only by virtue of the war power, namely, the right to conquer by the military force a public enemy of the nation.

The preceding view fully accords with the recent acts of Congress and with the circular of the Secretaries of State and the Treasury, which both confine the right of capture to property used, or intended to be used, in furtherance of the insurrection only; and the act of August the 6th employs the correct phraseology when it declares that all such property shall be "the lawful subject of *prize* and *capture* wherever found."

This places the right on its true foundation as a logical result of the war power; for the moment when property is appropriated, either in fact or intention, to purposes of organized hostility against a nation it loses its private character and becomes, instantly, public.

To avoid the constitutional difficulties which stand opposed to any general confiscation of Southern property another plan has been suggested, but one even more chimerical than those already considered, and this is to put forth a solemn declaration by Congress that the people of the seceded States are alien enemies, and then to treat them in accordance with such declaration.

Now, the first objection to this plan is that it proposes to recognize the very fact which the secessionists are waging war to establish, and which we are denying under arms before all the world, namely, that the so-called seceded States have *de jure* the political character of foreign powers, because there can be no alien enemies unless they be the subjects of foreign powers; hence if the United States by its legislation, concedes this fact, all the other nations of the earth would be justified in the immediate acknowledgment of the Confederate States as an independent government. cannot expect on the part of other nations a refusal to admit what we ourselves see fit to proclaim in the most public and formal manner, and especially when it is their desire and interest to make the admission, even against our strenuous opposition. But an equally fatal objection is that it would not give the supposed power of confiscation, because, as we have already seen, the usages of civilized warfare will not allow us to touch the mere private property of even alien enemies. We could not do it without denying at once our humanity and civilization and taking a voluntary relapse into barbarism.

Moreover, there is a third objection still more decisive, and that is that the act of confiscation, in a legal point of view, would be a mere nullity, because as soon as the war shall terminate with the restoration of the Union the traitors themselves must necessarily have the right to sue in the courts for the recovery of their property, and no plea can be imagined by which they could be barred, for certainly no one will pretend that they could be treated as alien enemies after the overthrow of the revolutionary powers, and therefore at the end of the war all their rights would stand again on the basis of the Constitution, and with no power in our system to divest them by any other means than a regular conviction and sentence under the guarantee of constitutional forms.

The Constitution expressly declares that no person shall be deprived of life, liberty, or *property* without due process of law and hence Congress can have no authority to take away a man's property by legislative action any more than to take away his liberty or his life. Any deprivation of either must be in pursuance of a judicial determination founded upon proper legal process.

It is true that during the continuance of the war, and so long as the rebels maintain their attitude of open hostility to the government, the latter may, for the time, treat then) as alien enemies *de facto* for belligerent purposes, and consequently may prevent them from using even their private property in any manner to aid in the movement of the insurrectionary forces; but this right of *prevention* in the government is one strictly appertaining to the military power. It is one of the rights incidental to martial law, hence it is one to be exercised by the President or his subordinate military agents and not at all by Congress.

It is also perfectly clear that this right of the President to prevent the rebels from employing their property in aid of the rebellion is but temporary, and since it is a power springing out of the war it must necessarily expire with the war. It is a mere power to prevent property from being used in a hostile manner against the government and not any power to *divest* or transfer titles.

Moreover, any attempt on the part of Congress to take away or transfer the title to property by mere legislative enactment would be the palpable usurpation of a power which the Constitution has wisely vested in a different branch of the government. To divest the title of property against the will of the owner is in no proper sense a legislative act, but one altogether judicial. But will anyone pretend that either Congress or the President can exercise judicial functions? Such a confusion of powers is characteristic of the worst forms of despotism. The most bitter denunciation of historians has always been levelled at such acts of the executive or legislature as assume to deprive the subject of his property without a regular adjudication of the courts.

It has even been proposed to take away the property of secessionists and bestow it upon loyal men by way of compensating the latter for loses which they have sustained at the hands of other secessionists.

Now, aside. from the consideration that such an act would be purely judicial, there may be stated a still more serious objection to its practical exercise. The punishment of any person for merely holding the opinions of the secessionists would be unprecedented barbarity. Opinion is not the subject of punishment at all with any but savages. Until thought has been evolved into action it can never be justly amenable to the censure of any human tribunal. Even the maxim *scribere est agere*, adopted by a judge whom the world regards with horror, in order to convict Algernon Sydney of treason, has been denounced by all subsequent lawyers as well as historians.

Shall it be left to free Americans to change that atrocious maxim for the worse by inscribing on their criminal records *cogitare est agere* or *dicere est agere?* At all events, if even *thought* or *speech* could be considered treason the question would not be for the decision of Congress but exclusively for the courts.

But a tendency to usurpation still more alarming, although in a different direction, has lately been manifested on the part of Congress in the attempt of that body to control the operations of the War Department in matters of a purely military character. The members of Congress who have participated in this revolutionary project seem to be acting under the delusive idea that the Federal Legislature has inherited all the sovereignty of the British Parliament, and may therefore adopt any precedent found in the history of the latter.

The British theory has been stated by Blackstone in this brief sentence:—

Sovereignty and legislature are indeed convertible terns—one cannot subsist without the other.

It is obvious, however, that our system is based upon an idea altogether different—that is to say, on the *distribution* of the sovereign powers, and not upon their *consolidation*, and hence with us it is axiomatic that no *branch* of the government can exercise any powers others than those which are expressly given or necessarily implied; and, therefore, those who deny a given power to any department are not required to show a positive inhibition of the power of the Constitution. It is enough to say that such power is not conferred in that instrument.

By what pretension of right can Congress then assume a supremacy over the War Power, to compel the latter to disclose secrets the revelation of which it deems detrimental to the success of our arms? Can we imagine a more flagrant act of usurpation than this? And would it not clearly justify the Executive in the exercise of martial law in respect to all such members of Congress as join in this new species of rebellion? The same rule must apply to members of Congress as to the judges of the courts. If either undertake to interfere with the appropriate action of the military power, they must be put out of the way until the war is over, or at least until they withdraw their mischievous opposition to the only authority which the sovereignty of the people has by the Constitution itself invested with the competency to conduct the war at all.

Another inquiry of extreme moment relates to the power of suspending the writ of *habeas corpus* in the case or persons who may be arrested in the loyal States for alleged complicity with the rebellion.

Now, it is plainly of the first importance to obtain a correct answer to this question, and for two special reasons: First, because in the early stage of the rebellion the exercise of this power afforded the only available means to prevent the insurrection from drawing large military resources from the very heart of the Union, and perhaps also from spreading the contagion of treason into territory then mostly free from it, and the peril may be again repeated, and, secondly, because it has been against the manifestation of this power that the advocates and friends of secession have been most clamorous in their outcries of denunciation, thereby proving its practical necessity by the very invective which denied its lawfulness.

The power of suspension, whatever may be its nature and extent, rests upon this clause of the Constitution:—

The privilege of the writ of *habeas corpus* shall not be suspended unless when in cases of rebellion or invasion the public safety may require it.

It is apparent that the language of the provision is perfectly lucid, as far as it goes, and the sole difficulty connected with it is that it does not indicate the depositary of the power limited, either in terms or by implicit reference.

The consequence has been that different opinions have been entertained on the subject, some jurists of eminent character asserting for Congress the exclusive authority of suspension, while others of equal reputation have attributed the exclusive power to the President, and a third party, of no less legal celebrity, has located it distributively in Congress and the President as a concurrent power in both.

In the absence of any decisive critical test for the inquiry and amidst such disagreement, it does not become any one, much less one not a lawyer, to speak too positively of the matter. Nevertheless, it does seem to the present writer, that one consideration has' been overlooked in the discussion which is capable of throwing upon it a very clear light. It would seem that the shortest and most certain method of ascertaining *who* is to exercise the power, since no department is especially designated, must be to determine the class to which the given power naturally belongs, whether that be legislative or executive; and if the latter, then of what species, namely, whether it be civil or military.

But, viewing the subject from this analytic point, the *discretion* to suspend the writ is seen at once to fall naturally under the class of military powers of those which appertain to the direction of the public force against an armed enemy, whether foreign or domestic, because the Constitution itself defines the prescribed occasions when the writ can be suspended at all to be "cases of rebellion or invasion," where the "public safety requires it." Here two things must concur to justify the exercise of the power: There must not only be rebellion or invasion, but also a necessity to suspend the writ imposed by the public safety.

But all these terms relate properly not to the functions of *legislation* but to those of *execution* in the control of military measures. It is the military force which cases of rebellion and invasion call into activity. It is the same force which great peril to the public safety puts in motion. It is this force, too, in the freedom of its evolutions, which the writ of *habeas corpus* may disturb and fetter, and therefore, by inevitable logic, it is the commander of the military force who ought to possess the power of setting aside the writ of *habeas corpus* when he finds it employed mischievously to defeat the operations of war.

Again, it would appear very difficult to determine beforehand, or for a numerous body of non-military persons, such as the members of Congress, to determine at all, the peculiar cases when and where rebellion or invasion may produce such danger to the public safety as to require the writ to be suspended. Rebellion may conceal its preparations so carefully as to come like the shock of an earthquake, without sign or premonition and at a time when Congress does not sit. An invasion, insignificant today, by changing the point of attack may become almost overwhelming tomorrow; and then the next day after the crisis of a single battle the peril to the public safety may be past; but it is obvious that as the peril to the public safety changes, either in time or place, so does the necessity which justifies the suspension of the writ of *habeas corpus*; hence if the power to suspend were vested exclusively in Congress the writ would probably seldom be suspended soon enough, and could hardly fail to remain suspended, at least in most instances, too long.

Moreover, the specific difference between legislative and executive power may be defined most accurately by a statement of their opposite functions. Thus, the former makes laws, the latter puts them into practice, or, as expressed by Rutherforth, "The legislative power is the joint understanding of the society directing what is proper to be done." "The executive power is the joint strength of the society exerting itself in taking care that what is so directed shall be done."

In a word, the characteristic of legislative power is to speak; that of the executive power is to act; but the suspension of the writ in a special case evidently appertains not so properly to speech as to action, and hence all the attributes of the power in question seem to class it with those of execution and to preclude any salutary exercise of it on the part of Congress.

It may be that Congress has some kind of authority over the subject, in a general way, under the constitutional grant "to make rules for the government and regulations of the land and the naval forces."

Nevertheless, if Congress can claim any such regulative authority its operation must necessarily be very much restricted by the fact that the supreme legislative power has in the Constitution defined the *occasion* when alone the privilege of the writ of *habeas corpus* can be lawfully suspended with as great a degree of particularity as the nature of the case admits and has left nothing to the discretion of Congress, nor is there any power in our system which can modify the constitutional definition by increase or subtraction of a single term, for surely no Federal authority can suspend the writ, unless "in case of rebellion or invasion;" but not even then unless the public safety may require it.

Are we not, then, obviously entitled to take another and bolder step in the analysis of this power?

Since it has been proved that the power of suspension arises only in special circumstances relating exclusively to the operations of war, may we not affirm that when these circumstances concur the writ *eo instanti* stands suspended by force of the Constitution alone, and that it then becomes not so much the right as the duty of the military commander to proclaim it. This view would confer on the chief of the military force in any district, as soon as the concurrence of the essential facts defined in the Constitution should become clearly manifest, a full authority to declare the occasion present for asserting the supremacy of martial law, for this martial law differs from civil law in the same manner as a state of war is opposed to a state of peace.

War has its own law as well as peace. The law of war is martial law, but martial law is nothing more than the application of military force to overcome the resistance of an enemy who acknowledges no other rule than that of force, and hence, in the presence of such an enemy, the military commander must necessarily have the power to set aside every civil authority which might assume to interfere in any way so as to control or embarrass the operations of the war.

A denial of this power virtually carries with it the denial of any power to render war effectual in any case whatsoever. If the civil judge can issue a *writ of ejectment* for the ground upon which a military encampment or fortress is situated, or *replevin* for the artillery horses on the eve of battle, or a *habeas corpus* to bring before him the bodies of soldiers or captives alleged to be illegally detained, then there is an end of all military authority, and the commander might as well raise the white flag and submit to the enemy at once. Hence it is unquestionable that the chief of any distinct military command must necessarily have the right to employ martial law; but that is the right to exclude the civil judge, and that again is *per se* a suspension of the writ of *habeas corpus*, and thus the old maxim, *Inter arma leges silent*, is as true now as it was the day when Cicero penned it.

It is the command of the military chief giving his orders to the military force which hushes the laws into so deep a silence.

But even the proclamation of martial law does not supersede the ordinary functions of judicial power to any greater extent than may be requisite to accomplish the special military purpose of the occasion which necessitates the measure. It does not confer upon the commander any authority to try offenses other than those against the usages of war. It does not invest him with a commission to determine civil suits between private parties. He is arbiter only in the great controversy of arms, and he applies to the issue before him not the rule of municipal jurisprudence but the stern law of war.

His sole office is to direct the use of military force so as to conquer a given resistance, and he removes out of his way whatever impediment may tend to prevent or obstruct the successful employment of that force. Hence if even judicial authority stands in the way he puts it aside for the time. But this definition of martial law obviously leaves the judge at liberty to sit in all cases which do not fall within the province of military command or otherwise affect such means as may be dictated by the policy of war.

We have now reached the last question appertaining to the general subject of power, and this refers to the authority of the President to arrest and imprison the persons of alleged friends and adherents of the rebellion in the loyal States.

If one examines this inquiry with proper attention and freedom from prejudice he cannot fail to be astonished that it should ever have been mooted at all, for can it matter, in the view of the Constitution, in what part of the United States the "public safety" may require the writ of *habeas corpus* to be suspended, provided the necessity results from a case of "invasion" or "rebellion" waged anywhere against the national flag? Or can it matter, according to the laws of war, in what locality an adherent of the public enemy may choose to carry on the work of a common hostility?

If a foe taken on the battlefield in Virginia may be imprisoned during the war, what rule of natural justice shall exempt from a like fate the friend of treason who is sending to its aid arms or information from Maryland? Is the character of a rebel spy more sacred than that of a rebel soldier? But neither the man of Virginia nor the man of Maryland can be said to be imprisoned merely because he is assumed to be a traitor, which would be a reason for detention under the civil authority only, but both of them are imprisoned because they belong to the revolutionary force, which is exclusively a military reason, and can this be represented as a matter of grave complaint? What I shall it be said that any person can plead as a cause of exemption from confinement the singular excuse that besides being an enemy he is a traitor also?

It is as clear as sunlight to all who are willing to see that the same provisions of the Constitution and the same laws of civil war which justify the government in imprisoning its foes taken in open fight will equally justify it in the capture and detention not only of those who may be on the march to join the enemy but also of those who may be secretly preparing to raise the colours of the enemy on any part of the national territory, and this latter was the precise predicament of the persons arrested and detained under the order of the President in the State of Maryland and elsewhere.

They were all, without a single exception, either pledged to the allegiance of the revolutionary power or else making preparations to strike in its favours and against the government; and the political authority of a nation, any more than any private person, is not obliged to wait until a blow impending is actually struck, which might perhaps then prove irresistible; but the government, like the individual, may anticipate the blow by disarming its antagonist and by holding him until he ceases to threaten hostilities, or at least until the force with which he has been in concert has been overcome or weakened so far as to have ceased to be dangerous, nor is there one writer upon natural law that does not recognise such a power of self-protection in every government.

What the right of self-defence is to individuals the war power is to nations; and in every case the necessary prevention of danger stands justified by the same reasons which justify resistance when the peril is present. Indeed, the only difference in rational principle between the case of an insurgent taken in battle and that of an unarmed *adherent* of the revolutionary force refers not to the question of right but to the question of evidence. In the case of those who are captured in fight there can be no doubt as to the fact of hostility, while in the case of others every degree of doubt may be possible.

There is, however, one criterion, the application of which furnishes a testimony as infallible upon the question of hostility as afforded by any belligerent acts whatsoever. and this criterion becomes decisive whenever in any case the oath of allegiance is demanded by the government and refused on the part of any citizen of the United States.

Allegiance is defined by Lord Coke to be "a true and faithful obedience of the subject due to his sovereign," or, in the words of Justice Story, "allegiance is nothing more than the tie or duty of obedience of a subject to his sovereign under whose protection he is;" but however the thing may be defined, it is manifest from its very nature, and all the authorities agree in this opinion, that every government has a right to exact from all citizens, at its discretion, a public pledge of their fidelity by taking the oath of allegiance or other formal or solemn declaration of loyalty.

Chancellor Kent says:—

> Every citizen may on a proper occasion be required to take the oath of allegiance.

This principle acquires a peculiar interest and importance for us from its pertinence to a case of insurrection. The civil war has divided the common country for a time, and raised up in it a revolution-ary power which asserts its independence by an appeal to arms; but what would be the result as to the *status* of individual citizens if this revolutionary power should be able to make good its claim and thus permanently dismember the nation into two separate and indepen-dent empires?

The case is simply this: a nation previously one divides itself in two. Then what rule does the allegiance of the individual citizen follow? As this allegiance was before one in reference to the one nation, how shall it be distributed between the two nations emerging out of the revolution? And here Chancellor Kent concurs with other eminent jurists in laying down the rule that during the revolutionary contest every citizen has the right of election and may transfer his allegiance to either of the rival governments at his option.

Of course, this rule is limited by the essential qualification that the right of election asserted remains merely *in fiere* while the war is progressing and can only become perfect when the nationality of the new government has been fully established. Hence it follows that whenever an insurrectionary force is organized in any country, and especially when it puts forth the claim to act as an independent power, then the lawful government has necessarily the right to treat such adverse force and all those who adhere to it by election as public en-emies, at least *ad interim*, and therefore to deal with them according to the established usages of war.

In other words, the government may choose to admit provisionally or for belligerent purposes the assertion of the revolutionary power and of its adherents that it is an independent public enemy, and there-fore may act upon that assumption not as an abstract truth but as a practical postulate granted on the other side, for certainly there can be no wrong or shadow of injustice in attributing to any person the very character which he claims, at the peril of life itself, to be his own. It is, indeed, very true that the government is not obliged to recognise this character of belligerents asserted by the forces of the rebellion. To do so is the concession for a time of a privilege and not the denial of any right even pretended.

The government, if it should see fit, may consider the matter in a far different light, and may treat it as a question of bald treason by turning over all captives taken in arms, as well as all active adherents of the insurrection, to be tried and punished in the criminal courts; and it must do either the one or the other. It must imprison or it must punish, or else renounce all pretensions of political authority and virtually abdicate its functions. There is no other imaginable alternative.

Now, suppose the government were to exercise its prerogative to try and punish while the war is going on and the event more or less doubtful. One general outburst of indignation would be heard from the whole civilized world against the barbarity of such a proceeding, and none would be louder in their censure than those pretended friends of constitutional freedom who now so bitterly assail the administration for employing the more humane and prudent remedy of imprisonment.

However, although it must be admitted that the government has the naked, legal right to try the captives it has taken for treason, such a course would not only be contrary to civilized usage, but also a great moral wrong, because so long as the forces of rebellion are able to keep the field there always will remain the bare possibility that they may ultimately prove successful. But what follows then? Why, that none of them can be considered guilty of any crime at all; for, in the view of all nations, success justifies from the guilt of treason, or, rather, transforms it into complete legitimacy.

And hence the epigram:

Treason never prospers. What's the reason?
That when it prospers none dare call it treason.

Therefore, there was but one course left for the government, namely, to imprison all captives until the question of their final guilt shall be determined by the result of the late war.

To ascertain by competent evidence who are adherents of the revolutionary power in the loyal States the government has applied the criterion of a tender of the oath of allegiance, discharging all who show themselves willing to pledge their fidelity to the nation as their fathers constituted it and detaining those only who refuse to acknowledge their subjection to Federal authority. Could anything be at the same time more just or more merciful than this? Besides, as an evidential test, the rule operates demonstratively, because whoever refuses to pledge his allegiance to the government under which he lives, by that act virtually denies its jurisdiction over him and voluntarily assumes the character of a public enemy. By the same conduct he also reveals the profound hostility of his heart towards the Federal authority and the obstinate determination of his will to resist it.

Shall the President, then, be reproached for conceding to these adherents of rebellion the very character which they willingly and even proudly assume? May he not well recognise them as what they are, *de facto*, though not *de jure,* enemies of the nation?

And if the President can do this he may deal with them while the war continues, not as criminals merely, but as prisoners of war; but if they can be deemed prisoners of war it must be admitted by all that no writ of *habeas corpus* can touch the case of their detention, because that rests exclusively in the discretion of the war power. To hold otherwise would be to transfer the authority of a chief command from the President and vest it in the judges of a hundred local courts.

It must be admitted, however, that any alleged adherent of the insurrection may renounce the benefit of this belligerent character at his pleasure. By taking the oath of allegiance he may recede from his voluntary attitude as a public enemy and then demand a trial before the courts; but this the Northern traitors have shown themselves utterly unwilling to do, because they are well aware of the fact, which many Union men have so strangely failed to comprehend, that the imprisonment complained of is a benefit rather than a burden, not an oppression at the hands of tyranny, but the privilege of exemption for a time at least from the merited punishment of treasons Hence, although the government has tendered a release to all these prisoners upon the condition of swearing allegiance, a condition so easy and also

In accordance with duty, they yet deliberately reject the boon of liberty. Each one carries the key to his own jail in his own pocket, but no one chooses to unlock the prison doors, because all are conscious that safety for them lies within and not without the walls.

The discussion thus far has related chiefly to the powers of the government in its dealings with the rebels in arms or with such adherents of treason as may be secretly giving them assistance, and a few words must now be devoted to the subject of its duty in respect to the loyal citizens, whose misfortune it is, but certainly not their fault, to have their homes within the limits of the seceded States.

In order to comprehend clearly this duty on the part of the government it may be necessary to define concisely the present political condition and relation of the hundreds of thousands in the South who still cling in firm allegiance of the heart to the Constitution, which has been annulled by the authorities of their States, and the Union whose protection is so far away.

Now, in the first place, it is true beyond all controversy that whenever a State withdraws from the Union wrongfully—that is to say, in a case where the Federal compact has not been broken by the General Government—such action on the part of the State is a breach of her own State constitution as well as of the Federal Constitution, because each of these constitutions is an essential part of that complex political system under which we live, and every citizen inherits different rights and is bound by different obligations under each, the whole of these together blending to make the sum of his civil liberties and duties.

Therefore, any action of either government, whether of the nation or of the State, which would take away the vested rights of the citizen of either must necessarily involve a violation of the general political compact which secures all his liberties though by different means; and that the secession of a State does thus directly tend to diminish the rights of its own citizens may be proved in the most conclusive manner. For example, the Federal Constitution guarantees a republican form of government to every State, and therefore to the citizens of every State; but the act of secession blots out forever that valuable political right of the citizen and leaves it to the caprice of the State government to establish either an aristocracy or monarchy, or what the seceded States have in fact established—a pure military despotism.

Again, the citizen of a State, by force of the Constitution, is virtually a citizen of every other State in the Union; but the act of secession obliterates this precious privilege also and leaves its victim an alien to one-half of the Federal territory, perhaps to the very State of his birth, even to the native mountain which was as a brother of his boyhood.

Again, the right of every citizen of a State in her appropriate constitutional relation is to have his liberty and independence from the control of foreign powers as well as from the lawless force of domestic revolt protected by the whole public power of the United States; but the act of secession tears this glorious right away, too, and places the citizen of a once great empire in a condition of despicable national inferiority. Hence, according to the settled principles of natural and political law, the act of secession by these gross and palpable violations of the social compact discharges all citizens from their allegiance to State authority, and therefore leaves them at perfect liberty to constitute a new State anywhere within the limits of their former State, now dissolved by the usurpation of a force hostile to the National Government, or if not possessed of sufficient numerical strength to maintain a State organisation to enter into the territorial condition under the full sovereignty of the General Government, if they choose to do so.

This latter alternative results necessarily from the premises, because the right of citizens to constitute a State, like all other rights, may, of course, be waived at their pleasure.

In the second place, since the discharge of the allegiance to their own State on account of its palpable violations of the Constitution cannot sever the tie which binds such citizens to the General Government, it follows necessarily that the latter is obliged by a sworn duty to interpose for the protection of their constitutional rights and to overthrow, if possible, those revolutionary powers which at once oppress the liberties of the individual and defy the authority of the nation; but if the United States should from any cause prove unable to expel the revolutionary force from every part of a seceded State, it is, nevertheless, a solemn national duty to put it aside as far as may be, and thus give the loyal citizens an opportunity to form a new State for themselves, at least in that portion of the former State which may be so freed from the sway of the insurgents, or to become a Territory under the sovereignty of Congress, at their option.

The duties of allegiance and protection are reciprocal. Hence if the supreme power of the nation should not within a reasonable time afford that protection, which is their Federal right, to its citizens of the South, they will be forever released from their allegiance, and thus will pass away, as if it had never been, that glorious Union which has been the centre of so many precious hopes, the subject of so many earnest prayers, the magical name which oppressed nations have so long murmured in all their dreams of liberty, and which had power to make tyrants tremble on the most ancient thrones. Gone forever will then be the most promising example of popular government which the annals of time have known, and perhaps ages of dreary darkness must roll away before humanity shall recover heart to repeat the example which has now so sadly failed! The misfortune will not be felt merely upon this continent or by the present age only. It will be as well the memory of a mighty loss to the world at large and to generations both near and far remote in the future years.

CHAPTER 3

Note by Miss Carroll to Accompany Republication of "The Constitutional Power of the President"

(In the spring of 1891)

Attorney General Bates, with whom I was intimately acquainted, said he would like my opinion in reference to the one he had just given, and wished it in writing. I therefore prepared the following, which met his approval and the cordial approval of the President and his entire Cabinet, and was largely circulated.

A. E. Carroll.

THE CONSTITUTIONAL POWER OF THE PRESIDENT TO MAKE

ARRESTS AND TO SUSPEND THE WRIT OF *HABEAS CORPUS* EXAMINED.

BY ANNA ELLA CARROLL.

SEPTEMBER, 1861.

The conflict of opinion which is expressed throughout the country by various editors and judges of unquestioned loyalty upon the power of the President to make arrests and to suspend the writ of *habeas corpus* seems to demand further discussion. I therefore briefly review the learned opinion of the Attorney General of the United States in order to show that the President in arresting persons in criminal complicity with the insurgents and in the suspension of this writ has only exercised the constitutional power vested alike in all his predecessors in office and does not require any apologist to defend him as an innovator of the Constitution.

Judge Bates grasps the entire system of our free government and admirably contrasts it with the governments of Europe. In European nations, the sovereignty resides not in the people, but in the government. Their governments exercise and possess absolute power; whereas, according to the American theory, the sovereignty resides in the people, and their government possesses only limited and delegated powers, not absolute. He adverts to the historic fact that the enmity of the American people of the Revolution was not against the legislative or judicial powers of the English government, but against the king. The reason was that the *crown* represented and assumed the exercise of this absolute power, making the people but the subjects or slaves of the individual man.

The American people, therefore, in making a government without a throne were scrupulously careful to reserve the sovereignty to themselves, and hence their government can exercise no other powers than those the *people* have conferred upon it. He ably shows that the people were equally precise in distributing the granted powers to three co-ordinate departments, each independent of the other; and the President, though in no sense a sovereign, is independent in his sphere and not subordinate to the other departments of the government. He presents the philosophic idea that our fathers never attempted to provide a common judge or arbiter in cases of conflict between the executive, judicial, and legislative powers of our system, and therefore deduces that the President cannot rightfully be called in question in the exercise of his power by the legislative or judicial departments.

Hence, in using his constitutional powers, he is in no way affected by their decisions to the contrary, each being limited in their spheres and co-ordinate and independent. That proposition being established; he proceeds to ascertain precisely what powers the President may constitutionally exercise. He proves conclusively that the President is only a civil magistrate, although by the Constitution he is made the "Commander-in-Chief of the Army and Navy and of the militia of the several States when called into the active service of the United States," and in directing the military power of the country he does so as a *civil magistrate and not as a military chief.*

This is the first time in our history that we have encountered the horrors of civil war, the first time we have felt that we were in contact with the physical force of the nation.

In our previous history, this *force* has been directed against *foreign* rather than *domestic* foes, and the novel spectacle of the exercise by the

Presidents of extraordinary military power has never been witnessed before by the American people! Hence they had not realised its nature or extent, which, nevertheless, is a constitutional power, and would have been exercised by every faithful chief magistrate who has administered the government under a similar emergency.

In making plain the important truth that although we have hundreds of thousands of men moving in vast armies in the field they move in strict subordination to the civic magistracy the attorney general has done an invaluable service to our constitutional liberty.

So long now as our legislatures and courts refrain from embarrassing the President in the exercise of his powers and so long as the vast military power remains subject to his control, just so long and no longer are our liberties safe!

If the time shall ever come when weak or over-zealous editors and corrupt politicians shall persuade judges or legislators to transcend their constitutional powers by attempting to circumscribe or restrain the President's legitimate action, or whenever a military chieftain shall acquire such an influence over the armies under his control as to disregard the orders of the President and set the military above the civil power, then are our liberties upon this continent hopelessly gone!

Judge Bates next notices the duties imposed on the President by the Constitution, which requires him to "preserve, protect, and defend" the same and to execute the laws over the nation. He argues that in case of rebellion or invasion, when the judicial power is weakened or overborne, so that the civil authorities cannot be exercised by the ordinary agencies of governments, it becomes the duty of the President to "take care" that the laws shall be executed, and for this purpose (as in the present case) it is necessary to use armies.

In such an extraordinary exigency, the President is made the sole judge of the manner in which it is most prudent to employ the powers entrusted to him. He must decide whether the rebellion or invasion exists to the extent of displacing the civil power, but *in executing the laws by the army he does not subordinate the civil or elevate the military power.* He holds the military ever *subject* and *subordinate* to the civil authority. He is *not* made a military dictator, a warrior, or a usurper in his constitutional exercise as "*Commander-in-Chief,*" but is required to stay at the capital, in the Presidential Mansion, and to hold in his hands the civil authority as *supreme over armies.*

The Constitution does not call on the gowned judges; they may sit unconscious of the fact that war exists, if they please, until the armed force comes within their presence, just as they did when the Capitol was on fire a few years ago. When the news reached the Supreme Court Judge Taney inquired where it existed, and being informed it was in the library, remarked that they would proceed with the case until it reached the Supreme Court room. So, I presume he will continue in the present struggle unless the fires of the rebellion should catch and consume his own chambers.

Under this branch of the argument the attorney general shows that the Constitution does *not* invest the judicial department of the government with the functions of determining whether rebellion or invasion exists, that being a political question, *its object being to destroy the political government of the nation and establish one upon its ruins.*

He frees himself with extraordinary ease from the mere technicalities of his profession and rises at once to the true dignity and comprehensiveness of the statesman.

He demonstrates that the President, as the political head of the government, is charged with the solemn duty of making war against the rebellion and of arresting and holding as prisoners those who in the exercise of his discretion he believes to be the friends and accomplices of treason.

He has and exercises no judicial, and the judiciary has no political powers and claims none; therefore, *no court or judge can take cognisance of the political acts of the President.* If, then, in time of rebellion the President, in the exercise of his powers (whenever the public safety may require it, of which he alone is judge under the Constitution), shall arrest any traitor or anyone found giving aid or comfort to the enemy, Judge Bates proves to demonstration that no *judge or court* can undertake to reverse this action on the part of the commander-in-chief.

He recurs to the common law for the true exposition of the writ of *habeas corpus.*

He shows that it is a high prerogative writ, and by our Constitution the country is at all times entitled to know *why* the liberties of any of its citizens are restrained, *"unless when, in case of rebellion or invasion, the public safety may require the suspension of the privilege."*

He felicitously reconciles the conflict of opinion, and shows that the power to suspend the *authority* of the judiciary to issue the writ is vested *alone* in the legislative department; but the power to suspend the privilege of the party arrested during the time of invasion or rebellion is *vested alone* in the executive department, which is charged with the *public safety.*

Now, should a judge assume to issue a writ of *habeas corpus* for the discharge of a political prisoner "when in case of rebellion or invasion," the answer is that the President has suspended the *privilege* of the prisoner, "*the public safety requiring it.*" Hence it is *no more necessary formally to suspend the writ of habeas corpus by a declaration of martial law* before arresting a traitor than it is to suspend the writ of *relievin* before seizing arms or munitions of war!

Here he strips the question of its fallacy and throws an achromatic light upon the subject.

He proves that all the powers of the President would be nugatory in suppressing rebellion or invasion by the capture of insurgents or the seizure of munitions of war if a judge might discharge the prisoner by the writ of *habeas corpus* or the munitions of war by a writ of replevin.

In short, that it would leave the enemy in entire power to war upon the government to the total subversion of our civil liberty.

This is the only government upon earth where the rights of the people are secured, and the attorney general shows its extreme humanity, as well as his own benignity of character, on the question of arresting political offenders.

The President, so far from violating, is *heroically defending* the rights of Americans in arresting criminals who are engaged in secret or covert war upon this government. *Instead of handing them over to the courts for trial, condemnation, and execution,* as he has the clear right to do and as every other government but ours upon earth unquestionably *would,* he only holds them as captives to prevent them from destroying the blood-bought rights which every citizen who remembers that he is a man and was born of a woman should fly to rescue and defend.

Anna Ella Carroll.

Maryland, September, 1861.

CHAPTER 4

Note by Miss Carroll to Accompany the Republication of "The Relation of the National Government to the Revolted Citizens"

(In the spring of 1891)

The subjoined document was written after a conversation with President Lincoln, who dissented from several remarks made in the Senate at the time, and to whom the pamphlet was presented for examination immediately after it was written by the author, and he gave it his full and unqualified indorsement. It was at once distributed in both branches of Congress.

A. E. Carroll.

★★★★★★

THE RELATION OF THE NATIONAL GOVERNMENT TO THE REVOLTED CITIZENS DEFINED—NO POWER IN CONGRESS TO EMANCIPATE THEIR SLAVES OR CONFISCATE THEIR PROPERTY PROVED.—THE CONSTITUTION AS IT IS THE ONLY HOPE OF THE COUNTRY.

BY ANNA ELLA CARROLL.

Congress has now under consideration the question of the power and expediency of abolishing slavery and confiscating the property, real and personal, of all or a large class of the rebels in arms. A question of more transcendent importance than any that ever before engaged the attention of the American people.

With an earnest desire that the country may not be led to the adoption of a mistaken and fatal policy, I propose now to contribute my best efforts to a further understanding of this vital subject.

No one doubts the power or the duty of the government to suppress the rebellion, to use the army and navy and all the military resources of the country to capture the rebels and kill them if they will not submit, and destroy their power to war upon us, but I do not think there is any grant in the Constitution, but rather an express inhibition upon the power of Congress to abolish slavery or confiscate the property of rebels.

There are two clauses in the Constitution which especially refer to the confiscation of property. The first defines the crime of treason and authorises Congress to prescribe the punishment, inhibiting, however, the confiscation of property beyond the life of the offender. The second is an absolute prohibition to Congress of confiscation altogether. The first defines the crime in these words:—

> Treason against the United States shall consist in levying war against them or in adhering to their enemies, giving them aid and comfort. No person shall be convicted of treason unless on the testimony of two witnesses to the same overt act or on confession in open court.
>
> The Congress shall have power to declare punishment of treason, but no attainder of treason shall work corruption of blood or forfeiture, except during the life of the person attainted.

Treason is not an offense against society, but an offense against its government, and in all ages a disposition has been evinced on the part of the governing power to construe everything as treason which opposed it, and this arises from the natural passion of revenge, the desire to punish for opposition to its authority, the rapacity common to all in the possession of political power, and the desire to obtain the money or estate of the convict.

Justice Story, in commenting on this clause of the Constitution, says:—

> The history of other countries abundantly proves that one of the strong incentives to prosecute offenses as treason has been the chance of sharing the plunder of the victims. Rapacity has been thus stimulated to exert itself in the service of the most corrupt tyranny, and tyranny has been thus furnished with new opportunities of indulging its malignity and revenge, of gratifying the envy of the rich and good, of increasing its means to reward favourites, and to secure retainers for the worst deeds.

This feeling is so strong in all governments that Montesquieu was so sensible of it that he has not scrupled to declare that if the crime of treason be *indeterminate, that* alone is sufficient to make any government degenerate into an arbitrary power.

The history of England is full of melancholy instruction on this subject, nor have republics been exempt from violence and tyranny of a similar character.

The *Federalist* has justly remarked that:

New-fangled and artificial treason has been the great engine by which factions the natural offspring of free government have usually wreaked their alternate malignity on each other.

It was under the influence of these admonitions, furnished by history and human experience, that the convention deemed it necessary to interpose an impassable barrier against arbitrary construction, either by *courts* or by *Congress*, upon the crime of treason. Hence it was that the authors of our Constitution guarded the rights of the citizen by defining specifically in *what* the act of treason consists and limiting the power of Congress in its punishment by absolutely inhibiting the confiscation of the estate of the traitor to the government, leaving it free to pass to his heirs.

The second clause of the Constitution in reference to confiscation is:—

No bill of attainder or *ex post facto* law shall be passed.

Now, it is to me a matter of great surprise that any should doubt but that the bills before Congress are in direct conflict with this clause.

These bills assume that certain parties have committed treason and ought to be punished; but, being beyond the jurisdiction of the United States, or in States where the civil authority has been expelled, they cannot be brought before the courts of the country for trial; therefore Congress shall adjudge them guilty of treason, forfeit their slaves and entire estates, and proceed directly to execute this legislative decree by deeds of manumission to the slaves and seizure and absolute forfeiture of all their estates as a punishment for the crime and as "indemnity for the past and security for the future."

If the object had been to have drawn a bill of attainder directly in *conflict* with the Constitution, I do not think one could have been made more efficient or more operative than some of the bills which have been pressed before Congress.

A "*bill of attainder*," as used in the Constitution, is a technical term, and we must therefore look to the common law and the concurrent history for the correct interpretation of its meaning.

Woodison in his lecture says:—

> But, besides a regular enforcement of established laws, the annals of most countries record signal exertions of penal justice adapted to exigencies unprovided for in the criminal code.
>
> Such acts of the supreme power are with us called *bills of attainder*, which are capital sentences, and bills of *pains and penalties*, which inflict a milder degree of punishment.
>
> In these instances the legislature assume judicial magistracy, weighing the enormity of the charge and the proof adduced in support of it, and then deciding the political necessity and moral fitness of the punishment.

Justice Story says:—

> Bills of attainder, as they are technically called, are such special acts of the legislature as inflict capital punishment upon persons supposed to be guilty of high offenses, such as treason and felony, *without any conviction in the ordinary courts of judicial proceedings*. If an act inflicts a milder degree of punishment than death, it is called a bill of *pains and penalties*; but in the sense of the Constitution it seems that bills of attainder include bills of pains and penalties, for the Supreme Court has said:—
>
> 'A bill of attainder may affect the life of an individual or may confiscate his property, or both. In most cases *the legislature assumes judicial magistracy, pronouncing against the guilt of the party without any of the common forms and guards of trial* and satisfying itself with proof, when such proofs are within its reach, whether they were conformable to the rules of evidence or not. In short, in all such cases the legislature exercises the highest power of sovereignty and what may be properly deemed an *irresponsible despotic discretion*, being governed solely by what is deemed political necessity or expediency.'

But the advocates of the policy of general confiscation, being unable to controvert this authoritative exposition of the term *bill of attainder*, assume the extraordinary position that the prohibition is *not binding* on Congress during a time of rebellion. I am unable to comprehend how anyone can assume this position, for nothing is more certain than that this prohibition was inserted in the Constitution *only* to prevent the exercise of this arbitrary power during a rebellion.

The authors of our Constitution never apprehended that Congress would assume to exercise *judicial magistracy* except in time of rebellion. They knew well that there never was any motive in time of *peace*, and even if there were that Congress would not attempt its exercise, for it is only in times of conflict between the public authority and the people that governments have ever attempted the exercise of this extraordinary and arbitrary power.

Justice Story says:—

Bills of this sort have been most usually passed in England in times of rebellion or of gross subserviency to the crown or of violent political excitement—periods in which all nations are most liable (as well the free as the enslaved) *to forget their duties and to trample underfoot the rights and liberties of others.*

. . . . Such acts have been often resorted to in foreign governments as a common engine of state, and even in England they have been pushed to the most extravagant extent in bad times, reaching as well to the *absent* and the *dead* as to the living.

The injustice and iniquity of such acts in general constitute an irresistible argument against the existence of the power. In a free government, it would be intolerable and in the hands of a reigning faction it might be and probably would be abused to the ruin and death of the most virtuous citizen.

In support of the policy of confiscation its advocates have searched universal history, from "the time when Ahab took the vineyard of Naboth, and David gave away the goods of one of the confederates of Absalom," down to the most arbitrary acts of Napoleon.

They have also cited the various penal enactments of the Colonies during the American Revolution in its justification.

It was unquestionably *these very acts* of confiscation by the Colonies which led to the clauses in the Constitution prohibiting it in Congress and the States.

Story, in remarking on these acts of the Colonies, says in a note:—

During the American Revolution this power was used with a most unsparing hand, and it has been a matter of regret in succeeding times, however much it may have been applauded *flagranto bello.*

228

Never were a people more jealous of liberty than our forefathers were at the formation of the Constitution, and naturally so, too, as upon that Constitution depended the fruits of the independence which they had just achieved at the cost of so much treasure and blood. To guarantee this liberty they provided in the Constitution *for trial by jury in criminal cases; the definition and Punishment of treason; the prohibition of bills of attainder, &c.*

But the people feared that these guarantees were not sufficient for the greatest protection of their liberties, and hence the fourth, fifth, and sixth amendments restricting the exercise of these grants of power in these words:—

The right of the people to be secure in their person, houses, papers, and effects against unreasonable searches and seizures *shall not be violated*, nor shall any person be deprived of life, liberty, or property *without due process of law*, nor shall *private property* be taken for public use *without just compensation*; the accused shall enjoy the right to a speedy and public trial by an impartial jury of the State, etc.

Story, in his comments on the vital importance of these amendments, which he characterizes as a bill of rights, says:—

It is not always possible to foresee the extent of the actual reach of certain powers which are given in general terms. They may be construed to extend (and perhaps fairly) to certain classes of cases which did not at first appear to be within them. A bill of rights, then, operates as a guard upon an extravagant or undue extension of such powers.

Besides, as has been justly remarked, a bill of rights is of real efficiency in *controlling the excesses of party spirit*. It serves to guide and enlighten public opinion and to render more quick to detect and more resolute to resist attempts to disturb private rights. *It requires more than ordinary hardihood and audacity of character to trample down principles which our ancestors consecrated with reverence*, which we imbibed in our early education, which recommend themselves to the judgment of the world by their truth and simplicity, and which are constantly placed before the eyes of the people, accompanied with the imposing force and *solemnity of a constitutional sanctity*. Bills of rights are a part of the *muniments of freemen*, showing their title to protection, and they become of increased value when placed under the *protection of an independent judiciary*, instituted as the appropriate guardian of the public and private rights of the citizens.

It is sad to witness Senators and Representatives in the great Republic of the United States, in contempt of the warnings of history, drawing their principles and precedents from the most cruel and revengeful tyrants, and displaying:—

> . . . a hardihood and audacity of character in trampling down the principles which our ancestors have consecrated with reverence, which we imbibed in our early education, which recommend themselves to the judgment of the world by their truth and simplicity, and which are constantly placed before the eyes of the people, accompanied with the *imposing force and solemnity of a constitutional sanction*.

We are not permitted to doubt but that these bills originate in the worst and most malignant passions of the human heart, and are pressed in utter *contempt* of our constitutional guarantees.

Listen to Senator Sumner's words, uttered on the 19th of the present month, in the country's Senate chamber:—

> With the *provision in our Constitution applicable to jury trials in criminal cases*, it is obvious that throughout the whole rebel country there can be no conviction under such statutes. Proceedings would fail through the disagreement of the jury, while the efforts of the counsel would make every case an occasion of irritation. For weal or woe, the gallows is out of the question; it is not a possibility as a punishment for this rebellion; nor would any considerable forfeiture or confiscation be sanctioned by a jury in the rebel country. . . . .
>
> Surely we ought to take all proper steps to avoid such failure of justice. . . .
>
> Strike down the leaders of the rebellion and lift up the slaves.
>
> But the tallest poppies must drop. For the conspirators who organised this great crime and let slip the dogs of war there can be no penalty too great.
>
> They should be not only punished to the extent of our power, but they should be stripped of all means of influence, so that, should their lives be spared, they may be doomed to wear them out in poverty, if not in exile. To this end their property must be taken; but the property of the leaders *consists largely of land*

owned in extensive plantations. It is just that *these should be broken up,* so that they can never be again the nursery of conspiracy or disaffection. *Partitioned into small estates,* they will afford homes to many who are now homeless, while their peculiar and over-bearing social influence will be destroyed.

Poor neighbours, who have been so long duped and *victims,* will become independent settlers of the soil. Brave soldiers who have left their Northern skies to fight the battles of their country, resting at last from their victories and changing their swords into ploughshares, will *fill the land with Northern industry and Northern principles.*

Here is a distinct proposition to set aside the most sacred guarantees of the Constitution, to uproot the social system of one-half of the American Union, numbering in the aggregate some twelve millions of souls, and to partition their land to the poor, and to the slaves, and to the soldiers of the other half of the Union, and to "fill the South with a foreign industry and foreign principles."

I cannot recall to memory any instance surpassing the atrocity of this proposition in all the annals of despotism. But the advocates of confiscation by Congress feel it obligatory upon them to find some support in the Constitution for the exercise of this power.

Senator Howard, in his argument, assumes that the power to declare war, to make rules concerning captures on land and water, to raise and support armies, to provide for calling forth the militia, to suppress insurrection and repel invasion *does by implication* give this right, and he claims it as a *war measure.*

He says:—

If Congress has not the power to confiscate the property of the enemy as a punishment and as an indemnity for the cost of the war that the American people have thrown away for all time to come the most efficient means of crippling and humbling the enemy.

This theory of Senator Howard has been adopted, I believe, by all who have spoken on this side of the question whose speeches I have examined.

The argument is this: Because Congress has the authority to confiscate the property of a subject of a *foreign* State in time of war and vest it in the United States, therefore Congress has the authority to confiscate the property of a citizen of the United States in time of civil war and vest it in the Government of the United States.

This, I apprehend, proceeds from a total misconception of the true nature of the Constitution and the principles of international law.

The right to punish an enemy and hold his property responsible for damages is inherent in all nations, but *how* this right shall be exercised depends upon the peculiar structure of their government. In ours the right to punish a *foreign enemy* and hold his property liable for damages is vested by the Constitution in Congress as the supreme legislative power of the nation; but the right to punish a domestic enemy and hold his property liable for damages is *exclusively* vested in the executive and judiciary departments.

Rutherforth says:—

> In a state of *equality*, after an injury is committed any who have suffered any damage by it are at liberty to make themselves amends at their own discretion and by their own force. They are at liberty *to take so much of the offenders' goods as if equal in value to what they have lost,* and the law of nature will give them property in the goods so taken; but in a state of civil society, if both the offenders and the sufferers are under the protection of the same society, their right of obtaining reparation *is restrained and becomes subject to the civil jurisdiction.*

Absolute governments may punish their subjects by the direct exercise of the sovereign power, but no government can do this which claims to be free.

For the punishment of crime the Constitution provides *civil tribunals* and has provided a civil force to bring the offender before its judgment bar, and if this civil force be insufficient by reason of the strength of the offender, then there is a military force provided to bring all offenders, *not collectively or by States,* but *individually, before the courts of the land,* and there they can be deprived of their property, their liberty, or their life!

Surely no one will contend that the grants of power in the Constitution authorising Congress "to declare war, to grant letters of marque and reprisals," &c., confers on Congress the authority to declare war against any State of this Union or any number of citizens of any State or to authorise any citizen of this Union to make reprisals upon another citizen.

We are left in no doubt upon this subject, for when the proposition *for authorising the exercise of the military force of the General Government against a delinquent State* was being considered Mr. Madison *opposed it, saying "that it looked too much like the power to declare war, and would probably be considered by the party against whom it was used as a dissolution of the compact."*

He moved the postponement of this question, which was unanimously agreed to, and was never again brought before the convention.

Could Congress use this power and declare war against any State or any citizen of the Union? Could it grant letters of marque and reprisal to war upon the citizens, one against another? Then, truly, as was forcibly expressed by a Senator, if this be our political system, it is not worth much; surely it is not worth the cost of a terrible war.

Before Congress can claim to exercise this power of war over any portion of the American people it must first recognise the rebellion as a success—*their revolution accomplished and the Union dissolved.* In short, must concede to the rebellion—what no European power has ventured to do— that they have achieved their independence and have established a firm and stable government, against which it is no longer proper to war with the view of suppressing it.

For Congress to take that position and treat the rebellion as a *foreign nation* and continue the war from malice or vengeance is to become allies of the rebellion and ourselves *traitors, like them, to the Constitution.*

Fortunately, however, for civil liberty the Constitution confers ample powers upon the government for its own preservation and just defence against all combinations of domestic foes.

While the Constitution withholds from Congress all power to declare war against any member of the Union, that instrument confers on Congress ample authority to provide and maintain a *military force*, and upon the *President* ample authority to *use* that force in the defence of the nation by the suppression of insurrection or rebellion whenever the civil force is not sufficient for that end.

War may exist between the General Government and a portion of the American people, but under the Constitution it never did and never *can* exist except by armed resistance to its authority. Citizens may "*commit treason against the United States in levying war against them,*" and thus (as in the present instance) involve the country in all the horrors of civil war; but they do not therefore become *enemies* in the sense of the law of nations—they are *still citizens of the United States* and *owe allegiance do this Government* and are *liable to punishment for their crimes, and they cannot escape from their allegiance nor their liability for punishment due their crimes* unless they flee the country of their birth, never again to look upon its flag! For, if *Congress is true to the Constitution*, they never *can* establish within the limits of the United States a government to protect and shield them.

If we will but comprehend the reason of the rule in the laws of nations, why one nation has the right to hold the persons and property of another responsible for the injuries inflicted by his government, I think it will be conceded that the rule has no application to a rebel in a civil war.

Writers on general jurisprudence have considered nations as independent, moral persons, living in a state of nature, where there is no common tribunal to settle controversies with other nations but that of force.

When an injury is inflicted upon one nation by another and reparation is withheld, there is no way to recover it except by war, because independent nations, from the very nature of things, are not subject to the civil tribunals of any other nation. A nation is in no otherwise responsible than through her people. There is no means of recovering reparation except by holding them and their property, public and private, responsible to the offended nation. *These* constitute not only the wealth of a nation, but are the nation itself.

> As a nation consists of an aggregate of individuals, the property of the nation is the property of all its individual members, and as a consequence a claim to indemnification for injuries sustained by a *foreign state* may be satisfied by a seizure of the property of any of the individual members of *that state*; that by the law of nations the whole property of the individual members of a state is responsible for the debts or obligations of the state or of the sovereign.
>
> A nation has a complete right by the law of nature to take possession of the property of an enemy as far as the purpose of equitable satisfaction or the necessities of just warfare require, so as to obtain, in the well-known phrase, '*indemnity for the past and security for the future.*'

As Rutherforth states with more clearness than any other writer the principle of this rule in the law of nations, I will cite him fully on this point:—

> But we acquire no right, corporeal or incorporeal, by the mere act of war, and it is a settled principle in the law of nations that without some natural or antecedent right, the mere taking of a

thing by war is no right at all.

In a war which is internally just, as a nation may take the person, so likewise it may seize upon the goods of the enemies, either movable or immovable, as far as such seizure is a necessary means to bring them to do what is right, but *what is seized only for this purpose does not become the property of the captors; the possession is just till the purpose for which the goods were taken is answered,* but as soon as the claims of the injured nation are satisfied the justice of the possession is at an end.

The surest way of trying whether it is the claim of war or the claim of a tacit consent in concluding a peace which gives us property in all such goods as are taken in war is to inquire what sort of right we have to them before peace is concluded.

There is no law of nations which forbids our enemies to continue a war when no other cause of dispute remains besides our detention of such goods as we have taken in the war beyond the equivalent for damage and expenses. As the law of nature will allow this to be a just cause for continuing a war, so there is no practice of nations and no general opinion of mankind that determines otherwise; but if any law of nations had given us property in such goods, the same law must necessarily condemn the adverse nation for continuing a war merely because we would not give them up, for the design of such a war would be to take from us what the law of nations had made us own.

This opinion that all goods which are taken in war are not strictly our own by any law of nations till peace is concluded— that is, till some consent, either express or tacit, has made them our own by the law of nature—seems to be the general opinion of mankind in respect to immovable goods, such as fortified towns or provinces which have been overrun in war.

The captors are looked upon, *while the war lasts, to be only in possession* of them, and though this possession may help them to make a better bargain for themselves in a treaty of peace than they could do otherwise, yet the property which they have in things of this sort is deemed to be precarious until a treaty of peace has ascertained and established it.

It is usual in treaties of peace to mention such immovable goods particularly, and the captors, if they acquire property in them, acquire it by express consent, may therefore reasonably conclude that the property which the captors have in all movable goods taken in war is likewise acquired in the same manner. The only difference is that immovable goods, which are generally the most important, are in the hands of the public and can readily be returned, whilst movable goods are of less consequence, are in private hands, and because they have either been consumed or have not been kept together cannot be returned so readily. For this reason, whilst the property in the former is adjusted by express consent, the property in the latter is left to pass from the original owners to the captors by tacit consent.

Here we perceive that this *right* gives to the captor only the *possession* and use of the property of an alien enemy during war, but the *title* does not pass, except by the *consent* of the nation to which the property belongs.

This *consent* is presumed in favour of movable goods on account of their perishable nature and the difficulty of identifying them; but this rule cannot be applied to *rebels* in a *civil war*, and for obvious reasons, because if the "rebels in arms" have not in fact dismembered the Union and formed an independent sovereignty they are today *citizens* of the United States and their property is a part of *its eminent domain*; therefore no law of war can confer upon the United States a higher claim to their property than it now has by the Constitution. To transfer the property from the citizens to the coffers of the government would not increase the national wealth it would add nothing to the national resources to take that which *is already ours*; but concede that the rebels have displaced the national sovereignty and become a *foreign nation*, then upon a reconquest of that territory our government would enter upon their rights of sovereignty, take possession of their national domain and national revenues, seize and detain their citizens as prisoners and their property to compel them to do what is right; but if we destroy that rebel power altogether and retain the territory our claim to indemnity for the past and security for the future is satisfied.

Vattel says:

> The conqueror who takes a town or province from his enemy cannot justly acquire over it any other rights than such as belonged to the sovereign against whom he has taken up arms; but if the entire State be conquered, if the nation be subdued, ... if the conqueror thinks proper to retain the sovereignty of the conquered State and has a right to retain it, ... reason

plainly evinces that he acquires no other rights by his conquest than such as belonged to the sovereign whom he has dispossessed, and on the *submission* of the people he is bound to govern them *according to the laws of the State.*

Chancellor Kent says:—

It is a settled principle in the law and usage of nations that the inhabitants of a conquered country change their allegiance, and their relations to their former sovereign is dissolved, but *their relations to each other* and *their rights of property* not taken from them by orders of the conqueror remain undisturbed.

And he cites the Supreme Court as deciding that:—

The laws, usages, and municipal regulations in force at the time of the conquest or cession remain in force until changed by the new sovereign.

It follows, therefore, that the rebel territory, with the rights of persons and of property not destroyed by the struggle, fall at once under the protection of the Constitution and municipal laws.

We have had in our history but two occasions to exercise this right against foreign nations. In our war with Mexico, in which we sent our armies to her capital for the purpose of obtaining indemnity, *there* we respected *private rights* and abstained from the seizures of *private property*, and, being unable otherwise to obtain indemnity, we took by conquest a portion of her territory, paying her in money for the excess over and above the amount of our claims for indemnity. Now, had a proposition been made in Congress to confiscate the property of the people of the conquered territory for the acts of the Mexican Government, its repugnance to the laws of nations would have shocked the moral sense even of the Congress of that day.

The first act which broke their allegiance to the Mexican Government and transferred it to the United States did, in the judgment of all publicists, bar all claim on them for the acts of their former government.

But in one respect this civil war does resemble a war with a foreign nation. The insurgents have subjugated some eleven States of the Union and have expelled all national and State authority and have enforced acquiescence and qualified allegiance to their arms and revolutionary government.

This calls for the exercise of new duties; *new,* I mean, from the fact that there was never before any necessity on the part of our government for their exercise.

But, though they are *new*, we cannot mistake our way if we will only consider the nature of this civil strife and how far the relations of the citizen is affected while the national authority remains displaced by the rebel force.

On this point Senator Sumner cites from Grotius:—

The first and most necessary partition of war is this—that war is *private, public*, and *mixed*. Public war is that which is carried on under the authority of him who has jurisdiction; private, that which is not so; *mixed, that which is public on one side and private on the other.*

And he says:—

In these few words of this great authority will be found that very discrimination which enters into the present discussion. The war in which we are now engaged . . . . . . is 'mixed'—that is, public on one side and private on the other. On the side of the United States it is under the authority of the government, and is therefore public; on the other side, it is without the sanction of any recognised government, and is therefore 'private.' In other words, the Government of the United States may claim for itself all belligerent rights, while it may refuse them to the other side.

This is a false inference from the *misapplied* principle of Grotius. Rutherforth, the recognised expositor of Grotius, in commenting upon this *very passage* in its application to civil war, says:—

If anyone should ask whether these internal wars of a civil society are public or private or mixed, we must certainly answer that, in the language of the law of nations, they are neither; for since this law takes no notice of what passes within a civil society—as far as what passes there has no reference to the rest of mankind—it has no occasion to mention wars of this sort, and therefore gives them no name. It does not so much as call them *wars*, and much less does it rank them under the head of *public* or *private* or *mixed*.

The law of nations does not call them wars, not because they are not wars but because they are such acts as do not come within its view, and as it has therefore given no name to. They have certainly the nature of war, for they are contentions by force. Common usage likewise has given them this name and calls them *civil wars;* 'and if we attend to the nature of the act we shall find that civil wars may be either *public,* mixed, or *private.'* A civil war may be called a public one when the heads of each party are respectively considered by their own people as *public persons.* A rebellion may be called a mixed war when one of the parties is under the conduct of a public person and the other consists of private persons. It may be called a private one when there is no subjection on either side.

According to this very principle of Grotius, a civil strife partakes of the nature of a public war whenever it is carried on against the Government by an organized force, acting through regular constituted authorities, regarded and accepted by the rebels as public persons. It is then a contest between the lawful government, on one side, and an *unlawful,* but *de facto,* government, on the other.

Now, to claim that this rebellion is "private" on their side because their government is not a "*recognised* government" shows a most singular confusion of principles in the mind of the Senator, for were their government "recognised" it would *then* cease to be a civil war at all and would become a public war between two foreign nations.

From the very nature of things, the claim to exercise a right is founded upon a corresponding obligation. Our government cannot claim belligerent rights without *conceding* the existence of a power (call it what you may) that is under an obligation to *yield them,* and an obligation to yield implies a corresponding obligation on the other side. While a rebellion remains within bounds, manageable by the civil force or by the military force acting in aid of the civil authority, there is no claim to exercise or duty to yield belligerent rights, and the relation of no one to his government in the theatre of the rebellion is affected in any way; but when a rebellion attains to such proportions as actually displaces all civil authority and subjects a portion of the territory to its dominion, the relations are purely *belligerent* and must remain *belligerent* until the civil authority is restored, for there can be no civil relations without authority to protect the citizen.

Our government can hold none whatever with the people of the subjugated States until the rebellion is suppressed and its authority re-established. The fact that these rebels possess the military power competent to displace and *have* actually displaced all civil authority elevates their struggle to the dignity of war. It calls for the exertion by the government of its military power, and it must deal with this strife for the present only with this military force.

Martial law may be applied to all the sections of country where the rebellion has displaced the civil authority, and every citizen of the United States may be subjected to martial law; their property may be seized and used by the military power if the public safety shall require it, but private property of the rebels which may thus be captured is not by any law of nations nor cannot be by any act of Congress vested in the United States, unless upon the recognition of their independence as a nation, for by the rights of *postliminium* upon the destruction of the rebel power every person is restored to his former rights, and everything that has not passed beyond the jurisdiction of the United States which can be found and identified returns to its former state under the Constitution.

Vattel says:

> The right of *postliminium*, is that in virtue of which *persons and things* taken by the enemy are restored to their former state on coming again into the power of the nation to which they belonged.
>
> The sovereign is bound to protect the persons and property of his subjects and to defend them against the enemy. When, therefore, a subject or any part of his property has fallen into the enemy's possession, should any fortunate event bring them again into the sovereign's power it is undoubtedly his duty to restore them to their former condition, to re-establish the persons in all their rights and obligations, to give back the effects to the owners; in a word, to replace everything on the same footing on which it stood previous to the enemy's capture.
>
> Among the Romans, indeed, slaves were not treated like other movable property. They, by the rights of *postliminium*, were restored to their masters, even when the rest of the booty was detained. The reason of this is evident, for it was always easy to recognize a slave and ascertain to whom he belonged.

The rights of *postliminium* are not under the cognisance of the law of nations.

Manning in speaking of usages of different nations, says:—

> Thus it will be seen that no general rule obtains regarding *postliminium*. Different States have different regulations on this

subject; and, as it is a question which concerns members of the same State rather than subjects of different States, its details belong to municipal law rather than the law of nations.

When, therefore, a rebel is brought again, either by force or by his own volition, under the power of the United States, the government is by the Constitution bound to re-establish him in all his rights and obligations, and, upon his submission to its authority, give back to him his property.

It is too clear for argument that, during the military occupation of any town, district, or State of the Union by an invading force of a foreign nation, Congress would have *no authority* to confiscate the property of any American citizen, inhabitant of that town, district, or State; and should the citizens, no matter from what motive, whether from instinct of self-preservation or from disloyalty, join the invading force and fight in its ranks against their country, they do not *thereby* become public enemies; they *do not forfeit their allegiance to the country*; they *cannot* defeat the country's claim to *punish them according the laws of the land*. They cannot plead upon the trial for giving aid and comfort to the enemy that they were traitors and fought *willingly* against their flag, though they may *plead*, and *plead successfully*, that the temporary inability of the government to protect them against the superior hostile force constrained their temporary submission.

True, the military generals of our country cannot distinguish the *nationality* of the enemy in arms, but will capture or kill all alike until they surrender to the authority of the government or flee beyond its frontiers; but the legislative power must distinguish a nationality, *must* recognise the American citizen, *must* recognise his constitutional rights to protection and his liability to punishment for crime. While it may hold the nation to which this foreign force belongs responsible for *indemnity* and security and may look to every citizen or subject owing allegiance to this power, it cannot look to its *own citizens, nor confiscate their property, nor hold them as hostages* in order to constrain a foreign government to make compensation for wrongs inflicted.

The same rules which apply to any portion of the citizens of the United States which may be subjugated by an *invading* force applies *now* to the citizens of the Southern States who are subjugated by the *rebel* force. The duty of allegiance and protection are reciprocal; therefore, when a State loses the power to protect any portion of its territory and inhabitants by reason of the superior force of a hostile power, the people so reduced necessarily must yield obedience to the *de facto* government. Their property and persons are claimed by the conquerors, but their allegiance is not severed from their government unless the conquest is confirmed by the consent of the conquered.

Castine, in the State of Maine, was captured and held by the British forces in September, 1814, and continued in their exclusive possession until the treaty of peace, in 1815.

The Supreme Court decided that the sovereignty of the United States was *suspended*, and that the inhabitants passed under a *temporary allegiance to the British Government*.

The Territory of Michigan was surrendered to the British Government by General Hull on the 16th of August, 1812, and continued in its possession until September 30, 1813. During this time the American laws were continued in force and the civil officers who remained in the Territory were continued in office. Judge Witherill and other officers of the Territory were paid their full salaries during the period of the British occupation.

The citizens and civil officers of Michigan who remained and submitted to British authority were not regarded by our government as enemies, but that was before the discovery of the theory of political *felo de se*.

Now, when a *revolted people* have actually expelled their lawful government and in its stead established a *de facto* one, the condition of the citizens is precisely the same as in the case of a lawful government expelled by a foreign force; therefore, while a government is unable to afford *protection* to its citizens, it *cannot* hold them responsible for any act they may commit *while under the pressure* of a usurping power.

What, now, are the *facts* in reference to this Southern rebellion?

Have not the rebels expelled every vestige of authority, both of the States and of the United States, and established over that territory their revolutionary government?

Have they not gibbeted, imprisoned in dungeons, or driven into exile all who would not submit to their despotism? For more than twelve months the Government of the United States has been unable to extend to these people the protection of its authority; *no flag* has been seen there—*no emblem of authority on the part of the United States to protect and shield them*. To punish these people for acts committed while under the dominion of this hostile force and while the Government of the United States was unable to protect them would be a flagrant violation of every principle of natural and political law.

It would place the authors and executioners of the injustice upon the scroll which bears to infamy the name of Jeffreys, the judicial murderer under Charles II.

No, no! what the United States may rightfully do is this: The President, upon the reestablishment of the civil jurisdiction, may bring to trial and condign punishment the authors and instigators of this rebellion. If the law against treason is not deemed sufficiently just, in view of the enormity of their crime, Congress may provide the punishment for all who do not lay down their arms so soon as they can receive the protection of their government. It may exclude them *forever* from all offices of honour or emolument; it may *fine, imprison, or execute them*; in short, it may declare any *punishment*, provided it works no corruption of blood or *forfeiture beyond the life* of the traitor.

Having established that the *responsibility of the people of the subjugated States* to the General Government *depends* upon *its power to extend protection over them*, I now propose to inquire *what are the relations of the General Government to the people where* the rebels have been subdued, but yet *before the civil authority has been re-established?*—a question, perhaps, of more importance than any which has ever engaged the attention of the American people.

We have effectually overcome the rebellion in some of the States and in many cities and districts of other States, and it is evident that within a short time, if Congress will but stop its career of violence against the Constitution, we will have overcome it in all the States.

It is not probable that the people will return within a short time to their allegiance or that the government will be able to extend the civil authority over the *whole* of that territory. It will be the work of time.

A large class of these people have become *thoroughly alienated* from the government, whether by the effort of demagogues or from whatever cause. A large class still love the Union and cling to the precious memories of its past history, who *honestly believe* it is *dissolved* and *never can be restored*. Then there is another class who, shocked by the terrible power of the rebellion, *have lost all hope and confidence in the power of republican institutions*.

If Congress will but abstain from all interference, there is no *doubt* about the ability of the President and his patriotic army to suppress the rebellion in every part of the territory; but the difficulties are in restoring peace to this distracted country *after* the rebel armies are overthrown. This requires the exercise of the highest and noblest qualities of statesmen. I would have Congress make no mistake *here*.

I would have them inaugurate no policy of *doubtful constitutionality*. Peace can only be restored to the country by extending to the people the shield of the Constitution. The union of these States *cannot* be restored under a *mutilated Constitution* or under a new or different one.

Now, until the protection of the Constitution is extended over the subjugated States and the civil authority is re-established the relations of the people to the government must necessarily remain *purely military*—that is, *martial law* is the only law the government can apply in the absence of civil authority.

The right to apply martial law to the citizens of the United States and subject them to military government is conferred by the clause of the Constitution authorising the suspension of the privilege of the writ of *habeas corpus*.

There are several instances in which this power has been exercised in the history of this government, and it was first used under the administration of President Washington during what was called the whiskey insurrection. It was used by General Wilkinson at the time of Burr's conspiracy, and by General Jackson in the war of 1812. General Scott applied martial law by military government in Mexico during our war with that country; but within the United States the public safety never required the application of martial law to whole communities of citizens until the present rebellion.

The establishment of a military government in the States of Tennessee and North Carolina indicates the President's policy for the restoration of the subjugated States to their rights in the Union, and is, as I believe, the *only* policy which can by any possibility effect it.

A military government, when established over a territory, holds the whole population, as it were, prisoners of war, subject to the rules of war. Its operations are confined to military questions and subjects all civil relations to its supervision and control, though, in fact, it exercises no civil *authority*, and Congress can confer upon it none, as its very existence depends upon the absence of civil authority.

It may exercise over the people of a district who are subjected to its authority all the rights which military commanders may exercise over their prisoners, according to the rules of modern warfare. It may provide for their rigorous imprisonment or it may parole them. It may exercise the extreme rights of the code of war over the life, liberty, and property of every citizen who *revolts* against its authority; but it has *no right* to take the life or *confiscate* the property of the people who have *submitted* to its authority any more than a commander has to *murder* or *plunder* his prisoners, and Congress can confer upon it none; for Congress has no more power to interfere with the conduct of a military governor than it has to interfere with the ordinary operations of the army before an enemy. It is not for Congress to pursue our generals in the field and say where to plant this battery or what house shall be battered down, what field ploughed up by cannon, what cities shall be burned, or what country shall be laid waste.

The direction of the operations of war belongs *not* to the legislative department; the Constitution has vested it exclusively in the *President as Commander-in-Chief.*

It is only for Congress to raise and support an army sufficient for the suppression of the rebellion. It is the President's duty to command and direct it.

And this military force, *directed by the President*, may employ every means known to civilized warfare. It may subject all persons to martial law "when the public safety may require it," and seize and use all property within the field of its operations to annoy, to weaken, or destroy the rebellion, and this without a regard to the ownership of the property, whether friend or foe, and leave to the political power to settle with the claimants, according to their respective rights under law.

This is a fearful power, but *without which* no government can *live*, and, unfortunately, by it most free countries have been destroyed.

The authors of our Constitution understood this *much better* than the men in *this day*. They placed this power exclusively under the control of the *President*. The danger of confiding the military power *exclusively* to his hands was fully considered by them. guarded against the *abuse* by vesting in *Congress* the exclusive authority to raise and support this military force, and they guarded against the abuse of Congress by withholding from it the authority to make appropriations for a longer period than two years.

Senator Howard asks:—

Have the people of the United States stripped themselves of all power to control the operations of the wars in which they may be involved? Is nothing left to their representatives but to furnish the men, the material, and the money, and are their orders as to the *mode* in which and the *purposes* for which these shall be used totally powerless and void? And does the Constitution subject to the will of the President exclusively the use of the military force in all the details of the service?

These very objections were urged by the opponents of the Constitution in the State conventions which adopted it.

Justice Story, in his commentaries upon this power of the President, says:—

> Of all the cases and concerns of government the direction of *war* most peculiarly demands those qualities which distinguish the exercise of power by a *single hand*. Unity of plan, promptitude, activity, and decision are indispensable to success, and these can scarcely exist, *except when a single magistrate is intrusted exclusively with the power*. Even the coupling of the authority of an *executive council* with him in the exercise of such power enfeebles the system, divides the responsibility, and not unfrequently defeats every energetic measure. *Timidity, indecision, obstinacy*, and *pride of opinion* must mingle in all such councils and infuse a *torpor and sluggishness destructive of all military operations*.

But the Senator takes another and a bolder step. He says:—

> The *President is our general and bound to execute our behests, subject to the will of Congress, and liable for disobedience to be reduced at once to the condition of a private citizen and incapacitated to hold any office of honour or emolument under the Government*.

The absolute supremacy of Congress is avowed by another Senator in these words:—

> There is no limit over the power of Congress; it is *supreme*, and the ordinary provisions of the Constitution must *yield* as resolved by Congress.

I do not charge that there is a conspiracy in Congress to grasp the sword and overthrow republican institutions and establish upon its ruins a legislative despotism; but certain it is that unless this claim is rebuked by the country it will end in one; for, if Congress can exercise this power during war, the war will never end except with the destruction of liberty. Grant the power during war, and Congress will continue the war for the sake of the power, for the annals of the world record no instances where the usurpers of power have ever voluntarily laid it down. When Congress emancipates the slaves, and confiscates the estates of the proprietors and apportions them to the poor and the slaves in order to fill the South with "Northern industry and Northern principles," it will continue the war in order to enforce its enactments.

Senator Sumner will not have Congress "fasten upon itself *the restraints of the Constitution*." He will not have it "repeat the ancient tyranny which compelled its victims to fight in chains." Unless wiser counsels shall prevail or unless restrained by the President, Congress, "*unchained by the Constitution*," will move its armies swiftly over the liberties of the country, both South and North. Our legislators who would disregard the constitutional guarantees of liberty may learn a lesson of Frederick the Great, who desired to remove a windmill which stood before the centre window of his favourite palace at Pozdam, but could not induce the miller to sell it. The king, irritated, threatened the owner to force him to consent. "There is a supreme court in Berlin," answered the miller. The king was silent, and the mill stands to this day, an annoyance to the palace, but one of the *best monuments* which an absolute monarch ever erected to himself.

The authors of our Constitution, witnessing the slavery of every people in every age by the union of all powers, legislative, executive, and judicial, in one body, and with a consummate knowledge of the philosophy of government, distributed its powers into three departments—legislative, executive, and judicial—defining the respective spheres of each with such precision that it is impossible to misunderstand it.

Despotism is inevitable wherever power is lodged in a single body, whether in one or in many, whether in a single executive or a numerous legislative body.

That "we, the people of the United States," do not exert our power directly, but by representative bodies, severally restricted by a written Constitution to certain specific duties, constitutes the *peculiar merit* of our form of government, and its successful working hitherto has been the proud boast of Americans as *their contribution* to the science of free government, the first and only one ever known in the history of the world. Shall it be the last? The last of all the ages, the last of all the lands? And shall our Union, rent by factions, after all pass away—pass like a star that sets to rise no more, no more forever?

★★★★★★

Henry Polkinhorn. Printer, Washington.

★★★★★★

Although Miss Anna Ella Carroll has lived and died without succeeding in collecting from the government payment for her nobly earned literary work, it would seem that simple honesty would require its immediate payment to her sister and heir, Miss Mary Henry Carroll, whose years of labour and devotion sustained and cheered our benefactress through all her declining years.

CHAPTER 5

Letters to Anna Ella Carroll

On receiving the paper on the *Relation of the Government to its Revolted Citizens*, being then absent from Washington, I wrote Miss Carroll that I felt rather dismayed at finding she had not used her influence for the freedom of the slave, but had rather brought forward the obstacles in the way. It seemed to me, as far as slavery was concerned, its abolition was obligatory, as the Constitution had made it the fundamental and paramount duty of the General Government to secure to every State a republican form of government, and that could not be a republican form of government where one class of its people held another class in slavery. However, at the time the discussion had been necessary, and the record was very interesting.

I asked her also whether some passages might not be construed somewhat as a personal attack on Sumner. I received the following reply:—

931 New Hampshire Avenue, July 7, 1891.

You are entirely mistaken, dear friend, as regards my writings. At the time they were written no one was able to predict the result of the war.

The essay to which you refer, in regard to Mr. Sumner and others, was, as stated in the memorial of '78, written expressly to meet the views of the President, and he was the first person to whom it was sent as soon as printed. I remember it perfectly. They came in late on a Saturday night. On Monday early I went up to the Capitol, handed Mr. Lincoln a copy, and received his very warmest thanks. It was then at once distributed in both houses of Congress.

Mr. Sumner, whom I well knew, so far from being offended,

paid me a very handsome compliment upon the pamphlet, and no one ever thought of anything but kindness in all I had done. At a great deal of personal sacrifice, I freed my own slaves before the war, and when the laws of the State of Maryland prohibited it from being done unless they were sent to Liberia, which I absolutely refused should ever be done in that case.

I wish I were able (as you suggest) to pen my biography, which, if properly executed, would, I know, be interesting; but at this time, I could not do it, owing to the extraordinary condition of my arm and hand.

Hoping to hear from you soon, I am most sincerely and affectionately, yours,

A. E. Carroll.

There is such a wealth of letters to Miss Carroll from distinguished political and literary men that to give even a portion of them would swell the volume beyond the proposed limits. Most of them can be found in the successive Congressional memorials. There is only space to add here a very few in addition to those given in the previous volume.

Among Miss Carroll's papers the following statement exists, in her own handwriting, of a conversation with General Grant, with whom Miss Carroll always remained on very friendly terms. The general never opposed her claim, but advised her to continue to bring it before Congress

Conversation Between General U. S. Grant and A. E. Carroll.
It was in December, soon after Congress met. I was introduced by Hon. Reverdy Johnson, then United States Senator, to General Grant. I told him my purpose in seeing him was to ascertain what he knew Of the Tennessee campaign, the plan of which I considered myself to have originated in the winter of 1862 and which was carried out in the following spring.

He told me he could in a few words. tell all he knew. He said Badeau, who was then writing his history, had been ill and obliged to abandon it for the present; that all he knew of the Tennessee plan was in that book; that he had never read a line of it and did not propose to do more than read what appertained to himself; that he knew nothing of the Tennessee until he was ordered up that river by the general then in command at St. Louis, General Halleck; that he would advise me to defer, or rather to wait the action of Congress, until the aforesaid book was issued, and that would contain all he knew of that campaign.

He was very cordial; seemed much interested, and wished me to make Mrs. Grant and himself a visit as soon as I could do so. I said I had thought it but just to claim in history the part I had taken. He said he thought I was right, and that I should be wanting in what was due to me if I did not do so.

This interview led me to delay any action by Congress. When the book came out there was nothing in it that impaired any statement I had made. When he was asked by a friend of mine to recommend the payment of my bill caused by great expenses incurred in going to the West, &c., he declined on the ground that he might be called on to express an opinion, which he wished to avoid, and so it went on until General Rawlings came into the Department of War.

A. E. Carroll.

Letter from Hon. J. T. Headley, the distinguished historian of the Civil War, to Miss A. E. Carroll.

Newburgh, February 6, 1873.

My Dear Madam: I am much obliged to you for the pamphlet you sent me.

I never knew before with whom the plan of the campaign up the Tennessee River originated. There seemed to be a mystery attached to it that I could not solve.

Though General Buell sent me an immense amount of documents relating to this campaign, I could find no reference to the change of plan. Afterwards I saw it attributed to Halleck, which I knew to be false, and I noticed that he never corroborated it.

It is strange that after all my research it has rested with you to enlighten me. Money cannot pay for the plan of that campaign. I doubt not Congress will show, not liberality, but some justice in the matter.

Yours very sincerely,

J. T. Headley.

Conversing with Miss Carroll concerning the loss of her papers, twice stolen from the desks of the military committees, as testified by Samuel Hunt, secretary of the Senate Military Committee, it was suggested that she should write concerning this loss to General Bragg, still living and residing in Wisconsin. She did so, receiving in response a most friendly letter expressing his astonishment that there could be any question about the letters. From this we give the following:—

Extracts from a Letter from General Edward S. Bragg to Miss Carroll.

Fond Du Lac, Wisconsin, April 26, 1891.

My Dear Miss Carroll: The authenticity of the letters of Assistant Secretary of War Scott, Senator Wade, and other men of prominence printed in your memorial to Congress in support of claim for compensation for services in the war is beyond question. They were before the Committee of Military Affairs (H. R.) and were examined and considered by them. The claim was scouted because it was to the War Department absurd to consider for a moment that a woman's knowledge of topography and strategic lines led the advance of the warriors, young and old, "who saved the country, in discovering the lines of the Cumberland as a most feasible one in making advance into the enemy's country, they having the command of the Mississippi River. Military men doff their hats with grace and pleasure to woman, but to surrender claim to anything in the way of personal glory in their profession to a woman—that is quite another thing!" That I may not be misunderstood, I repeat I have seen and read the originals of those letters when considering a bill for your relief in Military Committee of H. R. "The committee made a favourable report on the facts."

Wishing you a speedy restoration to good health, in which Mrs. Bragg joins me,

I am very sincerely your friend,

Edw. S. Bragg.

★★★★★★

Stanton summed up Miss Carroll's services tersely and truly when he said of her:—

Her course was the most remarkable in the war. She found herself, got no pay, and did the great work that made others famous.

CHAPTER 6

Closing Years

When I first made the acquaintance of Miss Anna Ella Carroll in 1890, though a confirmed invalid she was still bright and mentally active. Although she had almost lost her voice and had wholly lost her hearing, her intellect remained undimmed and her memory of past events, even in their details, was wonderful.

We could only converse by writing, but her clear intellect and large-heartedness were a constant delight, and the writing had the advantage that I could gather up the records of the conversation and keep them for reference.

When the first advanced sheets of the Biography were submitted to her she was greatly surprised, but after some demur as to publishing facts of her personal history, she gave her approval to the statements and desired that copies should be sent to members of her own family and a few intimate friends.

Thereafter I used to take her notices of the work and the letters of interest that we were constantly receiving, and she was greatly cheered by the warm expressions of regard and admiration that came to her even from the most distant States. Finding that the visits were a pleasure to her and eagerly anticipated, I fell into the habit of spending a short time with her every Sunday afternoon, a practice continued every winter up to the last. During the week, she read regularly and with avidity the New York *World*, and took great interest in all political questions.

The idea of suffrage for women was comparatively new to her, and we had many a discussion, often ending in a hearty laugh, when I turned upon her her own theories and assured her that I should make a good suffragist of her finally. She admitted that very possibly it might be so, but she lived largely in the past and in past ideas.

When the suffrage meetings and Society for the Advancement for Women held their sessions in Washington a lively interest for her was evinced, and prominent ladies would request the pleasure of an introduction to her, which was always willingly accorded. Each one came away delighted at the interview, wondering at the brightness and geniality preserved through so long an illness and at so advanced an age.

An account published in the *Inter-Ocean* in 1891 by Miss Isabel Howland gives a graphic account of one of these visits. It is as follows:—

Washington, May 30.

To the Editor:

No home in Washington offers to the visitor a more cordial reception than that of the Carroll sisters. On New Hampshire avenue, near its opening upon Washington Square, stands a block of houses with plats of green in front. One of these houses shelters the Carrolls. It was the good fortune of the writer on a certain afternoon lately to find herself, with a friend, pulling the door-bell of this house.

Admitted to the parlour, the time of waiting passed in admiring the taste and intelligence exhibited in the paintings and classic photographs upon the walls, the furnishings of the room, the books upon the table. These last silent witnesses for or against the culture of the family here bore examination. Among others, now forgotten, were Woodbury's Emerson and Keats' poems. The air of the room was made. sweet by a large bunch of syringa blossoms before the grate.

After a short delay summons came from the invalid and we went upstairs.

Is there anyone who does not know the name of Anna Ella Carroll? Shame to us it is that there are many who do not know it. Shame to us that Grant and Sherman and Sheridan and all the rest of the men who figured as leaders in our late civil war are familiar to every household in the United States, and Anna Ella Carroll is strange to those same households. Anna Ella Carroll, that big-brained Maryland woman, saved the Union. There is not the shadow of a doubt that it was she who planned the Tennessee campaign, the move which brought success to the government arms.

No one who takes the trouble to look into the proofs of this statement attempts to deny it. The Court of Claims does not. No Congressional committee has ever done so. They cannot. Letters of the men who had the conduct of the war are still in existence which declare that to Miss Carroll belongs the glory of the famous strategic movement; but for thirty years this woman has been sending in to the Congress of the United States her appeal for justice and for thirty years Congress has adjourned without taking action.

Hundreds of old soldiers, hundreds of old soldiers' wives have asked the government for help and it has been given to them lavishly. Miss Carroll, for her incomparable services of writing, publishing, and circulating war documents (following the direction of the President and the Secretary of War), and finally of proposing the Tennessee campaign, has never been granted a single dollar. In the thirty years she has grown old, has lost her health and the use of her limbs. She spends her days in bed. Her hearing is entirely gone and her voice is much affected, but her interest in the claim is as keen and fresh as ever.

We had heard all this and expected to be saddened by the sight of Miss Carroll in her present condition. The contrast of the reality with the anticipation was delightful. The invalid's room was bright and cheerful. A large bay window faced the west. From the bed, as we entered, there looked out a face irradiated with such a beautiful smile that one in the sunshine of it was ready to forget age, deafness, harshness of voice, invalidism—everything but its surpassing sweetness.

So long as the memory of that visit remains, the smile with which we were greeted will make a halo about it. The efficient coloured nurse, who is always beside her, brought chairs close to the bed and placed pencils and paper before us; Miss Carroll being too deaf to hear the visitor's voice. Sitting beside her, our eyes continuously wandered to the lovely hair, soft, white, and fluffy, which lay in little curls about her face, and was coiled in a loose knot high on the head.

She did not talk much herself, but eagerly received the papers upon which we had written. When anything especially pleased her she showed it by a warm pressure of the hand.

We spoke of her biography, which Miss Blackwell had written and which was just out, of the claim, and of their contemplated moving, which she was dreading.

On the wall opposite the bed hung an oil portrait of herself when a girl. There was surprisingly little difference between it and the older face upon the pillows in its setting of white hair and fascinating smile.

Before we left Carroll's sister Mary came in from her work at the Treasury Department. Miss Mary writes letters every day from 9 until 4, and with the salary thus earned supports the pleasant home. The affection between the two sisters is lovely to witness and is exhibited on Miss Mary's side in the most devoted care and unceasing attentions. Though always very weary, she never fails to spend an hour each evening writing to her sister. Miss Mary is a highly cultivated and delightful person, finding time between the hours of work at the Treasury to keep up with the thought of the times.

When we rose to go the Carroll hospitality, a relic of the free-hearted life of old plantation days, came to the front in the cordial invitation from Miss Carroll to repeat the visit. "Come again," she said; come and stay to dinner. You will be welcome any time, any day—always." And we left with an extraordinarily warm feeling about the heart for having made a half-hour's call upon strangers.

The biography above referred to has been published by Judd & Detweiler, of Washington It is warmly welcomed by the few who realise what Miss Carroll did at the time of the war and the way her claim has been disregarded by Congress. Others, who have pooh-hooed at the idea of a woman being equal to such work, will find in it plain statements which cannot be refuted without assailing the honesty and sincerity of such men as General Bragg, the Hon. Benjamin F. Wade, Thomas A. Scott, Reverdy Johnson, etc. No true history of our civil war will be written until the name of Anna Ella Carroll is given a place there. Time will prove her right to it; but we wish that justice might be done while she is living.

Isabel Howland.

Miss Carroll frequently referred to one and another of her friendly visitors and was delighted to hear news of them. During one of my last visits to her, in 1893, she called my attention to a sketch upon the mantelpiece of a quaint little country church, in whose cemetery her father, Governor Thomas King Carroll; her mother, and a brother and sister had been laid to rest. It was old Trinity church, on Church creek, about eight miles from Cambridge, on the eastern shore of Chesapeake Bay.

This interesting little church is said to be, with one or two exceptions, the oldest church in the United States. The kneeling-cushions and the ancient silver communion service sent over from England by "Good Queen Anne" are still in use. In that little cemetery, she now lies beside her father and her mother.

Almost to the close of her illness Miss Carroll remained wonderfully bright and able to enjoy the visits of her friends. Occasionally she spoke of herself as a very happy woman to have had secured to her a comfortable home and to have received all through her illness the devoted attention and tender care of her beloved sister.

Never a murmur, never a word of repining, but gradually her daily reading was intermitted and writing became more fatiguing.

An access of illness near the close of 1893 reduced her vitality, and in February of 1894 it became evident that she was failing. On the 17th she lapsed into an unconscious condition, from which she never rallied, but quietly ceased to breathe on the 18th without pain or struggle. The next day she lay beautifully arrayed in the little parlour of 718 Twenty-First street, her last home in Washington. The soft white curls still clustered about her lofty brow, a sheaf of wheat lay at her feet, a bouquet of fragrant violets were clasped in those beautiful hands that had done such noble work for her country at the time of its direst need. The warm patriot heart had ceased to beat. As I left her I turned at the parlour door for the last look. A friend stood at her head giving last fond touches with a face so transfigured with loving tenderness that it looked to me like an angel hovering over her.

Goodbye once more, dear friend and noble-hearted woman! You have joined the sacred army of the veterans and martyrs of our national cause. We will not forget you, and the future historian shall make known the undying glory of your life!

On the evening of the 21st, accompanied by two of her sisters, Miss Carroll's earthly form was conveyed to Baltimore, and on a beautiful moonlight night, on the steamer of the Eastern Shore, the sorrowing little party glided sadly down the Chesapeake Bay to Cambridge. There they were met by relatives and friends desiring to look once more upon the face of one who had always been to them a glory and a pride.

On the following day, the venerated form of the beloved sister and friend was conveyed to the ancient church, surrounded by its quiet cemetery. These grounds, at one time very lovely, are still in good preservation. Washed by the waters of the stream to which the church gives its name and framed in a circlet of huge oaks, even more ancient than the church itself, the sacred quiet of this lovely resting-place for the dead shed a soothing influence upon the sorrowing human hearts as they bade a final farewell to the beloved sister and left her in her chosen resting-place in the family burying ground beside her father and her mother.

And there she awaits the monument that will surely be erected at some future day in grateful remembrance of our National Benefactress.

www.ingramcontent.com/pod-product-compliance
Lightning Source LLC
Chambersburg PA
CBHW032039080426
42733CB00006B/132